D0897715

Beauty Will Save the World

Beauty Will Save the World

*Recovering the Human
in an Ideological Age*

Gregory Wolfe

Wilmington, Delaware

Library of Congress Cataloging-in-Publication Data

Wolfe, Gregory.
    Beauty will save the world : recovering the human in an ideological age / Gregory Wolfe.
      p. cm.
    Includes bibliographical references and index.
    ISBN 978-1-933859-88-0
    1. Aesthetics. 2. Christian literature—History and criticism. 3. Humanity. 4. Civilization—21st century. 5. Culture—21st century. I. Title. II. Title: Recovering the human in an ideological age.

BH301.C92W65 2011
111'.85—dc22   2011010876

Published in the United States by:

ISI Books
Intercollegiate Studies Institute
3901 Centerville Road
Wilmington, Delaware 19807-1938
www.isibooks.org

Manufactured in the United States of America

For Suzanne, my beauty

Dostoevsky once let drop the enigmatic phrase: "Beauty will save the world." What does this mean? For a long time it used to seem to me that this was a mere phrase. Just how could such a thing be possible? When had it ever happened in the bloodthirsty course of history that beauty had saved anyone from anything? Beauty had provided embellishment, certainly, given uplift—but whom had it ever saved?

However, there is a special quality in the essence of beauty, a special quality in the status of art: the conviction carried by a genuine work of art is absolutely indisputable and tames even the strongly opposed heart. One can construct a political speech, an assertive journalistic polemic, a program for organizing society, a philosophical system, so that in appearance it is smooth, well structured, and yet it is built upon a mistake, a lie; and the hidden element, the distortion, will not immediately become visible. And a speech, or a journalistic essay, or a program in rebuttal, or a different philosophical structure can be counterposed to the first—and it will seem just as well constructed and as smooth, and everything will seem to fit. And therefore one has faith in them—yet one has no faith.

It is vain to affirm that which the heart does not confirm. In contrast, a work of art bears within itself its own confirmation: concepts which are manufactured out of whole cloth or overstrained will not stand up to being tested in images, will somehow fall apart and turn out to be sickly and pallid and convincing to no one. Works steeped in truth and presenting it to us vividly alive will take hold of us, will attract us to themselves with great power—and no one, ever, even in a later age, will presume to negate them. And so perhaps that old trinity of Truth and Good and Beauty is not just the formal outworn formula it used to seem to us during our heady, materialistic youth. If the crests of these three trees join together, as the investigators and explorers used to affirm, and if the too obvious, too straight branches of Truth and Good are crushed or amputated and cannot reach the light—yet perhaps the whimsical, unpredictable, unexpected branches of Beauty will make their way through and soar up *to that very place* and in this way perform the work of all three.

And in that case it was not a slip of the tongue for Dostoevsky to say that "Beauty will save the world," but a prophecy.

—Aleksandr Solzhenitsyn, "Nobel Lecture"

Contents

Prologue

The Four Cultures and Me

A n old Albert Brooks film has been rattling around in my head of late: *Defending Your Life*. You may recall it. A divorced advertising exec fiddles with the CD player in his brand new BMW and plows into a city bus, only to find himself in Judgment City, where he has to account for himself in a jury trial in which the evidence consists of episodes from his life. The worst possible result isn't exactly hell; it's being sent back to earth for another attempt, rather than moving forward to a better planet and a better life.

In the version of the film playing in my head, the judges, prosecutor, and defender all bear a striking resemblance to . . . me. Now that I have arrived at that mid-way point of which Dante speaks, I find myself looking back, trying to figure out exactly how I got here. I may not be quite as lost as Dante's pilgrim in the dark wood, but I am beginning to realize one thing—just how wrong I've been in thinking I always knew what I was doing. The conscious choices I made now appear to me more like the iceberg's tip. The greater mass—my deeper self—has been below the surface, moved by currents of which I am only now becoming aware.

Reflections of this sort tend to accompany the task of assembling essays written over the course of a quarter century.

I've found some consolation in the thought that Dante's pilgrimage doesn't really begin at mid-life; in a sense, he's been on a pilgrimage all along. His youthful encounter with Beatrice, apprenticeship to the craft of poetry, and entanglement with the political vicissitudes of Florence—these and other chapters of his story shape the course of his voyage through the afterlife.

In other words, what happens when Dante the pilgrim sets off with Virgil is not so much a brand new life as it is an altered perspective on the life he already has. It is precisely through Beatrice, poetry, and politics that he will find the path toward redemption.

Gaining Perspective

Not long ago I came across a book that provided something of a roadmap for the pilgrimage I've been tracing: *Four Cultures of the West*. I hesitate to cast its author, John W. O'Malley, S. J., in the role of Virgil, but he has helped me to gain a sense of perspective on my journey—and on whatever coherence the essays in this book may possess.

Four Cultures of the West is a lively, wide-ranging, historical survey of the core styles of thought and vision that have shaped our civilization. O'Malley is a church historian specializing in the early modern period; he has written about the Council of Trent and the founding of the Jesuit order. As it turns out, *Four Cultures* is a book written in much the same spirit as I read it. In the introduction he says, "I was curious to understand better what had happened to me in the process" of being educated as a Jesuit.

I'm not a Jesuit, but in O'Malley's story I've begun to grasp an order in what formerly was inchoate. Though he is too modest a man to say it outright in the pages of his book, it is no exaggeration to say that the Jesuit order was founded in the Renaissance during a remarkable period in which all four of these cultures were synthesized by Ignatius of Loyola and his followers. At the outset of *Four Cultures*, O'Malley alludes to the early church father Tertullian's famous challenge: "What has Jerusalem to do with Athens?" In other words, what do the prophetic, religious cultures of Judaism and Christianity have to do with the "worldly" cultures of ancient Greece and Rome?

The answer given by the West, as it evolved through the medieval and Renaissance eras, was: plenty. Tertullian's prophetic culture was placed in a dynamic, productive tension with the other three cultures: the academic/professional culture of the philosophers and scientists, the humanistic culture of poets, rhetoricians, and statesmen, and the artistic culture of visual and performing artists.

Another way to look at this synthesis is through the ancient language of the "transcendentals": if the prophetic culture was fundamentally concerned with goodness and the academic culture with truth, then rhetoric and the arts sought to reflect beauty.

Father O'Malley is aware of the dangers of sweeping generalization. He concedes that there are a number of other cultures, such as the culture of business. But he makes a compelling case for the Big Four as fundamental to our development as a civilization.

In meditating upon the interplay between these cultures—sometimes harmonic and often antagonistic—I've come to understand a bit more about my own pilgrimage. Thanks to the love and generosity of my parents, I received an outstanding education, both in and out of the classroom. I was steeped from childhood in all four cultures, but as I came to maturity, I found myself inexorably drawn to the task of promoting two of them because I had seen what happened when the other two ran amok.

In his book Father O'Malley refrains from discussing any metatheory of how the cultures ought to relate to one another. Instead, he sticks to historically grounded description. At first I found this frustrating. I was hoping for some color commentary, some grand, unified theory. But I came to see the wisdom of his method: he hopes that the reader will "make application to your own milieu."

Wanting It All

As a child growing up in New York City, I attended a first-rate school, went to church on Sunday, had books read out loud to me in the evening, and was taken to Lincoln Center by my parents. The four cultures beckoned.

In school I was introduced to the academic method, which O'Malley notes is analytical and "never satisfied . . . critical of every wisdom . . . insatiably eager to ask the further question." I enjoyed that the method of academic discourse is, as O'Malley puts it, "agonistic and contentious."

In church I encountered prophetic culture, where the words of Jesus and the Old Testament prophets came from another language altogether, that of revelation—the transcendent slicing through our worldly expectations. Though its method was that of proclamation rather than reasoning, and paradox rather than syllogism, I felt instinctively that the prophetic complemented the academic, that revelation could stand up to reason, and that the foolishness of faith could prevent the mind from falling into excessive pride.

My introduction to cultures three and four came largely through my parents. As a former advertising executive, my father understood business culture, but in reality his heart lay in the tradition of what O'Malley calls "humanist culture," the province of "rhetoric, poetry, and the common good." When I was a child he turned away from business to throw himself into the realm of nonprofit causes. His gift as a writer was for the op-ed piece—language preoccupied with the first two cultures but aimed at persuasion, which is the essence of rhetoric. My father was less interested in poetry and fiction, which O'Malley notes are "more circular than linear" and glory "in ambiguity, in rich layers of meaning." Nevertheless, my father's love of words and good writing—his passion not only for argument but for the beauty of truth that can move the heart—helped awaken my interest in literature.

From my mother, who read stories and poetry to me at bedtime, I derived a fascination for culture four, the visual and performing arts. She took me to the Metropolitan Museum of Art and the Boston Symphony Orchestra before I could determine that these weren't cool things for a boy to like. And so they imprinted themselves on my consciousness. In discussing culture four, O'Malley notes the relationship between liturgy and "ritual performance"; certainly Seiji Ozawa, the legendary music director of the Boston Symphony Orchestra, had the aura of a high priest as he stood, baton in hand, before the orchestra.

In my innocence, I wanted it all, the whole blessed symphony of the four cultures. And of course there was something beautiful and right in that ardent desire. (I would have loved being educated by Jesuits.) But my fall from innocence was this: I hadn't yet understood my limitations and gifts, nor had I fully grasped the state of the world around me.

O'Malley rightly stresses that the differences and clashes between the four cultures are not always about content. They are in many ways about *style,* about forms of thought and discourse. The classic example he uses is the debate between Erasmus and Luther on free will. The two men shared many ideas, including a passion for reforming the church, and yet the clash between them was not merely about ideas. Luther spoke in the language of prophetic absolutes, while Erasmus the humanist preferred caution, nuance, and ambiguity—the accumulation of many small truths, rendered beautiful by art, to the monolithically proclaimed truth.

While each of the cultures has its virtues and vices, I came to fear the increasingly imperial claims of the prophetic and academic cultures—at least in the postmodern America in which I came to maturity. A number of the essays in Part One deal with my response to the "culture wars," which seem to me a conflict between politicized, ideological forms of the prophetic and academic cultures (which often used the arts as an arena in which to fight their battles). Those essays trace a journey that may appear, on the surface, to recount my flight from the conservative intellectual movement— the movement that nurtured me and gave me my start in the world. But I prefer to believe that the path I've trod remains true to the deepest wisdom of conservatism.

It may seem odd to criticize a postmodern academic culture that has called into question our capacity to know the truth. But the reality is that this academic culture has failed to take the best insights of postmodernism into account as an incentive to humility, preferring to smuggle its contentious, abstract claims to truth in through the back door. In any case, public discourse has increasingly come to be dominated by warring academic elites; there are fewer and fewer men and women of "letters"—non-academic artists and writers who balance a passion for truth and goodness with the concreteness that beauty demands—involved in the conversation.

At the same time, the acolytes of goodness—whether religious fundamentalists or intolerant secular advocates of tolerance—fire endless salvos from their moralistic fortresses. Just as we lack men and women of letters, so we are without true prophets. But scolds and do-gooders we have aplenty, on both left and right.

The Recovery of Christian Humanism

At a time when goodness and truth, faith and reason, were being so roundly abused, I found myself drawn to the common elements in cultures three and four: beauty and the imagination, which shun ideological abstractions for the realm of flesh and blood. O'Malley says of the Renaissance humanists I came to admire that their imaginative genius consisted in the way they understood *context,* the layers of historical circumstance and symbolic meaning in which ideas inhere. By studying languages and the way they change, the humanists developed the disciplines of history and textual criticism. They sought precision and clarity but they also understood the value of ambiguity, the difficulty of applying grand abstractions to the messiness of daily life.

The humanists also believed that rhetoric was the use of crafted language to speak to specific contexts. Unlike prophecy or analysis, the primary goal of rhetoric is to seek unity, common ground. Far from being ivory tower intellectuals, humanists frequently inhabit the political realm, but they do so as peacemakers, not firebrands. Finding the right word for the right occasion exemplifies this desire for points of connection. And as O'Malley notes, rhetoric aims not just at the head but at the heart.

But consider the low regard in which we hold terms like rhetoric and oratory today. Their meanings have almost become completely reversed, so that they now are synonymous with falsehood and verbal frippery. Such is the politicization of our times that I'm hard pressed to name anyone beyond Wendell Berry capable of bearing the title of orator.

The Renaissance humanists celebrated rhetoric but they also shared a passion for literature, which they called *bonae litterae*, "good letters." Literature and art are even more fully in the camp of beauty; they are in a profound sense, disinterested, without an immediate agenda to push. In art, beauty takes the hard edges off truth and goodness and forces them down to earth, where they have to make sense or be revealed as impostors.

Father O'Malley helped me to see why I've become an advocate for beauty as the necessary agent for rendering the claims of truth and goodness meaningful. To borrow the title of a recent book by Andy Crouch, I have chosen to pursue the task of "culture making" rather than merely critiquing culture.

So this life I'm defending has been spent in the realm of creative writing and the arts, though never in deliberate isolation from the other cultures. In particular, I've been drawn to the ways that prophetic culture can be placed in tension with the imaginative cultures, precisely because they need each other so much. What happens when prophecy meets art, heaven meets earth—when divine imperatives meet the tangled human condition? When two cultures meet, they challenge one another, preventing them from the excesses particular to their own natures. Faith asks art to be about something more than formal virtuosity and to consider that meaning itself is already inherently metaphysical, even religious. Art asks faith to become incarnate in the human condition without compromise—or evasion—and remain compelling.

When a character in Fyodor Dostoevsky's novel *The Idiot* says, "Beauty will save the world," the hyperbole seems over the top. And yet there just may be something profoundly *true* about it. The late Aleksandr Solzhenitsyn—as stern a moralist as the world is ever likely to witness—came to believe in the wisdom of Dostoevsky's insight, as he argues in his acceptance address for the Nobel Prize in Literature. So, too, another writer who experienced the ravages of totalitarianism in the twentieth century came to testify on behalf of beauty. Czeslaw Milosz, in his poem "One More Day," writes,

And though the good is weak, beauty is very strong.

Nonbeing sprawls, everywhere it turns into ash whole expanses of being,

It masquerades in shapes and colors that imitate existence
And no one would know it, if they did not know that it was ugly.
And when people cease to believe that there is good and evil
Only beauty will call to them and save them
So that they still know how to say: this is true and that is false.

Part One

From Ideology to Humanism

1

Beauty Will Save the World

Toward the end of my undergraduate days, I came across a passage in Aleksandr Solzhenitsyn's "Nobel Lecture" which I found startling and even a bit disturbing. Solzhenitsyn begins his address on the nature and role of literature with a brief, enigmatic quotation from Dostoevsky: "Beauty will save the world." Solzhenitsyn confesses that the phrase had puzzled and intrigued him for some time. And yet, he told the distinguished audience, he had come to believe that Dostoevsky was right.

For a young college student, possessed of a boundless confidence in rational debate and political action, the implication that beauty alone could harbor such redemptive powers was unsettling, to say the least. It was the kind of idea one would expect of an Oscar Wilde or some other fin de siècle decadent; it seemed perilously close to a hedonistic endorsement of "art for art's sake." What of truth and goodness, the other two "transcendentals"? And yet here were two great Russian novelists, known for their stern, prophetic, and intensely moral sensibilities, as well as for their stark depictions of nihilism and human degradation, applauding the redemptive force of beauty.

But the phrase stuck in my mind, and found corroboration in my studies of the role of the imagination in the social order. Like Solzhenitsyn, I have been won over by Dostoevsky's wisdom. Whereas I once believed that the decadence of the West could only be turned around through politics and intellectual dialectics, I am now convinced that authentic renewal can only emerge out of the imaginative visions of the artist and the mystic. This does

1

not mean that I have withdrawn into some anti-intellectual Palace of Art. Rather, it involves the conviction that politics and rhetoric are not autonomous forces, but are shaped by the pre-political roots of culture: myth, metaphor, and spiritual experience as recorded by the artist and the saint.

My own vocation, as I have come to understand it, is to explore the relationship between religion, art, and culture in order to discover how the imagination may "redeem the time." In the process of discovering this vocation, conservatism played a paradoxical role: it both inspired and hampered my search. On the one hand, conservative thinkers helped me to understand what culture is, and they introduced me to the riches of our Western heritage. But on the other hand I found that conservatives were so deeply alienated from modern culture that they had retreated from any serious engagement with it. This retreat, it seems to me, has had damaging consequences for the long-term success of the conservative mission.

For a time, I concurred with most conservatives in their wholesale rejection of modern culture. But eventually I saw this as a very un-conservative position to take. A culture is a delicate, organic thing; however ill it may become, we simply cannot stop caring for it and shut down the life-support machines. When a civilization truly dies, it cannot easily be resurrected.

In what follows, I'd like to retrace of few of the steps that led to my sense of vocation and current ambivalence about the conservative attitude toward culture and the redemptive power of the imagination.

Literature in the Waste Land

I was singularly fortunate in having two distinguished conservative scholars, Russell Kirk and Gerhart Niemeyer, as teachers throughout my undergraduate years. They took me—a raw youth very much caught up in the ephemera of the present—and provided me with a past. By grounding me in the Western tradition, they taught me, in M. E. Bradford's phrase, the importance of "remembering who we are." Only then was I prepared to return to the present. Armed with that knowledge, I became aware that the crisis of modernity was not merely the work of Democrats and Communists, but the product of a deeper spiritual malaise.

The essence of modernity, according to Kirk and Niemeyer, is the denial that man can know and conform to the transcendent order, so that he must therefore construct his own order, as an extension of his mind. The motto of the modern project was first uttered by Francis Bacon, who said that "knowledge is power." Later, Karl Marx would proclaim, "The philosophers have only interpreted the world in various ways; the point is to change it." The political expression of modernity, of course, is the ideological regime, founded on a rigid system of abstractions which are imposed on society by force.

But totalitarian regimes are not the only expression of ideology, or else the dissolution of the Soviet Union would signal the end of modernity. As Kirk, Niemeyer, and other conservatives, such as Richard Weaver, have pointed out, ideology also infects Western liberal societies. Though it can take many forms—logical positivism, deconstruction, and so on—ideology involves a fundamental alienation from being.

While ideology often claims the certainties of an absolutist intellectual system, its effects on the actual experiences of individuals tend to produce feelings of alienation and dislocation. The modern project, which began with the elevation of the self and the assertion of its nearly limitless power, has resulted in a world in which the individual self is a precarious fragment, without ties to true community or allegiance to legitimate authority.

Of course, the alienated self, wavering between dreams of power and bouts of angst, is the subject of most of modern art and literature. Given my love of literature, it was the work of the poets, novelists, and playwrights who explored the fallout of modernity that most attracted me. From Niemeyer I received insights into the novels of Dostoevsky, Solzhenitsyn, Arthur Koestler, and Thomas Mann. And from Kirk I was introduced to T. S. Eliot, Ezra Pound, and Wyndham Lewis—a group of extraordinary writers who were once known as the "Men of 1914."

The figure of Eliot, however, loomed largest in my mind. Eliot was not only the subtlest chronicler of the modern malaise, but also the most reliable guide out of the morass. In poems like "Gerontion" and "The Love Song of J. Alfred Prufrock" Eliot portrays, in dramatic monologues, the alienated, detached, and despairing modern self. Eliot's *Waste Land* gave the age its appropriate metaphor. Yet even in this poem of spiritual aridity, Eliot reveals his struggle for spiritual healing, listening to "What the Thunder Said." From the images of hell and limbo in the early poems, Eliot moves on to the experience of purgatory in *Ash Wednesday*. Finally, his *Four Quartets* speak of the irradiation of grace into the world, and of redemption through suffering. This final masterpiece records the journey of the isolated self toward integration, which includes a renewed sense of the presence of the past, and fleeting glimpses of union with God.

What gave added excitement to studying Eliot with Kirk was that he had *known* Eliot and Eliot's friends, Wyndham Lewis and Roy Campbell. I have always been fascinated by the literary and intellectual communities formed by writers with similar insights into their age, such as Samuel Johnson's "Club" and C. S. Lewis's Inklings. These meetings of the minds seem to me to be the essence of living culture, models of artists-in-community engaged with the challenges and opportunities of their time. Even though Kirk had known these writers only in their later years, I felt somehow touched by their vital presence, a fellow participant in their imaginative endeavors.

Modernity vs. Modernism

But there was a contradiction in my thinking at the time that slowly worked itself up to the surface of my mind. Like many conservatives I extolled Eliot as the supreme critic of the modern wasteland, which had produced art and literature characterized by chaos and fragmentation, squalor and ugliness, egotism, sensual excess, and an obsession with primitive paganism as opposed to Western Christianity. Yet I counted among my heroes Eliot and Wyndham Lewis, whose works were prime examples of the aesthetics of High Modernism. How could these facts be reconciled?

When I compared Eliot's works to those of Stravinsky and Picasso—two modern villains in the conservative hall of infamy—I could not help noticing striking similarities. All three employed the technique of fragmentation of time and space. One could plausibly argue that Eliot's *Waste Land* is a Cubist poem, a series of disjointed angles and multiple perspectives. Both Eliot and Picasso were aware that technology and ideology had fragmented our perception of reality; in their art, they used that fragmentation as a starting point, and sought to move through it to new visions of unity.

Another example of the conservative attack on "modern art" concerns the issue of paganism. Here, too, I found that the reality was more subtle than the caricature. Just as Stravinsky's *Rite of Spring* evoked a pagan ritual and Picasso's *Les Demoiselles D'Avignon* used African tribal masks, so Eliot in *The Waste Land* brought in primitive vegetation myths, as well as the insights of Buddhism and Hinduism. I found that all three artists were interested in paganism precisely because it seemed to possess the awe, sacramentality, and reverence for mystery that had been drained out of late nineteenth-century bourgeois liberal Christianity.

As it happens, Stravinsky, like Eliot, went on to become an orthodox

Christian and a self-described "classicist." Picasso did not make such a pilgrimage, nor did his life reflect a depth of spiritual understanding or moral rectitude. But to deny the imaginative insight Picasso possessed on the basis of his intellectual and moral failings, I came to realize, was both petty and closed-minded. Similarly, when I read D. H. Lawrence I found a penetrating critique of technology and the modern dichotomy between mind and body. Yet I have found that most conservatives prefer to dismiss Lawrence on the basis of his ideas about sexual liberation. Though it may seem a truism to most people, it eventually dawned on me that one can learn from an artist or thinker who asks the right questions, even if one may disagree with many of his answers.

Thus I was forced to account for the fact that many conservatives had succumbed to philistinism. Why did they utter these blanket condemnations of "modern art"? Why would anyone demand that art—a subtle medium, characterized by the indirections of irony, ambiguity, and hidden meaning—preach the "truth" directly? Why categorize artists and writers as good or bad in terms of ideology, rather than of imaginative vision?

The root of the problem, I believe, is a misunderstanding of, or aversion to, the nature of the imagination itself. Part of this can be traced to the Puritan and pragmatic strains in the American character. Conservatives have, by and large, focused their energies on political action and the theoretical work necessary to undertake action. The indirection of art, with its lack of moralizing and categorizing, strikes the pragmatic mind as being unedifying, and thus as inessential. Insofar as the great artists and writers of the past are admired, it is for their support of some idea, rather than for the complex, many-sided vision of their art.

The artist, like anyone else, is a representative of his time. His role, to paraphrase Hamlet, is to reveal "the form and pressure of the age." By "pressure," Shakespeare means impression or stamp. While it is true that some art can portray the ideal, the primary burden of art is to grapple with the reality of the present. Only by engaging the present can art achieve universal meaning. Modern artists create works that reflect modern conditions; they explore modernity, as it were, from the inside. The least imaginative of them merely reflect the surface of things. But the great artists dramatize the conflicts of their time, embedding meaning deep within their works.

It was Eliot himself who formulated the best response to those who want art merely to depict idealized forms of beauty. "We mean all sorts of things, I know, by Beauty. But the essential advantage for a poet is not to have a beautiful world with which to deal. It is to be able to see beneath both beauty and ugliness; to see the boredom, and the horror, and the glory." Eliot's perception is the natural extension of Dostoevsky's prophecy that "Beauty will save the world." Just as Christians believe that God became man so that He could reach into, and atone for, the pain and isolation of sin, so the artist descends into disorder so that he might discover a redemptive path toward order.

When it comes to culture, most conservatives are not conservative at all. As Burke, the father of modern conservatism, understood, the outward forms of society must change over time, but in such a way as to preserve the essence or underlying truth of human nature. So it is with art. New artistic styles begin in revolution (Gothic architecture came as a shock to those steeped in Romanesque), but such revolts are against a style that has ossified and lost its capacity to bear meaning.

Eliot, Picasso, and Stravinsky wanted to break out of a lifeless and complacent materialism. They wanted art to be able to do more than describe the surface of things or provide uplifting images of an ideal world. They wanted to shock, not merely to be sensational, but in the sense that the artist can help us see the world anew, as if for the first time, with a shock of recognition.

Ironically, I found that the conservative thinker Richard Weaver, with whom I agreed so thoroughly on most issues, represented the modern-art-is-degraded school of thought. In the chapter of *Ideas Have Consequences* entitled "Egotism in Work and Art," Weaver presents the classic notion of the West as experiencing a straight line of descent from the high point of the Middle Ages to the nadir of the twentieth century. His dismissals of Romanticism, Modernism, and jazz appear to stem naturally from his critique of modernity. But even Weaver seems oblivious to the notion that artists can burrow inside the reigning worldview, however decadent, and emerge with insights that offer visions of order. He can satirize the self-indulgence of Shelley's "I fall upon the thorns of life, I bleed," but he says nothing of Wordsworth's and Coleridge's attempts to recover a sense of the self's relation to transcendence. And his critique of jazz as mere incoherence is a colossal misconception of the high level of order embodied within improvisation.

Most conservatives think of culture as a museum, rather than as an organic continuity. They are all in favor of promoting the classics, but when it comes to contemporary culture, they have simply opted out. To be sure, the modern era has been cursed with a tremendous amount of shoddy, obscene, and meretricious art; everyone has his own list of the scandalous and sensational works that he is tempted to say represent the art of his own time. One can argue that High Modernism reached its limit and had to go the way of all artistic styles. But, to quote an ancient dictum, *abusus non tollit usus.* The abuse of a thing does not nullify its proper use. If conservatives would look about themselves, they would see that our century has also been blessed with a tremendous amount of superb art. It is perhaps another truism to say that art tends to flourish when civilizations are in crisis.

Politicization or Imagination?

There is another aspect to the conservative abandonment of culture I find distressing: the increasing politicization within the conservative movement. I have witnessed a movement which began with the insights of thinkers like Kirk into the primacy of imaginative vision, or what Weaver called "the metaphysical dream," turn into a highly politicized phenomenon in which there is more discussion of means than understanding of the ends of human existence.

Despite the gains which conservatives have made since 1980 in politics and economics, they have made precious little progress in the realm of culture. In other words, conservatives have not had much of an impact on the major cultural organs, such as the leading newspapers and magazines, nor have they made their presence felt in literature, criticism, and the visual and performing arts. Samuel Lipman's lecture at the Heritage Foundation, "Can We Save Culture?" (reprinted in an abridged form in *National Review,* August 26, 1991), has called attention to this problem. Though Lipman does not penetrate deeply enough into the causes of the conservative retreat from culture, I strongly agree with his description of the symptoms and his concern.

As Lipman argues, liberals have always known the importance of culture; conservatives have left culture in their hands by default. That is why the neoconservatives, who are ex-liberals, have produced *New Criterion,* the only serious journal of the arts emerging from a conservative perspective. The problem I have with *New Criterion* is that its raison d'être is ultimately political. It is bound together primarily because its contributors object to the excesses of the Left's cultural agenda. In other words, it does not arise from a shared aesthetic vision founded on a philosophical and theological understanding of human nature. On the other hand, I have to admit, with a good deal of chagrin, that traditionalist conservatives have been so beset by philistinism that they have produced no alternative of their own.

While such a state of affairs is distressing, it also implies that opportunities abound for conservatives—if they are willing to make the necessary investment of heart and mind. They cannot continue to trim the upper branches of politics while the roots of culture wither and die from inattention. Conservatives, above all, must once again put contemplation before action, or else their energies will be wasted.

No doubt this approach will strike most people as counter-intuitive: for generations now, our minds have been trained to stress the pragmatic over the beautiful. But the power of art to move the heart and thus, bring real change to the world might best be summed up in the words of a character in Mark Helprin's novel, *A Soldier of the Great War*. An Italian professor of aesthetics, a man who has been scarred by the cataclysms and tragedies of the modern world, tries to explain the power of art:

> My conceits will never serve to wake the dead. Art has no limit but that. You may come enchantingly close, and you may wither under the power of its lash, but you cannot bring back the dead. It's as if God set loose the powers of art so that man could come so close to His precincts as almost to understand how He works, but in the end He closes the door in your face, and says, Leave it to me. It's as if the whole thing were just a lesson. To see the beauty of the world is to put your hands on the lines that run uninterrupted through life and through death. Touching them is an act of hope, for perhaps someone on the other side, if there is another side, is touching them, too.

If art cannot save our souls, it can do much to redeem the time, to give us a true image of ourselves, both in the horror and the boredom to which we can descend, and in the glory which we may, in rare moments, be privileged to glimpse.

2

A Portrait of the Editor as a Young Man

I've been asked to relate my work as the editor of a quarterly journal of literature and the arts to the larger theme of this gathering: the patterns of Catholic civic engagement in America today. The more I thought about this assignment, the more convinced I became that the best way to address it was to attempt something of a self-portrait, to describe both the evolution of my ideas and some of the reasons for my conversion to the Catholic church.

You might say that I was born with the conservative intellectual movement's silver spoon in my mouth. As early as the 1950s my father was at the center of the emerging conservative intellectual movement. At that time he worked for a small foundation in a suburb of New York that promoted the virtues of the free market. He recalls that William F. Buckley Jr. came there to discuss the idea of starting up a magazine to be called *National Review*.

By the time I got to college age it was only natural that I would go to the academic mecca of conservatism in America, Hillsdale College in Michigan. In the late 1970s two great scholars taught there as visiting professors, Russell Kirk and Gerhart Niemeyer. More than fifty years after its publication, Kirk's *Conservative Mind* (1953) remains a brilliant, graceful synthesis of European and American traditionalist ideas from Edmund Burke to T. S. Eliot. Though the movement Kirk helped to launch would later degenerate into a large, fractious coalition dominated by Washington-based think tanks, his own thought manifests an amplitude of mind and heart that cannot be reduced to a manifesto.

Gerhart Niemeyer, an émigré political philosopher who had escaped from Nazi Germany, spent his life trying to understand the emergence of modern ideologies. Commuting to Hillsdale from Notre Dame, where he had taught for most of his career, Niemeyer would not only guide his students through the philosophies of Plato, Augustine, Rousseau, and Marx, but also through the literary visions of Dostoevsky, Musil, Trilling, and Solzhenitsyn.

After a one-semester flirtation with libertarianism, I quickly apprenticed myself to Kirk and Niemeyer. They established their conservative visions on a rich synthesis of literature, history, philosophy, and theology. In short, they espoused a form of Christian humanism that I found deeply moving. By comparison, the political and economic nostrums touted by others at Hillsdale as the practical manifestations of conservatism seemed brittle and thin. They were piping voices compared to the deep organ chords of Dante and Aristotle, Aquinas and Newman, whom I was reading with Kirk and Niemeyer.

A Cognitive Dissonance

Even with the help of these two great thinkers, I still experienced what I can only call "cognitive dissonance" in a variety of forms. This was particularly true when it came to literature and the arts, which I had discovered as my true passion. In my youthful ardor, I embraced the notion, espoused by many conservatives, that "modernity" was a monolithic, and very bad, thing. In the arts this entailed a repudiation of Modern Art (the words were always capitalized). It was well known that Modern Art was all about chaos and fragmentation, unfettered sexuality, the occult, and so on. It lacked order, unity, and nobility. So I decided that I would become a culture warrior whose mission was to go off and slay the beast of modernity.

Reading T. S. Eliot with Russell Kirk, the cognitive dissonances became more pronounced. I gravitated toward Eliot's conservatism, which he once expressed by declaring himself "a royalist in politics, an Anglo-Catholic in religion, and a classicist in style." This was a mantra ready-made for me. But the more I read his poetry, the more I found a disparity between his supposed classicism and the messy, fragmented, subjective dimensions of his poetic language. I discovered that Eliot came to regret that profession of his allegiances, and I tried to mature with him.

Since Eliot was clearly employing the fragmented modernist style that I had believed was part of the problem, further revisions in my thinking were necessary. It dawned on me that Eliot was seeking to embrace ancient truths, but in the artistic idiom of his day. Rather than impose a false classical order over his inner disorder, Eliot worked *through* his own chaos, shoring up fragments against his ruin.

As I pursued the implications of this line of thought, I looked around to see whether my fellow conservatives were engaging the culture of their own time. I found that they were deeply alienated from the world around them—that they had, in essence, despaired of conserving any cultural legacy. Whether consciously or not, they believed that Western civilization had died at some point in the past (some favored 1300, others 1832 or 1914). With the example of Eliot before me, I couldn't accept such a position.

I also noticed that with this form of tacit despair came rage, which explained why conservatives were always furious: they had no tradition left to conserve.

The more I studied literature and the arts, the more I realized that they show us that the world is far more ambiguous than we think. Under the tutelage of Kirk and Niemeyer I had learned that the conservative vision—shaped by the imaginative vision of the great writers and artists—was profoundly aware of the ambiguity of human life; it was precisely that awareness that led many conservatives to a sense of humility, of how difficult it is to change the world through direct political action. And yet it became more and more difficult to reconcile this truth with the ideological absolutism of the community in which I lived and worked.

I lost the last of my enthusiasm for conservatism as a political force soon after graduating from Hillsdale. I was at *National Review* in the summer and fall of 1980 during the final run-up to Ronald Reagan's election. For a time after the election I was caught up in the euphoria, but deep down I had moved on. A few days after the election, the phones at *NR* and other conservative organizations began ringing off the hook as people jockeyed for positions in the new administration, including jobs in departments these stalwarts had resolutely pledged to abolish. My euphoria evaporated and was replaced by something closer to moral revulsion.

The Tragic Sense of Life

I went off to Oxford University and immersed myself in literary studies and theological reflection. Throughout the evolution of my ideas about politics and culture, I had also been on a spiritual journey. Having moved through several Protestant denominations in my undergraduate years, I had arrived at the threshold of the Catholic Church.

Catholicism appealed to me because it offered a corrective vision to the individualism, triumphalism, and politicization of the conservative movement. I was drawn by many facets of Catholicism, including its communitarian ethos and sacramental vision.

But what ultimately drew me to the church was another facet, one about which too little is spoken. It's what the great Basque philosopher Miguel de Unamuno called "the tragic sense of life." At the center of this sensibility is a profound awareness of the ambiguities and divisions within the human heart, along with a stress on the importance of suffering and contemplation. I came to understand why Catholics venerate the crucifix, not the empty cross, why they are haunted by the words to Mary that "a sword shall pierce your side also."

There have been times when critics have confused the tragic sense with mere fatalism, but I suspect that is because Americans still suffer from the illusion that they can escape tragedy and remake themselves in the process. The truth, as I came to see it, is that the tragic sense of life is the ultimate antidote to religious arrogance and sentimentality, as well as to the ideological triumphalisms of Right and Left.

During my two years at Oxford, my instructors in the faith were the leading novelists of what has loosely been called the Catholic Literary Revival: Georges Bernanos and François Mauriac, Graham Greene and Evelyn Waugh, Walker Percy and Flannery O'Connor. For all their differences of personality, literary style, and politics, every one of these writers explored the tragic dimension of the Catholic worldview. Like T. S. Eliot, they synthesized modern concerns—from existentialism to scientism—with the truths of the ancient faith. Far from causing them to write safe, didactic tales, their Catholicism encouraged them to render in dramatic form the paradoxes of faith for an increasingly secular audience. Their characters—including the country priest and the whisky priest, Charles Ryder and Hazel Motes—learned the painful lesson that happiness and blessedness are not the same thing, that the church calls us to make a choice "costing not less than everything" (Eliot).

Where some saw only gloomy, depressing stories, I found liberation. "All is grace," Bernanos's country priest concludes, just before he dies. At the end of my time at Oxford, I was received into the church, embracing (I hoped) a costlier but more durable grace.

A Two-Edged Sword

A few years later I found a way to live out the best part of my conservative education *and* address the need for a deeper engagement between religious faith and contemporary culture. I launched a quarterly journal of literature and the arts called *Image,* whose purpose is to feature original creative work that grapples with the Judeo-Christian tradition. The journal is a two-edged sword: a challenge both to the secular critics convinced that religion can no longer inform great art and to those believers who, like my old conservative comrades, are convinced that the Western tradition is dead and buried.

Image is also a response to the hyper-politicization of our social order, a process that has been most visible in the so-called culture wars. There is some debate about just how deep the divisions of the culture wars go, but I think it's fair to say that at the level of public discourse, we have witnessed a slide into increasingly shrill, utopian ideological rhetoric on both sides of the aisle.

Politics may be a noble calling, but it is always in danger of becoming an end in itself. Political struggles take place over issues that are defined by the underlying culture. And culture, in turn, is nourished by art and religion. With all respect to my elders and betters, I think my generation, which grew up after the 1960s, is less interested in manning the ideological battlements and more interested in cultivating the spiritual and imaginative sources of our common life.

When I founded *Image* I feared that it would be nothing more than an obscure outpost. Little did I know that the culture was heading straight for us. When the Berlin Wall came down in 1989, Karl Marx was not the only modern thinker whose "master narrative" about human nature was discredited; Sigmund Freud also got demoted—at least the anti-religious Freud who wrote off religious faith as mere wish fulfillment. No longer do literary critics routinely assume that the appearance of religious experience in a novel short-circuits the drama and realism of the work. Religious writers and artists are gaining respect. *Image* is attempting to foster that process: in addition to publishing the journal we hold a summer workshop and an annual conference.

Of course, Catholics are playing a central role in this revival of art that grapples with faith. Think of writers like Oscar Hijuelos, Alice McDermott, Ron Hansen, Annie Dillard, Richard Rodriguez, David Plante, Tobias Wolff, Jon Hassler, and poets such as Dana Gioia, Paul Mariani, Brigit Pegeen Kelly, and the late Denise Levertov.

I take it as a healthy sign that there is no *school* of Catholic writers, that the group I've just listed is marked by a tremendous diversity of styles and sensibilities. We don't have figures today like Flannery O'Connor and Walker Percy who might be capitalized by the critics as Catholic Authors. While we should mourn that to some extent—O'Connor and Percy *were* profoundly Catholic writers whose works manifested philosophical depth and prophetic wisdom—there are plenty of reasons to celebrate the fact that fewer writers are being pigeonholed by their denominational allegiances.

Contemporary Catholic writers are in some ways less ambitious than their predecessors from the twentieth century. Today's Catholic writers are describing more intimate and familiar worlds. Instead of O'Connor's belief in the need to shout for a hard-of-hearing secular audience, we are more likely to find writers these days choosing to whisper. Alice McDermott's *Charming Billy* and Oscar Hijuelos's *Mr. Ives' Christmas* are both portraits of sanctity and suffering, but their take on the "tragic sense of life" is quiet and unassuming when contrasted with the stark, existential dramas of the whisky and country priests.

It goes without saying that many contemporary Catholic writers have troubled or anguished relationships with the church. The metaphor of Jacob wrestling the angel is frequently invoked these days. But this still represents a significant shift: there's less anger, less irony, and less willingness to turn one's back on the church in the leading Catholic writers today than was the case thirty years ago. If these authors are beset by doubts, they are also less likely to condemn the institutional church out of hand.

Beyond the Culture Wars

If I've had a recurring frustration over the years, it's been the difficulty of getting people to listen to good news. The relentless negativism of the culture wars and the suspicion of imagination that run deep in our American religious tradition remain potent forces. Despite the aesthetic richness of our tradition, American Catholics are not exempt from these forces. A great deal of education needs to take place. Seminaries should offer more courses in literature and the arts. The bishops could use a refresher course or two: their responses to controversial works of art like Martin Scorsese's film *The Last Temptation of Christ*, for example, have been inept at best.

Then there is the waste that comes with political posturing and name-calling. Conservatives fall back on blanket condemnations of modernity, promoting the sort of art that merely imitates the past (and does so badly). Liberals, while they are more open to contemporary culture, dance around the fact that most of the great modern Catholic writers and thinkers on aesthetics have been deeply traditional when it comes to theology. To quote the tag line from a Kurt Vonnegut novel: so it goes.

At a time when two of our most precious forms of communication—political discourse and reason itself—have been compromised by the divisiveness of ideology, art is one of the few things that can still bind us together. It should be no surprise that beauty—long vilified as hopelessly bourgeois or subjective by modernists and post-modernists alike—is making a comeback. From scholarly books like Elaine Scarry's *On Beauty and Being Just* to such films as *American Beauty*, it is clear that our culture is longing for the liberating and restorative power of creative intuition (to use a phrase of Maritain).

In her book Scarry laments the loss of a transcendent ground for beauty in modern thought. "[I]f the metaphysical realm has vanished, one may feel bereft not only because of the giant deficit left by that vacant realm but because the girl, the bird, the vase, the book now seem unable in their solitude to justify or account for the weight of their own beauty. If each calls out for attention that has no destination beyond itself, each seems more self-centered, too fragile to support the gravity of our immense regard."

Place this alongside this thought from von Balthasar: "Our situation today shows that beauty demands for itself at least as much courage and decision as do truth and goodness, and she will not allow herself to be separated and banned from her two sisters without taking them along with herself in an act of mysterious vengeance. We can be sure that whoever sneers at her name as if she were the ornament of a bourgeois past . . . can no longer pray and soon will no longer be able to love."

As forbidding as these two quotations may appear at first, I find them liberating. The problem that von Balthasar sets out—the danger of a social order in which truth and goodness are stressed at the expense of beauty—speaks directly to my own struggle to find an integrated vision in a polarized time. Taken together, these two statements suggest not only the enormous challenges facing our politicized society but also the possibility of a theological aesthetic that can heal and unite. The communitarian, sacramental, and tragic dimensions of the Catholic tradition grew out of a faith attuned to beauty. The effort to renew this tradition through literature and the arts shapes my own form of Catholic civil engagement.

3

Art, Faith, and the Stewardship of Culture

Has there ever been a time when the public has been more alienated from the world of contemporary art—the art being produced in its own day and age? It's hard to imagine. That alienation is obvious when it comes to the visual arts and classical music, but even to some extent respecting the serious literature of our time. The reasons for this estrangement are numerous and go beyond our era's love affair with pop culture and the general dumbing down of our society. There are more complex factors at work here, factors that include everything from the emergence of modern art forms a century ago to the changing roles of technology, media, and the economics of making and "consuming" art.

What I would like to focus on in this essay, however, is the more specific issue of the uneasy relationship between Christians and contemporary culture. I have spent a great deal of time reflecting on the role of art and the imagination in the contemporary church. While there are many hopeful signs in the church and in our culture as a whole, there are also some disturbing trends.

It is my conviction that the Christian community, despite its many laudable efforts to preserve traditional morality and the social fabric, has abdicated its stewardship of culture and, more importantly, has frequently chosen ideology rather than imagination when approaching the challenges of the present.

If this approach remains the dominant one, then the community of believers will be squandering a remarkable opportunity. There are innumerable signs in our society that people are hungering for a deeper spiritual life. Baby Boomers are aging and feeling guilty about their youthful abandonment of religion. There may be more genuine openness to religious faith—in the sense of curiosity and yearning—than at almost any time in a century. One of the powerful ways that believers can speak to that yearning is through the arts—and through faith that is leavened by the human imagination. Whether the church will respond or not will determine its willingness to be a steward of culture.

Christianity and Culture: Finding the Balance

There is no doubt that we live in a fragmented and secularized society— the polar opposite of the unified Christian culture that writers like Dante, Chaucer, and Milton took for granted when they penned their religious poems, or that Fra Angelico and Michelangelo assumed when they painted church walls and ceilings. The twentieth century witnessed art that frequently mocked religious faith, indulged in nihilism and despair, and engaged in political propaganda. Many artists have created works that are so difficult to apprehend that the disjuncture between the "elitist" art world and the "populist" world of art consumption has widened into a dark chasm. The estrangement between the creators of art and their public is one of the facts we all take for granted.

Within the Christian community there have been many different approaches to modern culture. Some of the mainline denominations have followed a liberal ethos that welcomes new trends in secular culture. Evangelicals and fundamentalists have moved in the opposite direction, retreating into a fortress mentality and distrusting the "worldly" products of mainstream culture—so much so that they have created an alternative subculture. To simplify somewhat, you might say that whereas liberals lack Christian discernment about culture, conservatives have just withdrawn from culture.

Among Christians who care about the arts, there are many who cling to the works of a few figures, such as J. R. R. Tolkien, T. S. Eliot, and Flannery O'Connor, who have forged a compelling religious vision in the midst of a secular age. But the danger in celebrating these Christian artists is that we isolate them from their cultural context, from the influences that shaped their art. There is a large body of believers who have essentially given up on contemporary culture; they may admire a few writers here or there, but they do not really believe that Western culture can produce anything that might inform and deepen their own faith. One might almost say that these individuals have given in to despair about our time. For me, the most depressing trend of all is the extent to which Christians have belittled or ignored the imagination and succumbed to politicized and ideological thinking.

The Dark Side of the Culture Wars

Perhaps the best way to get a purchase on this situation is by looking into the phrase that has come to describe the present social and political climate—the phenomenon known as the "culture wars." In his book on the subject, the sociologist James Davison Hunter describes the two warring factions as the progressives and the traditionalists (terms that are synonyms for liberals and conservatives). The progressives are, by and large, secularists who believe that the old Judeo-Christian moral codes are far too restrictive; they actively campaign for new definitions of sexuality, the family, and the traditional ideas about birth and death—the "life" issues. Traditionalists, clinging to what they see as the perennial truths of their religious and cultural heritage, wage a rear-guard action against the innovations wrought by the progressives. Issues such as abortion and euthanasia, homosexuality and the family, school prayer and other church and state conflicts lie at the heart of the culture wars. The stakes are extremely high and the struggle is fierce and bloody—and likely to become even more intense.

I do not wish to quarrel with this description of our cultural politics, nor do I want to suggest that these issues are not crucial to the survival of our social fabric. But I confess that I am astonished by the lack of attention most religious believers have shown to what I call the dark side of the culture wars. The dominance of the culture wars over our public discourse is a striking example of how politicized we have become. It was once a universally accepted notion that politics grows out of culture—that the profound insights of art, religion, scholarship, and local custom ultimately shape the terms of political debate. Somewhere in our history we passed a divide where politics began to be more highly valued than culture.

It is not difficult to find evidence for this assertion. Take, for example, the rise of single-issue politics and the plethora of political pressure groups and the lengths to which politicians go to court such groups. Above all, there is the shrillness and one-dimensionality of most political rhetoric. The quality of public discourse has degenerated into shouting matches between bands of professional crusaders. As James Davison Hunter has put it, the culture wars consist of "competing utopian politics that will not rest until there is complete victory." The result, Hunter concludes, is that "the only thing left to order public life is power. This is why we invest so much into politics."

Even in the circles where I grew to maturity—including the conservative intellectual movement and the many Christian organizations dedicated to defending religious orthodoxy—I have come to see a dangerous narrowing of perspective, an increasingly brittle and extreme frame of mind. Coverage of the arts in conservative and Christian journals is almost nonexistent. Again and again I have seen the emphasis in these circles shift to having the correct opinions and winning political victories rather than on cultivating a reflective vision and seeking to win the "hearts and minds" of our neighbors.

The very metaphor of war ought to make us pause. The phrase "culture wars" is an oxymoron: culture is about nourishment and cultivation, whereas war inevitably involves destruction and the abandonment of the creative impulse. We are now at the point in the culture wars where we are sending women and children into battle and neglecting to sow the crops in the spring. Clearly we cannot sustain such a total war. In the end, there will be nothing left to fight over.

Imagination and Cultural Renewal

Here is where the realm of literature and art comes into the discussion in two important ways. First, the changing attitudes toward art provide another case study in the narrowing effects of the culture wars. Second, it is my contention that the imagination itself is the key to the cultural and spiritual renewal we so desperately need.

As in any other arena, progressives and conservatives have very different attitudes toward literature and art. Modern progressives have been far more interested in the art of their own time than have conservatives; they have seen it as a subversive force, capable of undermining traditional values and making "alternative lifestyles" more acceptable. In taking this approach, the progressives have touched on one of art's most important functions: to force people to look at the status quo in a new way and to challenge them to change it for the better. From the satires of Euripides and Swift to the novels of Dickens and Flaubert and beyond, great art has engaged in the paradoxical activity of constructive subversion.

Unfortunately, the progressives have preferred art that is subversive without a corresponding vision of the deeper wellsprings of human and divine order. Being members of an elite class that is alienated from the traditional social order, they have become associated with art that is frequently nihilistic, or simply amoral. With less and less substance in their works, the artists supported by the progressives have resorted to irony, political propaganda, and sensationalism to elicit a response from their audience. Hence the passing celebrity of figures like Bret Easton Ellis, Karen Finley, Andres Serrano, and Robert Mapplethorpe.

On the other hand, conservatives have been deeply estranged from the art of this century. While they have celebrated artists who have shared their views, including such writers as Yeats, Eliot, Evelyn Waugh, and Walker Percy, conservatives have frequently condemned "modern art" as if it were a monolithic entity. The idea has been that modern art is somehow tainted by a predilection for nihilism, disorder, perverted sexuality, even an indulgence in the occult. Conservatives frequently mock abstract art, experimental fiction, the theater of the absurd, and functionalist architecture. They prefer art that provides uplift and lofty sentiment. Unlike the progressives, conservatives tend toward the populist attitude encapsulated in the phrase: "I don't know much about art, but I know what I like."

A corollary of this conservative alienation from modernity is the tacit assumption that Western culture is already dead. The stark truth is that despair haunts many on the Right. When conservatives turn to art and literature they generally look to the classics, safely tucked away in museums or behind marbleized covers. Ironically, many conservatives don't seem to have noticed that they no longer have anything to conserve—they have lost the thread of cultural continuity. They have forgotten that the Judeo-Christian concept of stewardship applies not only to the environment and to institutions but also to culture. To abdicate this responsibility is somewhat like a farmer refusing to till a field because it has stones and heavy clay in it. The wise farmer knows that with the proper cultivation that soil will become fertile.

The tradition of Christian humanism always held that the secular forms and innovations of a particular time can be assimilated into the larger vision of faith. That is why T. S. Eliot could adapt modernist poetics to his Christian convictions, or Flannery O'Connor could take the nihilistic style of the novelist Nathanael West and bring it into the service of a redemptive worldview. Only a living faith that is in touch with the world around it can exercise this vital mission of cultural transformation.

Because progressives and conservatives are so thoroughly politicized, their approach to art is essentially instrumentalist—as a means to an end, the subject of an op-ed column or a fundraising campaign. Of course, there is a deep strain of pragmatism in the American experience, and it does not take much to call it to the surface. In the context of American Christianity, the Puritan strain has shown a similar tendency toward pragmatism: art becomes useful insofar as it conveys the Christian message.

In a politicized age, constricted by the narrowness of ideology, few people really believe that art provides the necessary contemplative space that pulls us back from the realm of action in order to send us back wiser and more fully human. For Christians, the idea that contemplation and prayer ought to precede action should be second nature. How many of us have become unwitting disciples of Marx, who said that "up till now it has been enough to understand the world; it is for us to change it"? Marx's preference for revolutionary action over the classical-Christian belief in the primacy of contemplative understanding of transcendent order lies at the heart of modern ideology.

Art and Transcendence

Art, like religious faith in general and prayer in particular, has the power to help us transcend the fragmented society we inhabit. We live in a Babel of antagonistic tribes—tribes that speak only the languages of race, class, rights, and ideology. That is why the intuitive language of the imagination is so vital. Reaching deep into our collective thoughts and memories, great art sneaks past our shallow prejudices and brittle opinions to remind us of the complexity and mystery of human existence. The imagination calls us to leave our personalities behind and temporarily to inhabit another's experience, looking at the world with new eyes. Art invites us to meet the Other—whether that be our neighbor or the infinite otherness of God—and to achieve a new wholeness of spirit.

The passion to find reconciliation and redemption is one of the inherently theological aspects of art. Before the modern era, this passion often took the form known as theodicy—the attempt to justify God's ways to man. There are, to be sure, few full-blown theodicies to be found in bookstores and art galleries today, but the same redemptive impulse has been diffracted into dozens of smaller and more intimate stories. We may not have towering figures of intellectual orthodoxy like Eliot, O'Connor, or Walker

Percy living among us, but there are dozens of writers, painters, sculptors, dancers, filmmakers, and architects who struggle with our Judeo-Christian tradition and help to make it new. The renaissance of fiction and poetry with religious themes and experiences is in full swing, from older figures like J. F. Powers, Richard Wilbur, and John Updike to such gifted writers as Annie Dillard, Kathleen Norris, Anne Lamott, Ron Hansen, Louise Erdrich, Elie Wiesel, Larry Woiwode, Doris Betts, Reynolds Price, Chaim Potok, Frederick Buechner, Mark Helprin, Anne Tyler, John Irving, Tobias Wolff, and poets like Scott Cairns, Edward Hirsch, Paul Mariani, Geoffrey Hill, and Donald Hall.

But it is not only in literature that contemporary artists are returning to the perennial matters of faith. Take classical music, for instance. The three best-selling composers in classical music today are Arvo Pärt, John Tavener, and Henryk Gorecki. All of these composers were profoundly affected by the modern musical style known as minimalism. Yet they felt minimalism lacked a spiritual dimension—a sense of longing for the divine. So they returned to the ancient traditions of Gregorian chant and developed music that combines ancient and modern techniques, and which has brought back to contemporary ears the spirit of humility and penitence.

It is true that some of the artists that I've mentioned may not be strictly orthodox on all aspects of doctrine, and many of them remain outside of the institutional church. But many of these figures are faithful Christians or observant Jews. All of the artists I've listed treat religion as one of the defining components of our lives. I think it is fair to say that if this body of art was absorbed and pondered by the majority of Christians, the quality of Christian witness and compassion in our society would be immeasurably strengthened.

Above all, these artists and writers are neither baptizing contemporary culture nor withdrawing from it. In the tradition of Christian humanism, they are reaching out to contemporary culture and using their discernment to find ways to see it in the light of the Gospel. Just as Christ established contact with the humanity of the publicans, prostitutes, and sinners he encountered before he revealed the message of salvation to them, so Christian artists must depict the human condition in all its fullness before they can find ways to express the grace of God. In other words, Christian artists must be confident enough in their faith to be able to explore what it means to be human. At the heart of Christian humanism is the effort to achieve a new synthesis between the condition of the world around us and the unique ways in which grace can speak to that condition. That is how art created by Christians will touch the lives of those who encounter it.

Christian Humanism and the Incarnation

Behind this vision of Christian humanism stands the doctrine of the Incarnation: the complete union of Christ's divine and human natures. The Incarnation is the touchstone against which we can test the rightness of our efforts. That is because we must remember to keep the divine and human perspectives in a healthy balance. Emphasize the human over the divine and you fall into the progressive error; stress the divine over the human and you commit the traditionalist sin. To take just one specific manifestation of this, consider the need to balance God's justice with his mercy. If all the emphasis is on justice, you end up with a harsh, abstract, and legalistic view of the world. But if mercy is all you care about, compassion will become vague and unable to cope with the complex realities of a fallen world.

All great Christian art is incarnational because art itself is the act of uniting form and content, drama and idea, the medium and the message. If art is dominated by a moralistic desire to preach at the audience, it will become lifeless and didactic. We can easily spot didacticism when its message is different from what we believe, but no one who cares about art should confuse it with politics or theology. Art does not work through propositions, but through the indirect, "between the lines" means used by the imagination. We need look no further than the Gospels to be reminded of this fact. Christ's parables are marvels of compressed literary art: they employ irony, humor, satire, and paradox to startle us into a new understanding of our relationship to God. If we are too quick to boil these unsettling stories down to one-dimensional morals, they will no longer detonate in our hearts with the power that Jesus poured into them.

Many believers fear the imagination because it cannot be pinned down. But the imagination is no more untrustworthy than, say, reason. Like any other human faculty, it can be used for good or ill. Imagination, because it draws on intuition, can help us to see when reason has become too abstract, too divorced from reality. In a work of art the artist's imagination calls out to the audience, inviting the reader or viewer or listener to collaborate in the act of discovering meaning. Jesus's parables only find their fulfillment when we puzzle out their meaning, interpreting their ironies and paradoxes.

It is precisely this fear of the imagination that has led many Christians in America to create a subculture with Christian publishers, Christian record labels, and Christian art galleries. The underlying message conveyed by these products is that they are safe; they have the Christian seal of approval. But this is a devil's bargain: in exchange for safety, these products have given up their imaginative power. And this is just where the strangest irony of all emerges. This subculture has rushed to produce Christian versions of almost every secular trend: from Christian heavy metal bands to Christian romance novels to Christian self-help books. But because these products lack the transforming power of the imagination, they are little better than the pop culture trends they imitate.

Ron Hansen: Steward of Mystery and Culture

What is an example of a contemporary work of Christian imagination that truly synthesizes the realities of the culture in which we live with the timeless reality of God's grace? Almost anything by the writers and composers I've listed above would make for a brilliant case study. I could also draw on the work of visual artists, choreographers, singer-songwriters, and many other art forms I haven't yet mentioned. But I will stick to what I know best—literature.

Ron Hansen's *Mariette in Ecstasy*, published in 1979, is a haunting, enigmatic novel that is almost impossible to categorize. What makes *Mariette* especially fascinating is that it deals with a subject that must appear bizarre and esoteric to today's reading public. Set in a Benedictine convent in upstate New York around 1906, it is the story of a young girl who experiences the stigmata, the five wounds of Christ, in her own flesh.

Given the remoteness and abnormality of this world, the expectations and preconceptions of the reader undoubtedly play an important role in how the story is perceived. There is, of course, a long and undistinguished tradition of lurid, melodramatic tales of masochism and smoldering sexuality in the monastic enclosure. The genre, which probably began with Boccaccio's *Decameron*, moves on to nineteenth-century anti-Catholic novels such as *The White Cowl* to contemporary psychological fables such as the film *Agnes of God*.

But if Hansen works with some of the same materials, he has fashioned an altogether more serious and profound exploration of suffering and religious passion. The novel's protagonist, Mariette Baptiste, is the daughter of a possessive, hyper-masculine father; her mother died when she was young. Mariette is an intelligent and strikingly beautiful seventeen-year-old when she enters the convent. She is the type of woman who would cause jealousy, envy, and adoration anywhere she went, including the monastic enclosure.

Rather than using her intelligence and beauty in the more conventional modes of academic achievement and marriage, Mariette withdraws into an intense inner life. She becomes a spiritual prodigy. All of her sensual energy and vivid imagination is channeled into her courtship with her divine lover, Jesus.

Within her first year in the convent, Mariette experiences the trauma of seeing her sister, who is also a nun, killed by cancer at the age of thirty-seven. She undergoes a spiritual crisis in which she loses any sense of Christ's presence. Then, in the midst of this agitation, the stigmata appear on her body; she bleeds from hands, feet, and torso.

When questioned, Mariette claims that the stigmata were given to her by Christ Himself. It becomes clear that, far from being proud and ostentatious about these wounds, Mariette is embarrassed and troubled. The convent is thrown into a turmoil of conflicting opinions and emotional responses.

Here is a subject that is perfectly suited for Freudian analysis. If there was ever a paradigm of repressed sexuality, the apparently masochistic mysticism of the female religious would seem to be it. And yet Ron Hansen's novel makes no attempt to *explain* Mariette's experiences; there is no sense in which the author stands above and outside his protagonist's life, ready to share a knowing look with his reader about this sadly deluded girl. The story is open-ended, allowing the reader to interpret Mariette's experience in any number of ways. That is exactly what happens in the convent, where almost every possible reaction, from adoration to loathing and fear, are evoked by Mariette's stigmata.

The open-endedness of the narrative is not a copout, but a sign of Hansen's respect for mystery, that dimension of the Christian imagination championed by Flannery O'Connor. For the writer who acknowledges mystery, O'Connor held,

> the meaning of a story does not begin except at a depth where adequate motivation and adequate psychology and the various determinations have been exhausted. Such a writer will be interested in what we don't understand rather than in what we do. . . . He will be interested in characters who are forced out to meet evil and grace and who act on a trust beyond themselves—whether they know very clearly what it is they act upon or not.

O'Connor's words describe not only Hansen's vision but also his protagonist's significance. Mariette's psychology is more than adequate. The modern reader, consciously or unconsciously schooled by Freud, will note the eroticism of Mariette's spirituality and be tempted to think that in 1906 repressed sexuality led to religious hallucinations. But Hansen's narrative also takes into account the tradition, from the Song of Songs through Carmelite mysticism, of Eros as a metaphor for the soul's relation to the heavenly bridegroom.

The final level of ambiguity in the novel concerns the perceptions of those who must interpret Mariette's ecstasies. These perceptions are colored by the characters' deepest hopes, fears, and needs. Mariette's stigmata, like any intense and miraculous religious experience, act as a touchstone, revealing the inner lives of those around her. Though such revelations include jealousy, credulity, and anger, Hansen's compassion is broad enough to forgive nearly all of them.

Hansen seems to leave the reader free to embrace almost any explanation of Mariette's stigmata. But he is doing more than that. In leaving the narrative open-ended, the author is asking us to make our own judgments, and thus to confront and question our deepest beliefs and emotions. Despite the strong evidence for the truth of her experience, why is it so hard to let go of our suspicion that Mariette may be nothing more than a brilliant fraud? Is there something in us that refuses to accept such signs of God's grace irrupting into our world?

At the end of the novel, Mother Saint Raphael says to Mariette, "God gives us just enough to seek Him, and never enough to fully find Him. To do more would inhibit our freedom, and our freedom is very dear to God." Taken out of context, this might sound like a relativist's creed, but the prioress is talking, in simple and direct language, about the nature of faith itself.

Hansen draws on modern Freudian notions of human motivation only to suggest that there is a far more profound and satisfying answer to the mystery: Christian faith. Here is a work that truly synthesizes elements of the culture we inhabit with the perennial wisdom of the Christian imagination.

Ron Hansen is a true steward of Christian culture, as are the Christians who read and ponder his vision. His art is neither safe nor predictable; it requires, and rewards, a deep engagement of our imaginative faculties. Such an engagement requires us to invest our own time and passion. This brings me back to my central theme: how committed are we as Christians to nourishing our faith and renewing our society by becoming stewards of culture? Unless we contribute to the renewal of culture by participating in the life of art in our own time, we will find that the barbarians have entered by gates that we ourselves have torn down.

4

Christian Humanism:
A Faith for All Seasons

It is a curious fact that the artist who produced the most compelling and accessible vision of Christian humanism in the twentieth century was a multiply married, luxury-loving, alcoholic atheist by the name of Robert Bolt. It is worth noting that he came to this choice of lifestyle after a strict Methodist upbringing. And I might add that not long after throwing off his Methodist faith, he became a card-carrying member of the Communist Party. I am not sure what conclusions to draw from these facts.

But on a more serious note, I can say with a straight face that Bolt not only remained obsessed by Christianity his whole life, but also continued to think Christianly to the end of his days. He was what might be called a "flying buttress"—someone who remains resolutely outside the church, but who does a great deal to prop it up. In the divine economy, I suspect that there is a mansion in heaven for tortured Augustinian souls like that of Mr. Bolt, and perhaps in God's mercy it has room service.

I cannot remember precisely when I saw the film version of Bolt's play *A Man for All Seasons* for the first time. I think it was sometime during my high school years. But from the moment I first saw the actor Paul Scofield as Sir Thomas More, I was riveted. His masterful blend of gravitas and mirth, stoicism and vulnerability, piety and legal hardball was mesmerizing and energizing. In all my subsequent studies of More's life and thought, I have never had cause to doubt that Bolt caught something profound about the man in his play, however partial and biased a portrait it may be.

The story kept playing in my mind during a difficult transitional period in my life. I had been raised within the conservative intellectual movement. My first job after graduation was at *National Review* magazine, where I ,worked for William F. Buckley Jr. This was the summer and fall of 1980, which as you may recall was the triumphant march to the presidency of Ronald Reagan.

I should have been ecstatic during these weeks and months, and perhaps I was in fits and spurts. But I also frequently found myself depressed and conflicted. The reason was this: the core of my undergraduate education had been an introduction to the spiritual and intellectual depths of the Western tradition, but when I looked at those who claimed to be the defenders of that tradition, I saw only rigid ideologues who had become so politicized they had begun to undermine the very things they thought they were upholding. Slowly but surely I came to believe that the "culture wars," in which I had been trained to fight, represented a dangerous hardening of the national arteries. In short, I began to see the shrill slogans and nostrums of our politicized era like bits of plaque that were accumulating and choking off the flow of dialectic and deliberation, putting the body politic in danger of a heart attack.

I also sensed that religion was deeply implicated in the culture wars, and that disturbed me, because I was trying to forge a Christian worldview in those years. Too often, it seemed to me, Christianity was being reduced to mere polemics and apologetics. While I would grant that these forms of discourse have their place within a larger framework of religious life, I felt that they were choking out other forms of thought and expression, and that in the process they were becoming crude and blunt. They were being used as weapons. The result was that the faith was being stripped of its rich cultural heritage—a heritage that contained more humble, nuanced, and ambiguous understandings of God and man. And I was also developing an intuition throughout this time that there was an older, wiser religious vision that offered the antidote to our brittle, fragmented, polarized society—a vision I sensed in *A Man for All Seasons* and later came to know as Christian humanism.

Christian Humanism: Oxymoron?

Today the phrase Christian humanism sounds like an oxymoron in the ears of most people. The only word that most of us can remember being applied as a modifier is "secular." But it was not always so. Robert Bolt dropped a few breadcrumbs that I would later follow back to the original, and true, source of humanism—that source being the Judeo-Christian faith.

Bolt's play centers around the last years of Thomas More, the great lawyer, orator, and statesman who was eventually beheaded by Henry VIII of England for opposing Henry's divorce of his first wife, Catherine of Aragon. A true Renaissance man, More was not only steeped in the intricacies of the law and an eloquent orator, but he was also one of the leading thinkers of the day, fluent in Greek and Latin, the author of the enigmatic satire *Utopia*, as well as learned tracts on theology and spirituality. He had served as the king's ambassador on the Continent and eventually rose to the highest political post in the land, that of Lord Chancellor.

More was also a leading figure in Renaissance humanism, a movement that numbered among its members some of Europe's brightest stars, including the great Dutch scholar, Desiderius Erasmus.

In *A Man for All Seasons*, More is depicted as a man caught between two extremes, two implacable forces, which might be crudely summarized as church and state. On the one hand, he comes under pressure from his hotheaded future son-in-law William Roper to oppose the King on theological and ecclesiastical grounds. The Spanish ambassador, whose motives are a grab bag of principle and political expediency, urges More to defend Queen Catherine and uphold the decision of the Pope to refuse Henry's request for a divorce. The ambassador plays to More's Catholic loyalties, while also hinting that the Spanish king will reward him handsomely for services rendered. On the other hand, there is the Machiavellian politician Thomas Cromwell, who ruthlessly makes straight the way for Henry's will to power. Cromwell at first tries to enlist More on the side of the king, arguing in terms of Realpolitik, but when More resists, Cromwell resorts to any means he can to trap More, offering bribes, suborning perjury, and planting spies.

Thomas More, Forester

Bolt's play leaves us in no doubt that More is a man of adamantine principle, untouched by petty greed or vanity. A loving husband and father, he also proves to be ahead of his time by taking care that his daughter Margaret receives a superior education. (The need to educate women was, by the way, a key tenet of many Christian humanists of the period.) According to More's most recent (and best) biographer, Peter Ackroyd, Margaret was in fact "the most learned woman of her day." In *A Man for All Seasons*, More tries to fend off Margaret's suitor, William Roper, at first because of his impetuous attacks on corruption in the Catholic Church and his eagerness to join in the cause of Martin Luther's Reformation. What Bolt doesn't reveal in the play, perhaps for the sake of dramatic simplicity, is that More himself was an outspoken critic of meaningless religious superstitions, the selling of indulgences, and other forms of decay within the church.

Indeed, if you listen closely to the opening scene of the play—it is very easy to miss—More's servant enters into a room where More, his wife Alice and daughter Margaret, the Duke of Norfolk, and several others are laughing heartily. The subject of that conversation is the number of corrupt priests. Someone pipes up: "Bishop Fisher says every second bastard born is fathered by a priest these days." Then one member of the party says the priests in a particular region are very holy, to which someone replies, "and therefore very few." More laughs along with everyone else. In short, this group of sophisticated humanists harbors no illusions about the level of corruption in the church: the church is something one can joke about, even if there is a serious, and disturbing, point behind the jest.

Roper, on the other hand, is young, earnest, and keen on church reform. In the play More's attitude toward the impetuous Roper is far from harsh. He turns to Margaret at one point and says, "Nice boy. Terribly strong principles though." A few scenes later Roper reappears, but now he has abjured his Lutheranism and is equally hot to defend the Catholic Church from her enemies. When More objects to Roper's assertion that the enemies of the church are doing the Devil's work, reminding the young man that there are some things which as Lord Chancellor he cannot hear, Roper accuses him of a courtier's "sophistication." Moments later, when an embittered and ambitious man named Richard Rich seems to give away the fact that he is a spy of Cromwell's, More's family call on him to arrest Rich. Margaret calls Rich a "bad man."

> MORE. There is no law against that.
> ROPER. There is! God's law!
> MORE. Then God can arrest him.
> ROPER. Sophistication upon sophistication!
> MORE. No, sheer simplicity. The law, Roper, the law. I know what's legal not what's right. And I'll stick to what's legal.
> ROPER. Then you set man's law above God's!
> MORE. No, far below; but let me draw your attention to a fact—I'm not

God. The currents and eddies of right and wrong, which you find such plain sailing, I can't navigate. I'm no voyager. But in the thickets of the law, oh, there I'm a forester.

When More goes on to say that he would give the Devil the benefit of law, Roper is incredulous. More goes on to ask his prospective son-in-law whether he would cut through the forest of laws in order to get after the Devil. The answer, of course, is a resounding yes. Then More says, "And when the last law was down, and the Devil turned round on you—where would you hide, Roper, the laws all being flat? This country's planted thick with laws from coast to coast—man's laws, not God's—and if you cut them down—and you're just the man to do it—d'you really think you could stand upright in the winds that would blow then?"

Caught between the religious fundamentalism exemplified by Roper and the secular will to power represented by Cromwell, More seeks refuge in the law. The genius of Bolt's play is that we as viewers actually begin to become impatient with More's endless willingness to hide within the minutiae of the law. When even Margaret and Roper, who have demonstrated their support for More, seem to tire of the cat-and-mouse game, More gives one final defense of his tactics, this time with a theological twist. He says to Margaret,

God made the angels to show him splendor—as he made animals for innocence and plants for their simplicity. But Man he made to serve him wittily, in the tangle of his mind! If he suffers us to fall to such a case that there is no escaping, then we may stand to our tackle as best we can, and yes, Will, then we may clamor like champions . . . if we have the spittle for it. And no doubt it delights God to see splendor where He only looked for complexity. But it's God's part, not our own, to bring ourselves to that extremity! Our natural business lies in escaping.

In *A Man for All Seasons*, Bolt does not have the leisure to extrapolate the full range of subtlety of More's thought, and perhaps, as a working playwright, he only intuited the heart of More's philosophy. But from More's voluminous writings, it is clear that he regards the law as the product of human culture. It is, to be sure, an imperfect expression of God's law, but it serves as a mediating force between the abstract principles of heaven and the passions and follies of earth. Even when he said on the scaffold that he died "the king's good servant, but God's first," he did not compromise his belief that the Law of Succession passed by Parliament had essentially contravened legal tradition. According to his biographer, Peter Ackroyd, "He asserted the laws of God and of reason, as they had been inherited, and he simply did not believe that the English parliament could repeal the ordinances of a thousand years."

Bolt rightly has More use the law as his primary metaphor, given his legal and political experience, but it can be argued that many other products of human culture might also be used in much the same way. The brilliant scholar of comparative literature, Virgil Nemoianu, has written that for the humanists "Culture is seen as a kind of tumbling ground for the spiritual, the social, the historical and the psychological. For them the human being individually, and the human species collectively, act as a key, as the intersectional locus where all areas of the cosmos can meet." He continues: "Culture actually behaves as an enormous mediating force between the creaturely and the divine. According to [the Christian humanists], aesthetic culture is that which seeks to articulate the opening toward transcendence that appears as a human constant in all human societies known to us."

The elements of human culture that have drawn me are literature and the arts—another forest of human wit and imagination that softens the pride of abstract ideas and utopian politics. The centerpiece of humanist theories of education was literature—the study of classic Greek and Latin texts such as those of Homer, Aeschylus, Thucydides, Cicero, and Terence. And there was no more eminent champion of this passion for literature than the man who coined the phrase, "A Man for All Seasons," Desiderius Erasmus of Rotterdam.

Erasmus and "Good Letters"

In the summer of 1499, the young Erasmus came to England at the invitation of William Blount, the fourth Baron Mountjoy. During his studies at the University of Paris, Erasmus had supported himself by tutoring younger students, and Mountjoy had been one of them.

When he arrived in England, Erasmus had established only a small reputation, but Mountjoy sensed something extraordinary in his tutor and wanted him to meet England's leading lights. There is a tradition that at the dinner party where Erasmus met Thomas More for the first time, the Dutchman joked that he had come "*ex inferis*"—a Latin pun that could mean he had arrived from the cellar, the Low Countries, or Hell. Latin, of course, was at that time a living language, and would have been the language in which More and Erasmus communicated. But Latin was much more to these men than a way for Europeans of different national origins to converse; it was the foundation of the New Learning, the Renaissance passion for the literature and philosophy of the classical world.

A little later in his visit to England, Erasmus was visited at Mountjoy's Greenwich estate by More and a lawyer friend of More's named Edward Arnold. They invited Erasmus out for a walk. More led them to the royal palace at Eltham, where they met the nine-year-old Prince Henry, the boy who would become King Henry VIII. More and Arnold presented the prince with some "writings" (as Erasmus later put it in his memoir). Erasmus, embarrassed that he had nothing to offer to the young prince, hurried home and produced a poem in honor of England for the future monarch. Erasmus was impressed that More, an outstanding lawyer but not an aristocrat, had such easy access to the royal family.

In fact, the prince's father, Henry VII, had himself become a patron of this school of thinkers whose study of classical literature (*studia humanitatis*) earned them the name of humanists. Prince Harry would benefit from the new educational reforms and techniques instituted by the humanists. When he acceded to the throne, More and Erasmus had every reason to hope that their king, who could write music as well as theological discourses, would become an enlightened ruler, perhaps even the presiding spirit of a new golden age in which government would be more just and equitable and the church free of corruption and superstition.

There was to be no golden age. The approaching storm clouds—of Henry's tyranny, the sundering of the church, and a century of civil war on the continent—were just over the horizon. There can be little doubt, however, that that day in the summer of 1499 was a golden moment, the meeting of two great minds and the beginning of one of the great intellectual friendships of all time.

Myths and misperceptions about Renaissance humanism are legion, including the notion that it constituted a radical break from the Middle Ages, now a thoroughly debunked idea among scholars of those eras. But it is undisputed that the Renaissance was characterized by a passion for *bonae litterae*—literally, Good Letters (a phrase that has no real modern English equivalent), the study of the literature of ancient Greece and Rome. Latin, being the more accessible language, tended to dominate, but most of the major Renaissance humanists also knew Greek.

In a youthful manifesto, the *Antibarbari* (Against the Barbarians), the young Erasmus of Rotterdam argued that the pagan writers, far from being hostages to the Devil, constituted a *praeparatio evangelium*—preparing the hearts and minds of the ancient world for the Gospel message. He had little time for those who said that the pagan writers were demons who would corrupt the faithful. "These people say, 'Am I to carry books by damned men in my hand and in my bosom, and read them all over again and reverence them? Virgil is burning in hell, and is a Christian going to read his poems?' As if many a Christian were not burning there too, whose writing—if any good ones survive—would not be shunned for that reason by anybody."

Underlying the Christian humanist vision is a theological conviction that the Fall of man had damaged, but not obliterated, human nature. Thus the pagan writers, while they did not have the benefit of divine revelation, could approach, if not fully reach, the deepest truths about man's place in the universe. After the Fall, the image of God in man was marred, but not completely effaced. Another way of putting this is that *nature* bears witness to God, even if it needs to be completed and fulfilled by *grace*. This was not a view formulated for the first time in the Renaissance; it can be found in many of the great medieval thinkers, including Thomas Aquinas. It is also closely related to the Renaissance humanist focus on the dignity of man, a phrase that became the title of Pico della Mirandola's famous oration.

Rhetoric, History, and Reform

Three other key principles are associated with the humanist passion for Good Letters: the primacy of rhetoric, a return to the sources, and the development of a historical sensibility. From ancient times, rhetoric had been studied as the art of persuasion in public speech. The goal of education in rhetoric was to produce orators, men capable of participating in the civil discourse of their society. Over the centuries, rhetorical theory changed and expanded. By the Renaissance, the humanists began to shift the emphasis from persuasion in orations to elegance and correctness of style in a diverse range of literary forms, including letters, dialogues, and poetry. As Paul Oskar Kristeller has written, "The emphasis in rhetoric [in the Renaissance] had shifted from persuasion to style and imitation, and to literary criticism."

For More, Erasmus, and their fellow humanists, rhetoric was the centerpiece of educational theory. They had become convinced that the tradition of scholasticism, which reached its high point in the Middle Ages in the writings of Thomas Aquinas, had decayed into a dry, abstract system dominated by the form of discourse known as dialectics, which consisted of a seemingly unending series of logical distinctions and conundrums. The most infamous piece of scholastic dialectics is the question of how many angels can dance on the head of a pin. Taken out of context, such disputations sound far sillier than they actually were; for all their mockery of scholasticism, Erasmus and More tended to exempt the best medieval thinkers, such as Aquinas, from their satire.

But by the Renaissance the scholastic system had degenerated. In pressing for the reform of education Erasmus and his peers hoped that future generations would avoid the ethereal speculations of the scholastics and instead immerse themselves in the concrete particulars of literature as found in classical mythology, poetry, and drama. The humanists felt that literature was closer to life, that it provided a better lens onto the moral and spiritual life of man. In short, they elevated imagination to its rightful place alongside faith or reason as one of the fundamental faculties of human nature. Erasmus often vented his frustration when his comic and satirical works were attacked and misunderstood. Those "whose ears are only open to propositions, conclusions, and corollaries" are deaf to the more subtle literary techniques of irony and ambiguity.

The second principle behind the humanists' absorption in Good Letters was the belief that reform, the painful process of stripping away corruption and calcified practices, could only be brought about by returning to the sources. *Ad fontes!* (to the founts, or origins) became their motto. G. K. Chesterton, arguably one of the twentieth century's greatest Christian humanists, once said, apropos of this instinct, that any attempt at reform required, by definition, "a return to form." At the source of the river, the water is the purest. One step in this process was a mastery of the best that pagan culture had to offer.

The work that the young Erasmus was engaged in during and after his first visit to England came to be known as the *Adagia*. It consisted of 818 adages or proverbial sayings from the classical world, along with lively annotations by Erasmus. Throughout his life, in edition after edition, Erasmus added new adages, until the final edition, printed in the year of his death, 1536, contained 4,151. The *Adagia* is not a work likely to set a modern reader on fire—its form is something alien to our sensibilities—but it came to be one of his major claims to fame. Far from being an exercise in pedantry, it provided an introduction to a bewildering array of classical authors. Like a modern literary critic, Erasmus explored multiple levels of meaning in these

phrases—phrases that seemed to possess condensed and mysterious meanings. Moreover, as Peter Ackroyd writes, when Erasmus added his annotations to these maxims, "He invokes a long temporal perspective, in which the
implications and connotations of those phrases have changed; he is creating
a history of usage."

This awareness of the way language changes over time—the way words
accrete layers of meaning like geological strata— helps us to understand
why Erasmus cannot be accused of wanting to live in some past era. Some
Renaissance thinkers may have been naïve enough to believe that they might
return to an ideal classical order, but Erasmus and most of the humanists
were not that deluded. The whole thrust of the return to the sources was
not to restore a lost world but to find in the past the kernels of truth that
subsequent ages had obscured. As the late Cardinal Henri de Lubac put it,
"To get away from old things passing themselves off as tradition it is necessary to go back to the farthest past—which will reveal itself to be the nearest
present."

It is here that the third principle of the humanists' study of Good Letters
enters the picture: the development of a historical sensibility. By tracing the
usage of these adages, Erasmus took literature out of the ether and placed it
firmly in the context of history. This may have been the most controversial
of all his activities, since for many in his generation, the contextualizing of
literature seemed to open up the possibility of what we today might call historical relativism. But to think of Erasmus as someone out to deconstruct the
meaning of ancient texts would be to commit an egregious anachronism. His
goal was more modest, and a lot more profound: he and his fellow humanists
simply wanted to set the record straight. That is, they wanted to ensure that
all the textual errors and misreadings that had crept into the literary record
over the ages, as manuscripts were copied and passed from hand to hand,
were corrected or at least accounted for. They were the pioneers of modern
critical scholarship; they were editors, annotators, philologists.

Recovering the Biblical Text

What set northern humanists like More and Erasmus apart from the Italians
was a desire to return not only to the pristine texts of pagan antiquity, but
also to the Bible. An exemplar of this movement was the German scholar
Johannes Reuchlin, who had mastered Hebrew in order to emend the
received text of the Old Testament. On his first trip to England, Erasmus

had met John Colet, a theologian who had absorbed the Platonist philosophy of the Italian humanists and was applying it to the epistle of St. Paul in a series of lectures at Oxford University. Erasmus devoted several years to the study of Greek so that he could begin the next major undertaking after the initial edition of the *Adagia*: an annotated, corrected edition of St. Jerome's Latin Vulgate—the official version of the Bible for the past millennium. In the light of modern scholarship, Erasmus's edition can be seen as a rather primitive effort, riddled with errors; for all his encyclopedic knowledge, he was not fully equipped for the task. In fact, he saw his main achievement in the project as his commentary on the text, rather than in the editing process. But by daring to bring a critical sensibility to the Vulgate he established a principle that would lead directly to modern biblical scholarship.

Erasmus's edition of the New Testament made him a sensation through-out Europe. He dedicated it to Pope Leo X, who graciously accepted the dedication and commended Erasmus for his efforts. There were critics, of course. The more conservative humanist theologians at Louvain, in particu-lar, were scandalized that one man would tamper with the received text of the Vulgate. One of the Louvain scholars, Martin Dorp, had written Erasmus to dissuade him from moving forward. Erasmus and More responded to Dorp with long, eloquent letters that did much to moderate his opposition. But other conservatives were not so easily placated. They found his foreword to the New Testament, known as the *Paraclesis*, to be filled with danger-ous ideas, including the notion that the Bible should ultimately be trans-lated into vernacular languages and read directly by the common people. "I absolutely dissent," Erasmus wrote, "from those people who don't want the holy scriptures to be read in translation by the unlearned—as if, forsooth, Christ taught such complex doctrine that hardly anyone outside a handful of theologians could understand it, or as if the chief strength of the Christian religion lay in people's ignorance of it."

It is not hard to see why Erasmus was looked upon as a hero by many of those would become the leading lights of the Reformation. Between his scathing attacks on church corruption and superstitious practices, and his evangelical desire to make the Bible accessible to every Christian, Erasmus inspired a generation of reformers, including, at least for a time, Martin Luther. In their early letters to one another, Luther is respectful of the older man and Erasmus cautiously commends the German monk for his zeal and principle. When Luther famously nailed his ninety-five theses to the church door in Wittenberg, Erasmus was supportive. In the early days when Luther was first condemned by the Catholic authorities, Erasmus labored to get the reformer a fair hearing.

But the storm clouds were approaching. In the light of the tremendous forces unleashed by the Reformation, the moderation of an Erasmus may seem a negligible thing, a paper boat tossed about in a raging ocean that soon will swamp it. It is possible to see Erasmus as someone who helped to unleash forces he did not understand, or as someone who was ultimately irrelevant to the larger tectonic shifts of the time. There can be little doubt that in the increasingly tense and contentious atmosphere of the 1520s and '30s, Erasmus himself became testy and defensive. A favorite adjective to describe this side of his personality is "waspish." Some biographers have speculated that his illegitimacy made him abnormally sensitive to criticism. And yet, while such criticisms contain a large share of truth, they obscure a deeper truth: that Erasmus's moderation was based on something more than timidity.

The Benefits of Uncertainty

Both sides in the struggle worked tirelessly to recruit him. He steadfastly refused to become a spokesman for the Catholic Church (including that refusal, late in his life, of the cardinal's hat), but many of the reformers fundamentally misjudged his willingness to break with the church. As fierce as his attacks on the church might be, Erasmus was even more passionate about the need for unity and consensus. He preferred the slow processes of reform from within to outright revolution. And so, with great reluctance, he began to write against Luther.

Throughout his career, Erasmus went out of his way to denounce war and its consequences, whether the conflict be physical or merely intellectual. Writing to Luther, who had begun one of his pamphlets with the word "Assertio" (I assert), Erasmus replied:

> I am quite aware that I am a poor match in such a contest. I am less experienced than other men and I have always had a deep-seated aversion to fighting. Consequently, I have always preferred playing in the freer field of the muses than fighting ironclad in close combat. In addition, so great is my dislike of assertions that I prefer the views of the skeptics wherever the authority of Scripture and the decision of the church permit—a church to which at all times I willingly submit my own views . . . I prefer this natural inclination to one I can observe in

certain people who are so blindly addicted to one opinion that they cannot tolerate what differs from it.

Comments like this have encouraged the secular partisans of the Enlightenment to claim Erasmus for their own and prevented staunch defenders of Christian orthodoxy from warming to him. But the skepticism that Erasmus embraces does not indicate a lack of faith. On the contrary, it should be seen as an expression similar in spirit to the famous saying of St. Augustine: "In necessary things, unity; in disputed things, liberty; in all things, charity." What Erasmus contested was the tendency on both sides of the conflict to take disputed things and turn them into necessary things.

Some points need elucidating and some decisions have to be made, I don't deny, but on the other hand there are a great many questions which are better ignored than investigated, seeing that part of our knowledge lies in accepting that there are some things we cannot know, and a great many more where uncertainty is more beneficial than a firm standpoint.

Again, it would be wrong to think that Erasmus is advocating in this quote a sort of "know-nothing" attitude. What he feared was the obsession to push human reason beyond its limits, the drive to explain in abstract, propositional terms the great mysteries of faith. That explains why he ended up believing that the Reformers were just a new version of the scholastics: they, too, over-rationalized and abstracted, leaving the faithful wracked by fierce disputes over petty ideas.

In a 1527 letter to one of the reformers, Martin Bucer, Erasmus wrote: "I seem to see a cruel and bloody century ahead. . . . It is a long-drawn-out tragedy." Seven years later, with the conflict escalating into physical warfare, Erasmus heard the news that Thomas More had been executed by Henry VIII, the king who was to become the enlightened humanist ruler. He wrote to one friend: "In More's death I seem to undergo my own."

Men for All Seasons?

What was it, then, that made More "a man for all seasons" and caused a contemporary to say "Erasmus stands apart"? More was a man of principle who often chose not to stand on principle, a deeply spiritual man (always attracted to the monastic life) who was immersed in the public realm, a satirist of corruption in the church who staunchly opposed attempts to undermine church authority. More sought a third way between religious fundamentalism and secular politics and yet he could hardly be described as a compromiser. Erasmus was a deeply pious man who reveled in the pagan classics, a traditionalist bent on wide-ranging reform, a supremely cultured man who believed in the virtue of simplicity.

Where some have seen in these men only a series of contradictions, I came to believe that More and Erasmus exemplified the fruitful tension that the great religious minds have called paradox. In them I could see my own struggle to find a path between the Scylla of hyper-conservative Christianity and the Charybdis of secular liberalism.

More and Erasmus were central figures in the Renaissance movement that gave rise to the phrase Christian humanism, but the more I reflected on their lives and writings, the more resonances I saw with other thinkers from other times. I became convinced that this vision did not originate in the Renaissance but has always been present in the church's history. Christian humanism, I believe, rises to greater prominence in times when both the faith and the social order are wracked by fierce ideological conflicts, but its spirit has been present from the beginning.

On the face of it, the term "Christian humanism" seems to suggest paradox, a tension between two opposed terms—between heaven and earth. But it is a creative, rather than a deconstructive, tension. Perhaps the best analogy for understanding Christian humanism comes from the doctrine of the Incarnation, which holds that Jesus was both human and divine. This paradoxical meeting of these two natures is the pattern by which we can begin to understand the many dualities we experience in life: flesh and spirit, nature and grace, God and Caesar, faith and reason, justice and mercy.

When emphasis is placed on the divine at the expense of the human (the conservative fault), Jesus becomes an ethereal authority figure who is remote from earthly life and experience. When he is thought of as merely human (the liberal error), he becomes nothing more than a superior social worker or popular guru.

The Christian humanist refuses to collapse paradox in on itself. This has an important implication for how he or she approaches the world of culture. Those who make a radical opposition between faith and the world hold such a negative view of human nature that the products of culture are seen as inevitably corrupt and worthless. On the other hand, those who are eager to accommodate themselves to the dominant trends of the time baptize nearly every-thing, even things that may not be compatible with the dictates of the faith.

But the distinctive mark of Christian humanism is its willingness to adapt and transform culture, following the dictum of an early church father, who said that "Wherever there is truth, it is the Lord's." Because Christian humanists believe that whatever is good, true, and beautiful is part of God's design, they have the confidence that their faith can assimilate the works of culture. Assimilation, rather than rejection or accommodation, constitutes the heart of the Christian humanist's vision.

When the first Christians came to the realization that Christ's return was not likely to be imminent, they had to address the question of how to exist in the world, how to engage the cultures in which they lived. There has always been a tension at the heart of Christianity in which believers see themselves as called to be "in the world but not of it." The essence of the faith is that Jesus Christ, the son of God, took human form in order to redeem a fallen world through his sacrificial death and resurrection. To be of "the world"—or to use another New Testament metaphor, "the flesh"—is to remain unredeemed. In that sense, Christianity has always been grounded in an inescapable "either/or" question: to accept Christ or reject him, to strive to conform oneself to the holiness of God or to live in and for the self.

But if Christians are not to be of the world, they are still called to love it and to live in it. After all, John 3:16 begins with the phrase "God so loved the world." The world is not evil; that is a Gnostic idea. Of course, genera-tion after generation of believers have struggled to define what living "in the world" means. Some have interpreted their faith in such a way that they are only in the world as a ghost or a hologram might be: these are the conserva-tives who live in a world of abstractions, the harsh moralistic principles that keep them in orbit above the world.

Then there are those liberals who have sought to be so much a part of the world that they merge into it, losing their Christian identity.

It seems fair to say that the model of how to be in the world ought to be Christ himself. In the doctrine of the Incarnation Christians understand Jesus to be fully human and fully divine. All of the heresies and errors that afflict the church—and, I might add, in the individual believer's spiritual life—can be measured by their tendency to stress either the human or the divine dimensions at the expense of the other.

Ironically, this tendency to place one aspect of Christ's nature above the other presents itself initially as a distinct advantage. For example, those who focus on the human dimension of Christ's nature demonstrate the virtues of empathy for the human condition. At their best, they exemplify Christ's compassion and overriding concern for the poor and the oppressed. In their passion for social justice, liberals seek to alleviate suffering, break down barriers between people, and bring about an equality of results. When it comes to a conflict between the letter of the law and the spirit, liberals opt for the spirit.

Conservatives, who dwell on the divinity of Christ, have a vivid sense of the human propensity to error and evil. For them, the moral dimension is paramount: without law and order, society falls into anarchy. The conservative looks at the story of Christ's rescuing of the woman taken in adultery and instead of noting his leniency with her, compared to his damning attack on the Pharisees, points out that he reminds the woman to "sin no more." So long as the rules are fair, conservatives say, the only equality worth striving for is equality of opportunity.

Living within the paradox of the Incarnation is something we find very difficult to do. What should be a firm platform beneath our feet seems all too often to be a swaying tightrope. Down through the centuries Christian humanists have succeeded in staying on this tightrope more consistently than those around them. They refuse to collapse paradox in on itself, straining to keep the dualities of judgment and mercy, faith and reason, nature and grace, God and Caesar in a state of healthy tension. Their refusal to join in partisan battles often earns them the reputation of being aloof or pusillanimous. It's also why Christian humanists don't tend to found schools of thought or band together in cliques. More often than not, they choose to go it alone, communicating, perhaps, with kindred spirits across distances of time and space.

I like to think that in the history of the church Christian humanists are like the thirty-six just men of Hasidic belief: at all times, the Hasidic legend goes, there must be thirty-six *tzadikkim* or else the world will come to an end.

The Mission *as Metaphor*

In conclusion, I'd like to return to Robert Bolt and his other brilliant portrait of Christian humanism in the epic film, *The Mission.* The film recounts the story of the Jesuit missionaries who attempted to penetrate the rainforests of Brazil and bring the faith to the Guarani, one of the region's remotest and most inaccessible tribes. As the film opens, we see a missionary ejected from the tribe in a literal and gruesomely ironic fashion: he is tied to a cross and sent down the Parana River, only to tumble over the edge of the huge Iguassu Falls. This missionary had evidently tried to preach at the tribesmen and had been rejected. But the Jesuit priest played by Jeremy Irons enters a clearing near where the tribe lives, sits down on a rock, and begins playing an oboe. The Guarani were an intensely musical people, though the only instrument they played was drums. The priest's simple gesture appealed directly to the humanity of the tribespeople, enabling them to recognize what was human in him. The Guarani approach him with their spears raised but as he continues to play the spears fall to their sides. They soon accept him and, ultimately, convert to Christianity.

The themes of *The Mission* parallel those of *A Man for All Seasons*: the Jesuit mission, which became enormously successful, was brutally terminated by church superiors caught up in internal politics. Once again, the spirit of Christian humanism comes to a tragic end. But the indelible image of the priest playing the oboe remains the key moment in the film. It represents Bolt's return to the idea that human culture can become the medium through which heaven and earth meet. This time, instead of law, it is art that mediates grace, bringing communion where otherwise there would only be conflict and fear.

To the Christian humanist, culture and art can become analogues for the Incarnation. In particular, art is like a sacrament: a union of form and content, the inherence of divine meaning in the crafted materials of this earth. In a little-known essay entitled "Art and Sacrament," the twentieth-century artist and poet David Jones wrote that the Eucharist—the preeminent Christian sacrament—consists of bread and wine, not wheat and grapes. In other words, the gifts offered to God at the altar are not the untouched products of the earth, but artifacts, transformed by human hands through an art. As the literary scholar Virgil Nemoianu has written, "Christian humanism is nothing but reclaiming the basic inheritance of the world as it is: the natural and organic connection between the works of culture and the religious roots and vistas of the human being. It is the current separation that is artificial, not the other way round."

Seen in this light, it is possible to look into the history of the church and see that the Christian humanist response has always been to reach out and assimilate the works of culture into a new spiritual synthesis. As Nemoianu notes in his essay "Christian Humanism Through the Centuries," the third and fourth gospels, Luke and John, already show the disciples of Christ tailoring their story for a more cosmopolitan audience. The opening words of the Gospel of John—"In the beginning was the Word"—employ a metaphor with enormous philosophical and aesthetic depth. Within two hundred years of Christ's death, the faithful have moved beyond the ancient prohibitions concerning religious images, creating sarcophagus sculptures and wall paintings that transform late classical images of Apollo into the handsome young Jesus, holding the lamb over his shoulder. Apollo becomes the Good Shepherd. When the school of Neoplatonism arises, partly in response to the rise of Christianity, the Cappadocian Fathers—Gregory of Nyssa, Gregory Nazianzen, and Basil—boldly appropriate its insights into their theology.

The same process can be seen over and over again during the last two thousand years. Augustine and Aquinas, Melancthon and Calvin, Newman and Bonhoeffer, Eliot and O'Connor. It is a process whose importance cannot be underestimated, because it goes to the heart of the church's vitality and ability to communicate visions of truth, goodness, and beauty to the surrounding culture. After centuries of secularization, the West has exhausted the moral and spiritual capital of the Judeo-Christian tradition. The moral anarchy of our consumerist society cries out for vision. As fundamentalists barricade themselves into their fortresses and liberal believers hasten to baptize every passing secular trend, the need for Christian humanism is greater than ever.

It is my belief that we are living through a period when new Christian humanists are emerging to offer that vision without which, the Bible says, the "people perish." Think of the work of writers like Annie Dillard, Richard Rodriguez, Kathleen Norris, Gerald Early, and Anne Lamott; composers like Arvo Pärt, Henryk Gorecki, and John Tavener; filmmakers like Wim Wenders and the late Krzysztof Kieslowski. The list could go on and on.

Allow me to end with two quotations that seem to sum up the heart of Christian humanism. The Catholic writer Gerald Vann once wrote, "Today the old adage, 'Don't preach to the starving, give them bread,' can be given a new application: 'Don't preach divinity to the subhumanized; first give them back their humanity. . . . ' We cannot save others from subhumanity if we are subhuman ourselves." And Hans Rookmaaker, the Dutch Calvinist art historian, once said, "Christ didn't come to make us Christians. He came to make us fully human."

Part Two

Christianity, Literature, and Modernity

5

The Writer of Faith in a Fractured Culture

Ours is the long day's journey of the Saturday. Between suffering, aloneness, unutterable waste on the one hand and the dream of liberation, of rebirth on the other. In the face of the torture of a child, of the death of love which is [Good] Friday, even the greatest art and poetry are almost helpless. In the Utopia of [Easter] Sunday, the aesthetic will, presumably, no longer have logic or necessity. The apprehensions and figurations in the play of metaphysical imagining, in the poem and the music, which tell of pain and hope, of flesh which is said to taste of ash and of the spirit which is said to have the savour of fire, are always Sabbatarian. They have risen out of an immensity of waiting which is that of man. Without them, how could we be patient?
—George Steiner, *Real Presences*

After years struggling to launch *Image*, a quarterly journal that showcases contemporary art and literature which engage the religious traditions of the West—Judaism, Christianity, and Islam—I found myself overwhelmed by doubts about its mission.

The voice in my head went something like this: "Reflecting on the relationship between art and the perennial questions of man's origin and destiny is certainly a commendable occupation. But what does it mean to have a journal devoted specifically to this relationship? After all, through most of Western history, the intersection between religion and art has been at the center of the culture. Publishing a journal to highlight this intersection seems to relegate it to a specialty interest, like a hobby. Perhaps *Image* is really on a par with magazines like *Backpacker* or *Hot Rod*. Or worse, *Image* might be no better than one of those interminable scholarly journals, like *Sexual Semiotics Quarterly*. Publishing a journal where you can be guaranteed to find half a dozen poems about God in every issue seems artificial, perhaps even a little spooky. Are you doing justice to this material, or just creating a petting zoo for religious artists? Maybe you better bow out gracefully and let this material appear where it should, in the *New Yorker* and *The Paris Review*."

Now I'm not ashamed of these doubts, because they arise out of a sound instinct. Art that bodies forth religious themes and experiences should not be relegated—willingly or unwillingly—to the periphery of the culture. If *Image* were to become nothing more than a quaint sideshow in literary circles, I felt, it would be better to call the whole thing off.

But there is another inner voice reminding me that this process of marginalization has been going on for some time, as Western culture has become increasingly secularized and divided. We live in an age of fragmentation and discontinuity, and the response to that condition requires a certain element of self-consciousness. Indeed, the postmodern era in which we live is often said to be marked by a self-conscious awareness of our de-centered existence. Yeats sensed something like this when he wrote, with apocalyptic urgency, that "the centre cannot hold."

In the preeminent poem of the earlier generation of High Modernism— *The Waste Land*—T. S. Eliot sifts through the relics of an atomized culture, looking for meaning, and concluding: "I have shored these fragments against my ruin."

The danger of this approach, of course, is that the aesthetic hoarding of fragments can yield only a jumbled assortment of "found objects"—an imperfect synthesis, a failed fusion.

In any case, there is an analogy here for a journal like *Image*—and for the writer of faith today. Looked at in one way, *Image* may appear to be nothing more than a specialty publication, appealing to a few people on the fringe with certain interests—one shard among the many fragments of the culture. But there is another possibility, one that deliberately disturbs our sense of what constitutes center and margin, fragment and whole. It arises out of the biblical narrative, from the Genesis stories about the least and the youngest being elevated to the highest place, to the figure of Jesus, whose penchant for hanging out with the poor and the disreputable asks us to overturn our ideas about center and margin. When the center cannot hold, the margin is lifted up, becoming the source of a renewed order.

In that sense, *Image* might better be seen as a standing challenge to those at the center of the cultural establishment. The marginalizing of faith is perhaps due both to failures on the part of believers and secularist prejudice. Whatever the causes for that marginalization may be, a journal like *Image* can serve as a catalyst for changed perceptions: its value is not merely that as an end in itself but the role it plays in the larger conversation. It is a fragment, no doubt, but it yearns for, and points toward, a reconstituted wholeness. It's not about restoring a past order; it's about making connections that can draw us closer together.

The Postmodern Moment

But what of the writer of faith? To borrow a phrase from Walker Percy, how does the writer with religious concerns "insert" herself into the culture?

The postmodern moment offers her a measure of hope. For one thing, the "master narratives" of secular high modernism, such as Marxism and Freudianism, have themselves been de-centered, if not discredited. Each of these systems claimed that they possessed the ultimate form of reason, and in their failure to adequately explain the world, reason itself has been called into question. As Robert Royal has written, "Art has become more important in the postmodern world . . . because the truth claims of philosophy, theology, ethics, and even nature seem weak. The argument on many campuses over the canon has taken on added heat precisely because, where truth is assumed a priori not to exist, images and atmosphere will shape how most people think."

For the believing writer, who is likely to feel that faith and reason have historically been emphasized at the expense of the imagination, this will be a welcome development. Walker Percy reminded us that art—far from standing in opposition to reason—"is cognitive: it discovers and knows and tells, tells the reader how things are, how we are, in a way that the reader can confirm with as much certitude as a scientist taking a pointer-reading."

The other hopeful sign is that the grip secular modernism had on so many of our cultural institutions has now relaxed somewhat. In the decades after World War II, it was common to find critics dismissing literature or art with identifiably Christian themes. Under the influence of Freud, such critics argued that because religion was merely wish fulfillment it had no place in art, which ought to come to grips with the "real world." Dan Wakefield has written of the secular triumphalism of this period, when he and his generation echoed F. Scott Fitzgerald's claim: "All wars fought, all gods dead." In Wakefield's own case, this arrogance took many years to crack.

In recent years, other cracks have become visible in the bulwarks of cultural power, including the pages of the *New York Times Book Review* and the *Washington Post Book World*. The critics in these publications are increasingly open to the idea that religious belief often calls for a fierce and anguished grappling with the realities of life. Jewish, Christian, and Islamic poets and novelists such as Thomas Lynch, Reynolds Price, Khaled Mattawa, Andre Dubus, Mary Karr, Annie Dillard, Franz Wright, Larry Woiwode, Mark Helprin, John Updike, Marilynne Robinson, Rodger Kamenetz, Daniel Abdel-Hayy Moore, Paul Mariani, and Ron Hansen have received admiring reviews for their books in these publications. Another important sign that the times are changing is the number of authors who are turning toward explicitly religious themes for the first time, perhaps because they are less fearful of ostracism.

While there remains a great deal of secularist prejudice among the gatekeepers of culture—and sporadic eruptions of "New Atheism"—the writer of faith now has more opportunity for "a place at the table." Much of the impetus behind these cultural changes has come from the Baby Boomers, who are now in their sixties and suddenly seeing their mortality in the bathroom mirror. Just as they are shelling out for hair replacements, they are looking for the transcendence they left behind in Sunday school. They tend to want their religion with large doses of nostalgia and sentimentality, and many are partial to New Age pantheism and/or the therapeutic methodologies of the self-help industry. Nonetheless, openness is better than closedness, and the writer of faith should be grateful that he or she is once more heard in the public square.

From Hawthorne to Percy and O'Connor

The believing writer in America has always faced the same dilemma: how to find a way to heal the divisions running through the national psyche, including the community of faith itself. Nathaniel Hawthorne may have had an anguished relationship with Christianity but that was in part because his imagination hungered for a deeper faith than was available in his time. He confronted many of the same divisions that plague us today. To his right were the descendants of his Puritan ancestors, whose lack of imagination pushed them in the direction of philistinism and fundamentalism; to his left were Ralph Waldo Emerson and his followers, whose religious commitments had evaporated into a pantheistic liberalism.

Hawthorne's response was to evoke the power of evil and locate it squarely in the human heart, in opposition to an age that wanted either to deny evil or place it within human institutions or see it in the face of some scapegoated group. Instead of extolling Emerson's gnostic self-reliant man, Hawthorne held up for admiration Hester Prynne, a woman who is radically dependent on others. After she is scorned and abandoned by the conservative Christian community, she learns through penitential suffering and sacrificial love to turn outward again. Hawthorne strove to articulate a theology of suffering and solidarity in *The Scarlet Letter*. Toward the end of his career, in *The Marble Faun*, he felt his way toward a more thoroughly sacramental vision, which he hoped would counter the forces of individualism and foster a deeper sense of community.

From Hawthorne it is possible to trace a line of literary descent that runs through T. S. Eliot to Flannery O'Connor and Walker Percy. All three of these twentieth-century writers attempted to address the divisions that Hawthorne struggled to reconcile. Eliot spoke of the "dissociation of sensibility" whereby faith and reason, head and heart, had been separated by Descartes and the rise of modern scientific rationalism. Eliot was all too aware of the fragmentation of Western culture. Eliot's ambition was to create a body of poetry that would not only dramatize the major episodes in the decline of Christendom, but also discover how grace could be found in a fractured culture.

At first Eliot sought to oppose the romantic egotism of modern art by proclaiming his allegiance to classicism and the pursuit of objective truth. When he first began to speak of faith in his work, it was through indirection and allusion; the exhaustion of traditional religious language made him fear the deadening effect of cliché and the resistance of secular readers. In the end, however, Eliot found that it was only by reaching into his experience and speaking in a personal voice—in *Ash Wednesday* and *Four Quartets*—that he could discover the timeless moments of grace that touched the "still point of the turning world." For Eliot, the road to transcendence could only be found through a process of probing the immanent—in this he was akin to Dante, whose *Divine Comedy* demonstrated that the way down is the way up. In Eliot's late poetry this process led to a redemption of the romantic impulse, a synthesis that still resonates half a century after his death.

O'Connor and Percy retained the philosophical depth of Eliot, but they chose smaller canvases for their art, in O'Connor's case the Georgia backwoods and in Percy's the country clubs and suburban subdivisions of the New South. O'Connor's parables took the modern Nietzschean "will to power" and incarnated it in the lives of wandering preachers, salesmen, and middle-aged society ladies. The pride of these folk had to be shattered by a collision with the world, and in that moment grace was offered to them. Percy's world is less violent and dramatic than that of O'Connor, for the good doctor from Covington was interested in the ways we have domesticated our despair. Drawing on European existentialists such as Kierkegaard, Marcel, and Camus, Percy gave us alienated seekers who tried to become anonymous, disappearing into the backwaters of a crassly materialistic culture. Because they were genuine seekers they could run but not hide from the Big Questions.

Contemporary Writers of Faith

What of our contemporary religious writers, those who have been published in the last thirty years? Like Percy and O'Connor, they have chosen to work on smaller canvases. Working from the concrete particulars of time and place, their imaginations reach out to the universal truths. Significantly, they have not felt the need to employ indirection and irony to the extent that Eliot, Percy, and O'Connor often did. Moreover, O'Connor's notion that "for the hard of hearing you have to shout, for the nearly blind you have to draw large and startling figures" no longer seems appropriate to postmodern writers. In a time where all master narratives are under suspicion, they have taken a quieter and more intimate path. By and large, contemporary writers have felt more freedom to depict their characters' religious experiences and tensions directly, and more often in whispers rather than shouts.

In the brief survey that follows, I will mention a few of the most distinguished writers in a number of somewhat arbitrary categories, focusing in on a younger, promising writer in each area. The three categories I would like to touch upon are historical fiction, regional fiction, and contemporary lyric poetry.

Perhaps because we have become so cut off from the past, Jewish and Christian writers are turning more and more to historical fiction. By placing the story in a historical period in which religion is woven into the fabric of life, and where it has not suffered from trivialization, these writers can explore the life of faith and examine the conflicts that lie in our past. Ron Hansen's *Mariette in Ecstasy*, set in a New York convent at the beginning of the twentieth century, tells of a young postulant who receives the stigmata, the wounds of Christ, and of the tumultuous aftermath of this event. Mark Helprin's *A Soldier of the Great War* returns to World War I to examine a turning point in the modern world; it is suffused with many startling insights into the nature of love and art. Denise Giardina has written of the West Virginia coal miners and their plight in the first half of this century. Frederick Buechner's novels about medieval saints Brendan and Godric at once debunk traditional hagiography and give us more moving portraits of sanctity than any conventional saint's life could.

If I may be allowed to speak of a colleague's work, I would like to single out Harold Fickett's novel *First Light*. Fickett set himself the goal of chronicling the generations of a prominent American evangelical family from the eighteenth century to the present. *First Light* introduces us to Abram White, who as a boy experiences grinding poverty in Ireland. Abram hears of the opportunities available to those who emigrate to the New World, and he decides to run off and do just that. His goal is to make his fortune and return to Ireland to rescue his family. In New York, after years at sea, he meets and marries a woman named Sarah. The choice of names is deliberate, of course: Fickett maps his story on the biblical narrative of Genesis.

The historical and cultural territory Fickett has marked out is vast and uncharted. *First Light* attempts to recover one strand of American religion from obscurity and to invest it with the dramatic weight and dignity that it deserves. Yet it does not sentimentalize its subject: unlike most of the historical novels that have been released by Christian publishing houses, *First Light* is not populated by impossibly heroic and virtuous plaster saints. Abram and Sarah struggle with their faith. Abram's desire to rescue his family and establish a new life is balanced on a knife's edge, where pride and cruelty lie dangerously close to sacrifice and love. *First Light* is a rescue operation in and of itself, a recovery of memory that pays tribute to a central religious tradition in America, while at the same time showing us its flaws. By telling us where we came from, Fickett helps us to struggle with our identity as a people. The restoration of memory helps heal the fragmentation that occurs when we are cut off from the past.

The Regional Novel

Another category where outstanding work is being done might be called the regional novel. This is a highly unsatisfactory label, because it covers a multitude of different narrative styles and subjects, but it will serve for the moment. What I mean by "regional" is that the author gives us a richly detailed picture of life in a specific place, either in the present moment, or reaching back into the recent past and moving toward the present. Religion is not necessarily the center of attention in these novels, but it is a part of the characters' lives, and plays an important role in the dramatic conflicts depicted in the story. Among the writers that might be placed in this category are Larry Woiwode, Louise Erdrich, Andre Dubus, Garrison Keillor, Kaye Gibbons, Doris Betts, and Marilynne Robinson. The South and the Plains states (including the Dakotas and Minnesota) have been among the most fruitful regions in this genre.

One of the most intriguing regional writers to emerge in recent years is Elizabeth Dewberry. Her first novel, *Many Things Have Happened Since He Died*, deserves to be more widely known. This first-person narrative is told by a twenty-year-old Alabama woman. She is pregnant, married to an abusive loser, and alone in the world. Though she is almost unbelievably naïve, her passion for a better life is fierce. The resemblance may be faint, but she is the descendent of Hester Prynne. Let down by the Pharisaical fundamentalists in her community, she must forge her own theology in the midst of suffering she barely understands. Late in the novel the narrator, heavily pregnant and thoroughly isolated, fears the ordeal that is soon to be upon her. She is worried about her unborn child, whom she plans to put up for adoption, and about the pain of birth and death. She addresses God directly:

> Dear God maybe I am coming to You soon maybe when the baby is born.
>
> It wasn't suicide I just couldn't make myself go to the doctor I don't know why. Maybe because I know what is coming and I don't want the doctor to confirm it. Maybe because I am afraid the baby is a monster and he would tell me. I don't know. But now I feel that You are preparing me for death so I wanted to talk to You about that.
>
> Please save me. I don't necessarily mean don't make me die I just mean take me to Heaven. And please let Malone and Daddy be there

when I get there. I haven't been real religious lately I haven't been to church in a while. But if I had more time I think I would have come to some sort of peace with You. I will do this I am not that scared of dying but would You please help me would You stay with me or send an angel of Malone or somebody to be with me. And would you please take care of the baby don't make the baby die please give it a nice home and parents and let it take piano lessons and be in the school band and grow up and go to college and be happy and get married to somebody nice and have good healthy children and when it dies please let it come to Heaven and be with us. I think she is a girl. I would name her Elizabeth. When you write her name in the Book of Life could you possibly put Elizabeth in parentheses beside it. If not that's okay.

Dewberry's novel has a breadth that can draw readers from all sectors of our fragmented culture. The novel's central concerns revolve around what might be called "women's issues," and yet the religious dimension cannot be downplayed. This woman does not wallow in self-pity or sublimate her anger in political activism. The narrator's fundamentalist upbringing may have let her down in many ways, but it does enable her to carry on a running debate with God which gives meaning to her suffering.

The Lyric of Doubt . . . and Faith

Among America's most distinguished poets are a number of believers, including Richard Wilbur, Denise Levertov, Donald Hall, Mary Karr, Franz Wright, Richard Chess, and Paul Mariani. Their mode is primarily the lyric, though a number of them have tried their hand at longer sequences.

I'd like to say a brief word about a Southern poet named Andrew Hudgins. His collections include *Saints and Strangers, The Never-Ending,* and *Ecstatic in the Poison.* His book-length narrative, *After the Lost War,* uses the voice and the life of the Southern poet Sidney Lanier to address such matters as Southern history, mortality, and the role of poetry. In his shorter poems, Hudgins often deals with Christian subjects without excessive self-consciousness. One of his favorite approaches is to write an ekphrastic poem (a poem about another work of art) based on a medieval or Renaissance painting of a New Testament subject. But a number of his poems are themselves like these paintings: Christ and Mary and John and other biblical figures seem to be set against a background that is contemporary, just as Van Eyck put Flemish castles in the background of his paintings. The final poem from one of his collections is called "Psalm Against Psalms." It begins this way:

> God had Isaiah eat hot coals,
> Ezekiel eat shit, and they sang
> his praises. I've eaten neither, despite
> my childhood need to test most things
> inside my mouth. . . .
> Isaiah ate the blood-red ember.
> Ezekiel ate the dung. It went in fire
> and came out praise. It went in shit
> and came praise from his mouth. And this
> is where I stick. I pray: thank, ask,
> confess. But praise—dear God!—it clings
> like something dirty on my tongue,
> like shit. Or burns because it is a lie.
> And yet I try: I pray and ask
> for praise, then force the balking words
> out of my mouth as if the saying them
> could form the glowing coal—cool,
> smooth as a ruby—on my tongue.
> Or mold inside my mouth the shit
> that melts like caramel—and thereby,
> by magic, change my heart. Instead
> I croak the harsh begrudging praise
> of those who conjure grace, afraid
> that it might come, afraid it won't.

The poet concludes that he is not capable of embodying the absolute purity of either spirit (fire) or flesh (dung).

> I'm smaller, human, in between,
> a leavening of dirt with fire,
> and I must be, with every passing day,
> more careful of what goes into my mouth,
> more reckless of what issues forth.

Hudgins does not conceal his doubts or the self-consciousness that is so much a part of the modern era: they are incorporated into the piercingly honest voice of the poem. Here is poetry that is truly confessional: not a barbaric yawp of self-indulgence but an effort to measure the self against the larger realities of the soul.

The Prophetic and Philosophic Modes

To return to the broad spectrum of American letters, there are two modes of the imagination that lack many practitioners at the moment. The first I would call the prophetic voice. Prophetic writers, like Eliot, have moral intensity and a deep sense of history. They can be scathing, full of Swiftian "savage indignation," but their attacks are launched in the name of preserving moral and spiritual standards. Two of the most compelling prophetic writers of our time are the British poet Geoffrey Hill and the Southern man of letters Wendell Berry.

The other type of writer that we are missing at the moment is the philosophical kind, such as O'Connor and Percy. This, I think, is our greatest lack, because the philosophical artist, at his or her best, possesses the ability to link the foreground action of particular characters and settings to the deep currents flowing beneath the surface of a culture. While we will have to wait for authentically prophetic and philosophical writers, we can rejoice in what we have.

But what of the literary and religious communities into which these works are launched? They too are divided. When it comes to their choice in books, Catholics and mainstream Protestants have been least affected by the phenomenon of cultural separatism. With a healthy instinct, they have not sought out specifically Christian novels or publishers. When they show an interest in serious literature at all, they tend to want to read the best writers, not merely the safe or acceptable ones. At the same time, many of them have accepted the dichotomy between art and faith that perpetuates cultural divisions. There is evidence that that dichotomy has begun to narrow, as the recent success of Robinson's *Gilead*, Tyler's *Saint Maybe*, and Hansen's *Mariette in Ecstasy* indicate.

The most interesting development in recent years has actually been occurring in the group broadly known as evangelical. A number of evangelicals have grown tired of the legacy of cultural separatism, of treating only some authors and publishers as officially approved and therefore safe.

Though I cannot quantify this movement (some insist that it is very small), it is certainly having some impact. There are signs that many evangelicals are abandoning a brittle and triumphalistic stance, and searching for a vision that encompasses mystery, ambiguity, sacramentalism, and even tragedy. Bret Lott's fiction comes to mind here.

Our culture is caught between a vision of pluralism and the reality of tribalization. Of course, diversity has its virtues; cultural homogenization is fraught with problems. But our mission now must be to dismantle the barriers. The religious traditions of the West—those known as the "People of the Book"—must once more be seen and heard in the public square. The faith must be made to speak, and not in the hectoring voice of the reactionary or in the attenuated and embarrassed tones of the liberal. Transformation is what faith and imagination have in common: they take the stuff of ordinary life and place it in the light of the ultimate questions of sin and redemption.

As Andy Crouch has pointed out in his book *Culture Making*, the work of social change is not so much about critiquing culture as it is about making *new* culture. And there is no more fertile ground for this than the place where faith and art meet. Faith and imagination reach out to explore the mysteries of heaven and earth and then return to the community with the symbols and stories that help us know who we are. It is time to move beyond the stale politicized debates between fundamentalists and relativists and return to the sources of creativity. The goal should be to renew the tradition of Hawthorne, Eliot, O'Connor, and Percy. Of course, art in itself cannot save a single soul, much less a nation, but in this postmodern era, when reason has become suspect, the imagination helps us to see and speak the truth. It reminds us, in George Steiner's words, that we are on "the long day's journey of the Saturday," that Good Friday is behind us and Easter Sunday before.

6

Ever Ancient, Ever New: The Catholic Writer in the Modern World

The . . . tradition [of Christian culture] exists today, for though the Church no longer inspires and dominates the external culture of the modern world, it still remains the guardian of all the riches of its own inner life. . . . If society were once again Christian . . . this sacred tradition would once more flow out into the world and fertilize the culture of societies yet unborn. Thus the movement toward Christian culture is at one and the same time a voyage into the unknown, in the course of which new worlds of human experience will be discovered, and a return to our own fatherland—to the sacred tradition of the Christian past which flows underneath the streets and cinemas and skyscrapers of the new Babylon as the tradition of patriarchs and prophets flowed beneath the palaces and amphitheaters of Imperial Rome.
—Christopher Dawson, *The Historic Reality of Christian Culture*

Whenever I have had the chance to visit secondhand bookshops in recent years—whether they be converted barns in Pennsylvania, decaying mansions in the Corktown section of Detroit, or dank corridors in Oxford or London—I have found myself shouting out discoveries to my friends. More often than not, my finds have been books by Catholic thinkers which have been out of print for twenty or thirty years. On their frayed dustjackets and faded paper covers, the praise of critics whose names are all but forgotten today testifies to the excitement these books once generated. The prices have been hard to beat: Romano Guardini's *The End of the Modern World* for a buck, Christopher Dawson's *The Historic Reality of Christian Culture* for thirty pence, Chesterton's *Manalive* for a quarter. Many of these books come from libraries—predominantly Catholic libraries. In fact, I have personally profited from the closing of dozens of seminaries and convents in the Anglo-American world. With a feeling that is at once elated and guilty, I run off with spoils that once lined the shelves of cavernous Gothic buildings.

In reflecting upon the topic of this conference, "The Catholic Writer," it occurred to me that my book-hunting adventures might serve as a metaphor for the sweeping changes in Catholic intellectual and cultural life over the last half-century. The writers whose works I was collecting were those who constituted what was once called the Catholic Intellectual Renaissance, an outpouring of philosophy, theology, history, and literature which combined fidelity to the ancient teachings of the church with considerable sophistication of mind and spirit. Here were the works of the minds who dominated Catholic letters for the first half of the twentieth century, gathering dust, rejected by the current establishment, only to be discovered and then hoarded as treasures by a small segment of a younger generation.

The Catholic historian James Hitchcock has termed the eclipse of these writers in the 1960s and '70s "the slaying of the fathers." But in cocktail parties at most Catholic universities today, the mention of names such as Maritain, Gilson, Mauriac, or Waugh would very likely evoke not so much hostility as an amused condescension for individuals who are considered thoroughly passé. Relegated to that zone of weeping and gnashing of teeth known as the "pre-Vatican II" world, the Maritains and Mauriacs are thought of as apologists for an order that has been largely left behind in our progress toward a more enlightened dispensation. "To be sure," the cocktail chat might go, "they were men of cultivation and learning, even of wit, but, you know, they were positively medieval."

Of course, many of the writers of the Catholic Renaissance would have been flattered to be associated with the Middle Ages, a time which to them connoted not barbaric darkness but a remarkably integrated culture, a world of light and grace, where flesh and spirit could be merry beneath the canopy of Heaven. But leaving the virtues of the High Middle Ages aside for the moment, I would like to suggest that, in the long run, the thinkers who made up the Catholic Renaissance will prove to be the most authentically modern and original of all. Scratch a progressive and more often than not you will find, just beneath the language of "liberation" and "dialogue," notions that made their first appearance during the debates of the Patristic era. But show me a thinker who has faithfully grappled with the achievements of St. Augustine or St. Thomas, and you will likely find someone who has the ability to grasp the real challenges of the modern world.

As will be evident by now, I am pursuing a paradox about the spiritual and intellectual life of the church. Chesterton, that modern master of paradox, has come very close to the matter in his discussion of the term "reform." For Chesterton, the word "reform" is both meaningless and dangerous unless we recover its literal definition. The liberal conceptions of reform as either a gradual evolution away from an older doctrine or practice, or as a revolution against tradition, are misguided. True reform, he says, involves a *return* to form. Only in subjecting oneself to the rigors of the original form—a term which itself reminds us of something ordered, coherent, and specific—can the detritus of time and human folly be washed away and vitality return.

But just as one might step in at this point and argue that Chesterton's definition is really nothing more than a slavish imitation of the past, notice how the paradox executes its boomerang turn. By returning to the original form from the standpoint of the crisis of the present, the resulting reform might well take on a radically different path when compared with the immediate past. In other words, the return to form may yield results which are startling, but which remain true both to the distant past and to the conditions of the present. (Chesterton loved his self-proclaimed role as a "conservative radical.") As the brilliant orthodox theologian, Cardinal Henri de Lubac, puts it in his *Paradoxes of Faith*: "To get away from old things passing themselves off as tradition it is necessary to go back to the farthest past—which will reveal itself to be the nearest present."

Beyond the paradoxes of intellectual history and institutional reform, of course, lies the fundamental paradox of the divine nature itself, which St. Augustine described as beauty "ever ancient, ever new." It is also the paradox of the Gospels, which remain continuous with the Old Testament even while ushering in the New. The thinkers we group under the heading of the Catholic Intellectual Renaissance embodied that paradox in their writings. It is what makes them at the same time profoundly traditional and strikingly modern. Few of these figures could be called tame or timid; ever the servants of the church, they nonetheless were bold, occasionally shocking figures, who were suspected by some of their less imaginative contemporaries of being imprudent or even heretical. At times, the accusations of the hyper-orthodox

led to excruciatingly bizarre situations, as when Evelyn Waugh, that staunch-
est of Papal Catholics, was accused by a prominent priest-editor of writing
a novel that would corrupt the morals of the faithful. Waugh's long letter
of justification to the Archbishop of Westminster, with its patient explanation of his harshly ironic satire against modern secularism, makes for grimly
comic reading. But these attacks from the extreme Right balance those of the
Left, and offer further proof of the wisdom and vision of these great minds.

The Catholic Intellectual Renaissance

In theology, there is a principle which states that the bigger and more mysterious a being is, metaphysically speaking, the harder it is to describe its
nature in direct terms. When it comes to understanding God Himself, it has
often been said that it is better to attempt to say what He is not, and in this
way inch closer to a perception of what He is. I'd like to borrow this technique to describe the modern Catholic Renaissance.

First, the Renaissance was not an expression of anything that might be
called an "Establishment." The single most striking fact about the majority
of its writers is that they were converts. In the earlier generation one could
point out Leon Bloy, Jacques and Raissa Maritain, Paul Claudel, Gabriel
Marcel, Charles Peguy, Evelyn Waugh, Graham Greene, Christopher
Dawson, G. K. Chesterton, Ronald Knox, Edith Stein, Dorothy Day, and
Adrienne von Speyr. The younger generation included such converts as
Louis Bouyer, Thomas Merton, and Walker Percy. Add to this such near-
converts as Henri Bergson and Simone Weil, as well as the Anglo-Catholic
converts T. S. Eliot and W. H. Auden, and you have a sense of a vision that
could attract many of the leading minds of the age.

Conversion is an experience that is in some sense unique to every convert, but it inevitably involves a process of discovery—the feeling, to quote T.
S. Eliot, of arriving home and knowing the place for the first time. Ironically,
many of these intellectual converts did not find ready acceptance in official ecclesiastical circles. All this goes to show that the converts were hardly
submitting themselves blindly to authority figures in order to assuage their
anxieties about sex, guilt, and death (a common charge of their secular critics). Rather, they were engaged in a protracted mental and spiritual struggle
that ended in a willing embrace of the central mysteries of the faith. To all of
them, their faith was an asset, a key to understanding both the highest truths
and the most pressing problems of the moment. They would undoubtedly

share Flannery O'Connor's belief that "there is no reason why fixed dogma should fix anything that the writer sees in the world. On the contrary, dogma is an instrument for penetrating reality. Christian dogma is about the only thing left in the world that surely guards and respects mystery."

If the Renaissance intellectuals were not creatures of any establishment, neither did they form a "movement." There were, of course, "schools" of thought, including Thomism, the Catholic existentialists, and the Neo-Patristic "Ressourcement" theologians, but even within these schools there were widely divergent views. This point may seem a truism, but it is, to my mind, an important corroboration of the intellectual honesty of these thinkers that, while they shared a common faith, their explorations of the world took them down disparate paths.

Finally, it is worth noting that these writers were predominantly lay people, not clerics. We take the leadership of lay intellectuals in the church today somewhat for granted, but it has largely been a modern development. It is a development which recent popes and the Second Vatican Council itself have strongly endorsed, seeing it as a necessary consequence of an increasingly secularized society, and also because the specific character of the laity is to know the natural goods of various forms of worldly endeavor.

The leading figures of the Catholic Renaissance moved easily and naturally in secular professional circles—a fact we may tend to forget. This is not only a testament to the greater openness of secular intellectuals in the earlier decades of the century, but of a positive rejection of the fortress mentality on the part of the Renaissance thinkers. Their place, as they saw it, was on the frontlines of culture, and if they encountered some hostility, they also found a great deal of respect. As James Hitchcock has pointed out, the Catholic Thomists helped to spur a neoscholastic movement that was taken up by such teachers as Mortimer Adler and Richard McKeon at the University of Chicago, where the joke was that "atheist professors taught Catholic philosophy to Jewish students."

It has been said that orthodoxy develops only in response to the challenges posed by heresy. But if the great orthodox thinkers have received their impetus from the need to oppose a narrowing and distortion of the faith, it is equally true that they always manage to rise above merely defensive postures to achieve a vision which reawakens in us a sense of the beauty and wonder of the world. One need only think of a work like St. Augustine's *City of God*, which was written as a response to the pagans who claimed that Christianity was responsible for the fall of the Roman Empire. This magisterial book not only refuted those charges but became the blueprint for the political and social order of medieval Europe for nearly a millennium. I would like to suggest that the greatest of the Catholic Renaissance writers in the modern era accomplished this twofold mission of critique and imaginative vision. Of the many themes which run throughout their writings, I have chosen to single out three: the recovery of the sacred, the critique of the world, and the assimilation of modernity.

The Recovery of the Sacred

In the age dominated by Darwin, Marx, and Freud, human nature appeared to be determined by evolution, the means of production, the unconscious, or, in the case of a few creative scholars, a combination of these forces. Few of the thinkers of the Catholic Renaissance dismissed entirely the insights into the workings of the mind and the social order which came in the wake of modern psychology, sociology, and natural science. Catholic existentialists like Gabriel Marcel adopted the Freudian and Sartrean notions of alienation, but placed them in the context of the traditional Christian understanding of man as a stranger and pilgrim on the earth. Marcel preferred to speak of *Homo Viator*, Man the Wayfarer.

Like Marcel, the Renaissance writers retained the conviction that man's life, far from being mechanically determined, was inherently dramatic, poised between sin and grace. It should come as no surprise that the Catholic novelist was in a particularly strong position to reawaken the transcendent dimension of human experience. As Flannery O'Connor put it,

> Drama usually bases itself on the bedrock of original sin, whether the writer thinks in theological terms or not. . . . The novelist doesn't write about people in a vacuum; he writes about people in a world where something is obviously lacking, where there is the general mystery of incompleteness and the particular tragedy of our own times to be demonstrated, and the novelist tries to give you, within the form of the book, a total experience of human nature at any time. For this reason the greatest dramas naturally involve the salvation or loss of the soul. When there is no belief in the soul, there is very little drama.

Where the Catholic novelists of the twentieth century have succeeded in providing us with intimations of grace, they have revealed it in experiences which seem to confound our normal expectations for revelation. Greene, Mauriac, Bernanos, and O'Connor, among others, have depicted grace in the lives of seemingly odious and pitiful individuals, in moments of violence, and in quiet, almost unnoticeable ways. Though these novelists were accused of being obsessed by dark visions of sin, they replied that if grace means anything, it must be the presence of the divine *within* a fallen creation.

Walker Percy is a case in point. A Southerner and Catholic convert, Percy had a profound knowledge of modern philosophy, psychology, and linguistics. Influenced as a young man by Dostoevsky and Kierkegaard, he developed a form of Christian existentialism that is at once sympathetic to, and critical of, the modern temper. Percy, like another of his mentors, Marcel, found the metaphor of *Homo Viator* compelling. Trained as a doctor, he was passionately interested in science, and yet he opposed the type of scientism that reduced the sacred dimension of our humanity to mere biological determinism.

Percy's last novel, *The Thanatos Syndrome*, is set, like the old sci-fi TV series Max Headroom, "twenty minutes into the future." The protagonist is Thomas More, psychoanalyst and lapsed Catholic. He has just returned from two years at a minimum security prison for having sold mild doses of amphetamines to truck drivers to help them stay awake on their long cross-country runs. But, on his return to the prosperous Louisiana parish of Feliciana, More notices something odd about several of his former patients. Before his prison term these patients exhibited the classic anxieties and quirks of alienated and fearful human beings. But they now appear contented, sexually supercharged, gifted with total recall and mathematical genius. To More's alert eye, however, these people seem somehow less than human: strangely docile, incapable of speech beyond two-word sentences. Soon More is off in pursuit of the conspiracy behind this sweeping change in human behavior.

More's investigation uncovers suspicious behavior on the part of two leading scientists. Bob Comeaux, a psychiatrist, is the director of the Qualitarian Center at Fedville. The Qualitarian Center, which seeks to promote the "quality of life," performs operations known as "pedeuthanasia" and "gereuthanasia." These terms, covering what we would call abortion, infanticide, and euthanasia, are possible thanks to the Supreme Court ruling, *Doe v. Dade*, which stipulates that a fetus or newborn does not acquire rights as a human being until it is eighteen months old. Then there is John Van Dorn, a Renaissance man—scientist, nuclear engineer, educator, Olympic soccer coach, bridge champion. Both Van Dorn and Comeaux travel in the professional jet stream where science, federal bureaucracy and funding, and research-sponsoring foundations combine to create the therapeutic state.

It turns out that Comeaux and his colleagues have secretly been dumping quantities of heavy sodium isotope into the Feliciana water supply (although not that of Fedville). Ironically, it is the research done by More into the effects of heavy sodium on cortical function that leads Comeaux to his experiment in altering human behavior. When he is found out, Comeaux candidly admits his responsibility, but challenges More to criticize the good achieved by the experiment.

> What would you say, Tom . . . if I gave you a magic wand you could wave over there [Baton Rouge and New Orleans] and overnight you could reduce crime in the streets by eighty-five percent? . . . Child abuse by eighty-seven percent. . . . Teenage suicide by ninety-five percent. . . . Teenage pregnancy by eighty-five percent. . . .

More is incapable of arguing against Comeaux; he refuses, however, the lucrative offer to "join the team." The only voice that speaks up against the forces represented by Comeaux and Van Dorn is that of Fr. Simon Smith, a crazy, alcoholic priest who runs a hospice for AIDS patients, deformed infants, the elderly, and the terminally ill. Fr. Smith is no paragon of virtue, but his own youthful admiration of the Nazis, and for several brilliant German psychologists who subsequently committed atrocities against children, has led him to be deeply distrustful of abstract schemes to benefit something known as Mankind. In fact, Fr. Smith sees an incipient Holocaust in the policies of Fedville. "Do you know where tenderness always leads?" he asks. "To the gas chamber."

The words are intentionally shocking; indeed, they are meant to be a form of shock treatment. Like Tom More, who experiences both discomfort and embarrassment on hearing these words, we are more complicit with evil than we would like to admit. Along with Malcolm Muggeridge, Percy is convinced that the West is afflicted with a death-wish. "In the end, one must choose—given the chance," says Fr. Smith. "Choose what?" More replies. "Life or death. What else?"

The Thanatos Syndrome probes the effects of the Faustian will to power which characterizes modernity. How is it that Renaissance men can combine intellectual brilliance and seeming altruism with inhuman brutality? The answer is much the same as that given by the Grand Inquisitor in Dostoevsky's *The Brothers Karamazov*: better to bargain with the Devil, exchanging human freedom, with all its anxieties and attendant responsibilities, for the "peace" of a humanity without free will. The twist to this arrangement, which the Devil is careful not to divulge, is that by reducing man to the level of cattle—taking away the sacred dignity of human personhood—men become as expendable as cattle.

The Critique of the World

The second theme, which I call "The Critique of the World," is admittedly somewhat amorphous. What I wish to focus on is the fact that Catholicism reminds us that we can never allow ourselves to become too closely identified with the order of worldly goods. I have chosen to focus on a less frequently discussed theme, namely, the association of Christianity with bourgeois materialism in the modern age, but I could just have easily explored the Christian critique of totalitarianism, as in Solzhenitsyn, or the reemergence of Gnosticism.

We are told in the Gospels to be in the world but not of it. From the time of the Apostles down to the present, the tension between "Christ and Culture," as the Protestant theologian H. Richard Niebuhr put it, has remained constant. The writers of the Catholic Renaissance faced strong challenges from modern novelists and political philosophers who accused Christianity of being nothing more than a prop for a decadent bourgeoisie. Philosophers as different as Kierkegaard and Nietzsche had railed against a complacent, bourgeois Christianity in the nineteenth century, and in the twentieth, novelists like James Joyce and D. H. Lawrence portrayed organized religion as hypocritical, repressive, and out of touch with human needs. Writers such as these have been called anti-Christian, but their depictions carried the conviction of experience and should not be dismissed.

Catholic social thought, both in the tradition of papal encyclicals, and in the works of Renaissance scholars such as Jacques Maritain, Yves Simon, and, in a later generation, John Courtney Murray, steered a middle course between the extremes of radical capitalism and revolutionary socialism. Stressing the importance of a recovery of the notion of the common good, these thinkers avoided baptizing any current political system. In this sense, they followed the wisdom of returning to form—that is, to the Augustinian understanding of the tension between the City of God and the City of Man—in order to achieve true reform.

If the problem of a too ready identification between Christian values and the bourgeois life seems less applicable to contemporary Europe, it certainly retains its bite for America in the present day. Despite our secularized public institutions, America is a nation awash in religion and religious expression. But American Christianity has always suffered from a chameleon-like tendency to become identified with civil religion and popular culture. From the gospel of success preached by certain strains of fundamentalism, to the New Age pantheism which characterizes much of progressive Catholic thought these days, the faith is often of the world, but not quite in it, if I may be permitted to reverse the metaphor.

Once again I would like draw my illustration from the realm I know best, literature. The French Catholic novelists—Leon Bloy, François Mauriac, and Georges Bernanos—succeeded in continuing the tradition of the fictional critique of bourgeois society which had been pioneered by Gustave Flaubert and Emile Zola. Whereas Flaubert could only see Christianity as a beautiful dream that had been corrupted by complacency and provincialism, the Catholic novelists managed to depict the same symptoms while preserving a vision of the radical transcendence of true faith.

François Mauriac's *Viper's Tangle* appears to stack the decks against Christianity. Written in the form of a diary, it is the testimony of a lawyer named Louis, who quickly reveals himself to be a thoroughly nasty figure—a moral monster, in fact. Louis is a peasant who has risen in the world, becoming a wealthy landowner, and is now facing death. Estranged from his wife for over forty years, and possessed of a loathing for his children, Louis masterminds a scheme to disinherit his family, which, he thinks, waits like a pack of vultures to descend on his carcass and divide up his fortune.

Louis frankly confesses to being a hate-filled man. One of his abiding hatreds is for religion itself. Part of this stems from his upbringing. Louis's mother represents the kind of smugness to which the peasant mind is often prone. "My mother never talked to me about religion, except to say—'I am quite easy in my mind: if people like ourselves are not saved, then nobody will be.'" His wife, who comes from a higher social plane, maintains a piety which he finds maudlin and superstitious.

But one fact about Louis soon becomes evident: "I have never possessed the power of self-deception which is most men's stand-by in the struggle for existence. When I have acted basely, I have always known precisely what I was doing." Indeed, Louis's caustic comments about the world around him are often true; he has a remarkable capacity for sensing hypocrisy and, in a word, sinfulness. In his negation, he often hits targets that deserve to be hit.

As his confessions proceed—for that is what they really are—chinks in Louis's misanthropic armor begin to appear. His plot eventually breaks down, and the dream of revenge which he had nursed for so many years leaves him vulnerable. His wife dies, without any real reconciliation between them, and he discovers among her papers evidence that her shallow piety had deepened into a sacrificial, even ascetic, form of suffering. He realizes that the one thing he had deceived himself about all these years was his need for love, human and divine love. Just before he dies, he accepts what he once called the "sublime lunacies" of Christianity.

In summary form, the plot of *Viper's Tangle* will hardly sound convincing. But the underlying irony of the novel is that, contrary to everyone's assumptions, Louis is driven not by the love of money, which he uses merely as a form of insulation, but by a hunger for the absolute. What separates Louis from most of those around him is that he is not lukewarm; his very coldness contains within it the possibility for reversal, for white-hot passion. The intensity of his desire for something more than riches becomes his path to salvation. Ironically, the book ends with a letter from his son, who plans to use his inherited wealth by investing in a Cinema and a new liqueur—the two symbolic drugs of the modern materialist world. Only a niece recognizes that Louis was "the only truly religious person I have ever met."

François Mauriac's astringent vision offers little comfort to those who seek uplift from art with religious themes, but his lack of sentimentality is precisely what makes him a master of what Flannery O'Connor called "Christian realism." His depiction of a restless heart is a powerful indictment of a culture that has lost touch with the demands of supernatural faith.

The Assimilation of Modernity

The final theme I want to touch upon may appear to be another truism. It is simply this: that these twentieth-century Catholic writers were, in fact, modern men, and that they participated fully in the unique opportunities and difficulties of the modern world. It is worth saying because among those who consider themselves orthodox, there is a persistent tendency toward nostalgia and a provincialism that brands everything "modern" as decadent, or even demonic. Flannery O'Connor once said that "smugness is the Great Catholic Sin," one to which we are all prone. Cardinal de Lubac puts it this way:

"'Know the moderns in order to answer their difficulties and their expectations.' A touching intention. But this way of projecting the 'modern' into an objective concept, of separating oneself from them to consider them from the outside, makes this good will useless."

The church, because it embraces the truth about human nature and human destiny, has always been able to assimilate new ideas and new cultural patterns, finding in them redemptive possibilities. To quote Cardinal de Lubac again,

> No longer to believe, in fact, in the assimilating and transforming power of Christianity; to divert the exercise of Christian prudence so as to make of it an entirely negative and defensive prudential system: such is one of the most fatal forms of lack of faith. It is to believe no longer, in fact, in Christian vitality. It is to refuse confidence in the Holy Spirit. It is to justify as if on principle those who think that Christianity has grown old for good.

The leading figures of the Catholic Renaissance did not think this way. Philosophers such as Gabriel Marcel and Dietrich von Hildebrand established a healthy dialogue with Existentialism and Phenomenology, respectively. The painter Georges Rouault drew inspiration from the Fauvist and Expressionist movements in art. Even Chesterton, seemingly the most defiantly anachronistic of writers, employed Joycean literary techniques in *The Man Who Was Thursday* to convey the chaos of modern relativism.

An apt illustration of this assimilative capacity is the aesthetic theory of the twentieth century's two leading Thomists, Jacques Maritain and Etienne Gilson. Cultivated and urbane scholars, these men devoted a large portion of their philosophical study to aesthetics. Throughout their careers they asserted that the appreciation of works of the imagination was essential to the fulfillment of our humanity. Both were unabashed champions of modern art. Maritain maintained a close personal friendship with Rouault; his wife Raissa was a poet. Gilson's daughter, Jacqueline, was a painter in the semi-abstract style.

In their description of the history of art, Maritain and Gilson claimed, contrary to most people's intuition, that painting began to go downhill after Giotto "discovered" perspective and ushered in the era of representational painting, and only began to recover with Cezanne and the revolution of modern art. The reason for this hinges on the definition of the purpose of art. The common belief is that art should be an imitation of reality, rendered with a faithfulness that approaches that of the camera. But Maritain and Gilson countered that the end of art is not the mere repetition of reality through imitation, but the creation of beautiful objects that enable us to see through nature to deeper meaning. No artist creates pure representations of reality: we tend to admire artists precisely insofar as they possess a unique style that moves away from imitation and communicates a penetrating vision of reality.

Gilson's difficult but rewarding book, *Painting and Reality* (the Mellon Lectures of 1955), contains this explanation:

> During the long episode that lasted from the end of the fifteenth century to the beginning of the nonrepresentational art, painters, instead of remaining firmly established on the ground of nature, progressively or regressively shifted over to the ground of imitation, representation, and, in short, exchanged making for knowing. Imitation—that is, representation of reality as it appears to be—stands on the side of science or, to use a more modest word, knowledge. Reduced to its simplest expression, the function of modern art has been to restore painting to its primitive and true function, which is to continue through man the creative activity of nature. In so doing, modern painting has destroyed nothing and condemned nothing that belongs in any one of the legitimate activities of man; it has simply regained the clear awareness of its own nature and recovered its own place among the creative activities of man.

Based on this line of reasoning, it should come as no surprise that Gilson was also a champion of abstraction, that form of art which so many people assume to be the expression of nihilism and despair about human life. Gilson's use of the word primitive is not accidental either: the modernist painters deliberately returned to primitive cave paintings and tribal masks in order to recover a sense of the mythical and sacred in the midst of an industrial, bourgeois society. Rouault went back to the naïve representations of medieval stained glass in his struggle to convey man's spiritual destiny. Great artists have always known that the need to attain freshness and vitality can only be achieved by returning to the farthest past, which, as de Lubac reminds us, "will reveal itself to be the nearest present."

The creation of beautiful objects, for their own sake, Gilson insists, is a direct analogy to the creative power of God. Of course, man cannot create something out of nothing, but in making new "beings," the artist "will know the exhilarating feeling of finding himself in contact with the closest analogue there is, in human experience, to the creative power from which all the beauties of art as well as those of nature ultimately proceed. Its name is Being."

The Relevance of the Renaissance Writers

What, then, is the relevance of the writers of the Catholic Intellectual Renaissance to the present, and to the future? In the twenty-first century, our situation as Catholics seems even more perilous and uncertain than in the heyday of these thinkers. The church has been plunged into a crisis of identity and confidence in the upheaval which followed the Second Vatican Council. Those who wish to defend the faith may naturally feel that in the present we do not have the luxury for novels, paintings, and works of scholarship. Understandably, there is a drive toward activism, to the launching of sorties from a well-defended fortress into the hostile territory of secular culture.

What would these writers advise us to do, were they here today? Though many of them expressed deep concern near the ends of their lives about the direction of certain movements in the church, I am convinced that they would counsel us to do just as they did. They would exhort us to confidence in God's providence, to reach back into the richness of our tradition and find ways to apply it to the present. In the words of the Dominican writer, Gerald Vann,

> It is for us Christians, then . . . to do these two things. First, to learn to be receptive of life before plunging into activity; to learn to be possessed of life, of truth, of love, to be possessed by God. Then secondly, to learn to face the squalors of life as they come to us—and we do not grow into the light by trying to escape the darkness but by meeting it—with courage and tranquility, as we shall then be enabled to do: trying to make sure that the deeper our knowledge of it becomes, the deeper also becomes our sense of oneness with the redemptive pity of God, and therefore the less our danger of coming to terms with evil. . . . In that way we shall incidentally integrate ourselves; for we shall find that, in a world which is so largely uncreative and so largely hopeless, we for our part shall find always a renewal of life and of hope, through

our sharing, however humbly, however fumblingly and imperfectly, in the re-creative, the redemptive, work of the Word who was made flesh and dwelt amongst us in order precisely that we might have life and have it more abundantly.

In short, our task is to redeem the time, to be inspired by the one who said: "Behold, I make all things new."

7

After This Our Exile:
The Christian Poet in the Modern World

By the rivers of Babylon, we sat down, yea, we wept when we remembered Zion. We hanged our harps upon the willows. . . . How shall we sing the Lord's song in a strange land?
—Psalm 137

When their Babylonian captors required of the Israelites a song of Zion, they undoubtedly meant well. But the request could only leave a bitter taste in the mouths of the exiles. How can one sing of home when one has been torn from its nourishing immediacy? And how can the foreigner feel the poignancy of those special, shared recognitions among countrymen? The plight of the Christian artist in the modern world can best be understood, I believe, in terms of the metaphor of exile. The crisis of Christian culture in the West since the Renaissance has been characterized by a process of secularization that has developed to such an extent that we now hear the West described as "post-Christian." It is only within the last century that the public truths and institutions of society have been radically severed from their Christian roots and the full force of modernity has been felt in mind and heart. In the cultural public square the Christian has come to be in the minority, to live as an exile from the major artistic and intellectual institutions. But unlike the Israelites in Babylon, modern Christians have suffered an internal exile because they inhabit a society that still retains the stamp of its origins in faith.

For the Christian artist, the awareness of exile is particularly acute. First, the pervasive pressure of modern consciousness has made it increasingly difficult to maintain a Christian worldview. Then there is the problem of audience: to sing a song that the majority of people will not comprehend becomes problematic. In the past, the Christian artist assumed the complete permeation of society with religious belief and was free to pursue his craft and subject without self-consciousness. In the secular world, however, the Christian artist must also convey his religious perception, and his temptation is to turn the art object into a vehicle for propaganda—a choice that inevitably destroys the integrity of art itself.

In our time, the challenge for the artist who grapples with Christian faith has been to fully incarnate his belief, by uniting vision and judgment, and by speaking directly to the modern mind. It is a challenge that has been met by a few outstanding figures whose vision has reconciled faith and the modern condition, and thus given new vitality to Christian culture, even though it is a culture in exile. I propose to discuss the work of three such figures, all modern poets writing in English.

The Burden of the Self

The cultural fragmentation of Christendom, as it has been felt in the widespread secularization of our social and political institutions, presupposes a prior spiritual and mental crisis, which I shall call the crisis of modernity. Originating in the late Middle Ages, the nominalist assertion that the mind could not apprehend nature led to Descartes's empiricism as the only valid form of knowledge. During the eighteenth century, modernist rationalism spawned dreams of society run according to abstract schemes, and in the realm of art, strict metrical regularity and conventional subjects formed the basis of a neoclassical aesthetic.

In reaction to rationalism, the Romantic movement asserted the primacy of emotion, freedom of form, and the imagination as a redemptive force. But romanticism was not simply a reaction to modernity; it was in many ways an extension of it. For though the Romantics spurned empiricism and mechanism, they too believed nature to be unknowable. It was not a long step from the romanticism which believed nature to be benevolent and the source of all virtue to the romanticism which saw nature as violent—indifferent at best and hostile at worst. The individual is then seen against the backdrop of fate, forging his own destiny through the power of his genius.

The most significant aspect of the Romantic movement was the emergence of the self as the center of consciousness. The residual deistic belief in a trans-human world enabled Alexander Pope to write a poem entitled, "An Essay on Man." But when Wordsworth decided to write an epic poem, he chose not the Fall of Troy or the Fall of Man as his subject, but William Wordsworth. And soon a rather exuberant American named Whitman would be singing a "Song of Myself." The romantic self may have been guided by intuition rather than reason, but it was a creature of modernity in that it failed to integrate the self with being. The subsequent history of art is really a playing out of the romantic ego: late romanticism emphasizes the dreams of power in which supermen conquer fate, as in Wagner, and eventually the existentialists come to regard nature as absurd, and resort to the strange comforts of despair.

The point I want to emphasize is that the emergence of the self as a problem in Western art has been central and remains with us. However much we may deplore the burden of self-consciousness, it is not something that can be willed away. Nor has it been a complete bane for art. As Jacques Maritain once wrote: "Art cannot return to ignorance of itself, cannot abandon the gains won by consciousness. If it succeeds in finding a new spiritual equilibrium, it will be, on the contrary . . . by still greater self-knowledge."[1]

It is one thing to say that we can regain a philosophical synthesis that will restore our apprehension of being; it is another thing to expect that the artist in the modern world can climb out of the skin of his self-awareness. Even if an artist can and should order his own soul, it does not follow that his art can disregard the structure of the life around him. Flannery O'Connor, perhaps this century's greatest Catholic artist, wrote to a friend: "I am a Catholic peculiarly possessed of the modern consciousness, that thing Jung describes as unhistorical, solitary, and guilty. To possess this within the Church is to bear a burden, the necessary burden for the conscious Catholic. It's to feel the contemporary situation at the ultimate level."[2]

The reconciling mission of the modern Christian artist is to "feel the . . . situation to the ultimate level" and to move through that experience to a new spiritual equilibrium. There is no simple way to say how the artist achieves this, since the artistic process involves the search for a form that dramatizes and enacts vision. But it is likely to involve a journey toward order on the part of either a fictional protagonist or a poetic persona.

The cultural fragmentation that has occurred under the pressure of modernity has made the artist's quest for form even more difficult. Without

the shared beliefs, mores, and traditions of a unified culture, there arises
the problem of what the Christian poet and artist David Jones has called
"unshared backgrounds." Many of the greatest modern artists, including
James Joyce, W. B. Yeats, and D. H. Lawrence, sought for a myth adequate
to create a communion with a disparate public. But most writers found that
no single myth was adequate, and they were forced to more or less exotic
varieties of eclecticism.

For the Christian writer the loss of common symbols has two consequences. On the one hand, traditional religious symbols have become opaque,
no longer shining forth the spiritual experiences which they are intended to
mediate. On the other hand, a vast ignorance about the rites and dogmas of
Christianity has developed as twenty-first-century man has turned his back
on the past.

Paralleling the loss of unifying myth has been the decay of language, our
most elemental symbolic system. Words become utilitarian, politicized, and
incapable of expressing a wide range of human experiences. T. S. Eliot once
used the phrase "dissociation of sensibility" to refer to the modern dichotomy between mind and heart as it had been manifested in literary language.
In that context, he goes on to discuss why modern poetry is so "difficult."
"Our civilization comprehends great variety and complexity, playing upon a
refined sensibility, must produce varied and complex results. The poet must
become more and more comprehensive, more allusive, more indirect, in order
to force, to dislocate if necessary, language into meaning."[3]

Thus the use of exaggeration, allusion, and distortion becomes necessary in order to preserve meaning. Flannery O'Connor noted that she used a
drowning to symbolize a baptism, such was her need to convey the nature of
spiritual death and rebirth in the sacrament to a pagan audience. The final
pitfall that the decay of language may entail for the artist is simply this: by
unskillfully using a decadent language he will be implicated in the very confusion and evil he seeks to combat. We will see that the contemporary poet
Geoffrey Hill is particularly concerned about the poet's role in perpetrating
what he calls "the tongue's atrocities."

In order to outline the way in which the Christian artist has spoken to
the modern age, I will discuss three English poets. First, Gerard Manley
Hopkins, who wrote in the late Victorian period, just as the crisis of Christian
culture was becoming acute. Then I will treat the poetic journey of T. S.
Eliot, who represents the high-modernist tradition. To conclude, I will examine the achievement of Geoffrey Hill, a postmodern poet living and writing

in England. Though I could have chosen other artists, such as David Jones and Flannery O'Connor, my selection is intended to provide an overview of the changing conditions during the last century, including an awareness of our situation at this point in time.

Gerard Manley Hopkins and Inscape

There are two common assumptions about the life and work of Gerard Manley Hopkins that are responsible for a partial and misguided understanding of his intellectual and poetic accomplishments. The first is that Hopkins is predominantly the poet of simple, lyric joy in God's creation, and that while his "terrible sonnets" and *The Wreck of the Deutschland* display a darker side of existence, his special gift was unclouded praise. The second misconception is related to the first: Hopkins, it is said, was an isolated figure out of touch with his time, who wrote what now seems to be almost modernist verse straight off the top of his head.

It is true that as a Jesuit priest in a country in which Roman Catholicism was a minority, Hopkins was not near the center of English political and intellectual activity. But he was profoundly aware of the nature of the time in which he lived and struggled against the forces he thought to be inimical to Christianity and a vibrant social order. The rigorous linguistic, philosophical, and theological training he received at Oxford and as a Jesuit enabled Hopkins to become a stalwart opponent of positivism, materialism, and psychologism. He believed modern science was compromised by its excessively abstract and methodologically narrow focus; many scientists, he wrote, "seem to end in conceiving only of a world of formulas, towards which the outer world acts as a sort of feeder, supplying examples for literary purposes." From Ruskin he learned to eschew abstraction and to remain keenly sensitive to the concrete details of nature. From Pater he drew a strong belief in the concreteness of artistic detail. At a time when the modern mind was conceiving nature in gnostic fashion as something to be conquered and manipulated, Hopkins remained intimate with nature as ontologically given—in short, with the world as creation. He feared the growing number of "generations" that "have trod, have trod, have trod" on nature's freshness.

As Hans Urs von Balthasar points out in a brilliant discussion of Hopkins's relevance to theological aesthetics,[4] the poet rejected the scientific and philosophical movement that dissolves the unique natures of species into a "chromatic transitionalism" that blended all forms with one another (for example, in Darwinism). Instead, Hopkins reaffirmed the fixed differences between natures. In his reading of the scholastic philosopher Duns Scotus, Hopkins found confirmation of something he had long believed. Scotus held that all beings contained a principle of individuation or *haecceitas* (that is, "thisness" as opposed to *quidditas*, or "whatness").

Hopkins called this unique, individual essence in each created being its "inscape." Inscape is sustained and held in tension by "instress," a concept somewhat analogous to the idea that God constantly maintains the created world in existence. Contrary to popular belief, Hopkins did not find inscape solely among natural phenomena; he always held that man was the king of creation and many of his finest poems celebrate particular people he met in his pastoral work. One critic has noted that Hopkins, in appreciating his human subjects, "wished to [see them] functioning not only characteristically but intensely, violently, dangerously. . . ."[5]

Inscape must not only be perceived; it must, in von Balthasar's words, be "en-selfed as person." The apprehension of instress, von Balthasar continues, requires "in the subject an answering stress, so that it can hold communion with the stress of things and experience them from within and can also through a prepossession of their nature find the word that exactly expresses it."[6] In this process man discovers not only the unique "selving" in nature but the mystery of his own self. But this "selving," as Hopkins called it, cannot derive from anything more vague or shallow than the human self. In his philosophical writings, Hopkins rejects chance or the Hegelian "World Spirit" as potential sources for selving, and concludes that its origin is in the triune God. And as Christ, the Second Person of the Trinity, is the Logos, by whom the worlds came into being, the universe is seen to have a christological form.[7] That is why the constant motion of Hopkins's poetry is from the intuition of being to the need for praise and right action; in short, the movement is from "is" to "ought."

Though much condensed, this sketch of Hopkins's theological aesthetic makes a deeper reading of his poems possible. First, it will be seen that the problem of the self disappears in the poet's preoccupation with the answering stress of poetic utterance and the love of being expressed by it. In "Henry Purcell," Hopkins celebrates the powerful inscape of the composer's music: "It is the forged feature finds me; it is the rehearsal / Of own, of abrupt self there so thrusts on, so throngs the ear."[8] Purcell is then compared to a great stormfowl opening his wings in the wind as if he were to take flight:

Let him oh! with his air of angels then lift me, lay me! only I'll
Have an eye to the sakes of him, quaint moonmarks,
to his pelted
plumage under
Wings: so some great stormfowl, whenever he has
walked his while
The thunder purple seabeach, plumed
purple-of-thunder,
If a wuthering of his palmy snow pinions scatter a
colossal smile
Off him, but meaning motion fans fresh our wits with
wonder.

Though the bird is not paying attention to himself, the "quaint moon-marks" on his feathers "scatter a colossal smile" as the wind opens his wings and displays his beauty. So the unselfconscious artist may show forth God's goodness.

It is the use of language that distinguishes Hopkins, but however firm his own theological grounding, the nature of the times and the decay of language itself lead him to place great burdens on words and word-order. For all its formality and artificiality, Hopkins's "sprung rhythm" is meant to be a heightened form of colloquial speech. Thus the Jesuit sought to keep poetry close to the vitality of language as it is commonly spoken, steering literature away from the decadence of aestheticism or the pomposity of Parnassian diction. His poetic diction is packed with the short, sharp, guttural Anglo-Saxon words of Teutonic origin, skillfully played off Latinate words. In his use of language Hopkins takes the route of many modern Christian poets: he reaches into history to restore life and meaning to words.

Through the use of compressed syntax, assonance, and internal rhyme, Hopkins attempted to write incarnational poetry. Perhaps the best example of this comes from the poem "That Nature is a Heraclitean Fire and of the Comfort of the Resurrection." Hopkins notes the power and beauty of nature as it undergoes numerous transformations—dying in one form only to be born in another, as clouds become rain, falling to the ground, only to return through evaporation. But the poet recoils at the thought that man dies and is seen no more. Suddenly the thought of the Resurrection brings comfort, for in Christ we have died and will rise again.

> In a flash, at a trumpet crash,
> I am all at once what Christ is, since he was what I am, and
> This Jack, joke, poor potsherd, patch, matchwood, immortal diamond
>   Is immortal diamond.

The Incarnation means that man, a mere "Jack, joke," will be transformed from dust to the diamond of an immortal soul. The sharp, harsh rhymes suddenly give way to the verbal transformation, as "what I am, and" is rhymed with "diamond" to show the link between our mortal and immortal states. At his best, Hopkins achieved a fully sacramental vision that triumphed over the alienation of modernity to recover the experience of Christian faith.

T. S. Eliot and the "Significant Self"

The poetry of T. S. Eliot presents a special problem to the critic because it is essential to see his corpus as whole. I agree with scholars such as Russell Kirk and Marion Montgomery, who see Eliot's life and work as a journey or pilgrimage. Like any great artist, Eliot never repeated himself; as he said late in life, every poem is a "new beginning . . . a raid on the inarticulate." Moreover, it is extremely difficult to break Eliot's career into phases, for just as one is about to talk about his Symbolist/decadent period, one realizes that during this time he was also studying the thought of conservative thinkers like Irving Babbitt and Charles Maurras. Again, it is the Eliot of the *Four Quartets* who reminds us that "In my beginning is my end." Though secular liberal writers see Eliot as betraying true modernism by cravenly embracing fascism and religion, it is more likely that the early Eliot was not the agnostic relativist they believed him to be.

Born six months before Hopkins's death, Eliot was to experience as a young man not only late Victorian aestheticism but the literal fragmentation of European society in the First World War. It is evident that, in one sense, the breakdown of Western culture manifested itself as an inability to discover order and relationships between things. The Symbolists and Imagists Eliot found appealing in his youth seemed to be free of the need to wrench meaning out of words; perhaps the image-in-itself would restore some sense of the immediacy of experience. But it was not long before Eliot became dissatisfied with the image-in-itself. As Marion Montgomery writes,

We may observe, as Eliot increasingly did, that in the absence of meta-physics, the worship of things for themselves becomes the sign of a new romanticism. Keats's things of nature—urn or nightingale—suggest the infinite through the decay of things. His use of nature is replaced by things considered in themselves infinite. The poet's responsibility then becomes the infinite proliferation of imagistic assertions of things.[9]

The final cry of the imagistic poet, if he has the honesty of an Eliot, is expressed in *The Waste Land*: "On Margate Sands. / I can connect / Nothing with nothing." The dissimilitude and separateness of things becomes an agony.

As early as his doctoral dissertation on the idealist philosopher F. H. Bradley, Eliot had elaborated a psychological theory that would eventually be transformed into a spiritual discipline. It has been called "the dialectical conception of the significant self and its temporal becoming," and arises out of the attempt by idealist philosophers to bridge the gap left by Kant between the phenomenal and noumenal selves. Anne Bolgan has written that the core of Eliot's thought rests in the "continuity of the phenomenal or personal self with the noumenal or impersonal self and in the conviction that the first of these enters into the becoming of the other in time."[10] In the words of Gabriel Marcel, Eliot knew man to be *Homo Viator*, man the wayfarer, and would eventually come to see the wayfarer as pilgrim.

The concept of the "significant self" is an aid especially in our read-ing of the early poems. The personae of these poems reveal the danger of solipsism, a retreat from reality into fantasy. That the poems gain much of their strength from Eliot's own temptations we need not doubt, but as poet he never lost control of his material. "Prufrock" is not only a hollow man, but in his timidity we sense a willingness to deceive, even to the extent of deceiving himself. "Gerontion," a later poem, depicts the consciousness of an older Prufrock, a man who has withdrawn into the sterility of his own head, but Gerontion asks: "After such knowledge, what forgiveness?" *The Waste Land* represents a further step: in "shoring these fragments against my ruin," the persona of the poem at least attempts to sift the rubble of his own life and that of Europe. I follow Cleanth Brooks in seeing *The Waste Land* as a conscious and complex process of locating identity in difference, a struggle against the inability to connect. The poem falls short of any pat resolution, but it does appear to have a virtue crucial to the spiritual life: hope. The poet senses that in "the awful daring of a moment's surrender" the self may be lost and found again, only transfigured, caught by "Christ the tiger."

Hopkins pursued a more traditional path in seeking to lose his self-consciousness in the contemplation and praise of God's grandeur. Eliot, more fully a modern, finds order and rest precisely where Maritain claimed modern men would need to find it, through "still greater self-knowledge." Eliot's directly Christian poems, *Ash-Wednesday* and *Four Quartets*, gain much of their poignancy and persuasiveness because they heighten and resolve the themes in what has gone before, especially those two perplexing realities which Eliot in *The Waste Land* calls "memory and desire."

Ash-Wednesday is a deeply personal poem, meditative and penitential. It is shot through with Dantean, biblical, and liturgical allusions, which are rescued from cliché through the power of personal feeling and Eliot's ability to give them existential meaning. We may not be able to follow the poet into his private world, but we hear a chastened voice and sense a renewed vision. Desire has found an object worth desiring, and memory is freed from the early Eliot's attempt to find a "tradition" and can dwell in the timeless moments that have been vouchsafed to it.

In *Four Quartets* Eliot freely returns to those places that historically have given meaning to his life. In memory he visits the homes and landscapes of his ancestors: "Burnt Norton," "East Coker," and "The Dry Salvages." Eventually he makes his way to "Little Gidding," where the Anglican Nicholas Ferrar made prayer "valid" by renouncing worldly power and establishing true community. Eliot's penitential discipline is now guided by the Negative Way of St. John of the Cross. The world and its desires he relinquishes, but in the sudden illumination, the piercing beauty of contingent being is restored to him in all its immediacy. The modern poet has relinquished the role of high priest that the secular world has invested him with; the "words don't matter," because poetic vision in the end must open to something beyond itself. The end of exploration is to find the place where we started from, and to "know the place for the first time."

Eliot's quest, and his achievement, were directed toward the creation of the poetry of personal knowledge, a bridge between subjective and objective worlds. I take the phrase "personal knowledge" from the work of a modern philosopher of science, Michael Polanyi. It is the burden of Polanyi's seminal study to prove that science does not operate by impersonal or "objective" actions on the mind; rather, according to Gerhart Niemeyer's reading of Polanyi, "all knowledge involves an element of intellectual passion, a tacit component of previous beliefs, as well as a personal commitment."[11] Though this argument was originally related to modern science, it applies with equal force to the poetic sensibility. Since the Romantics, and Wordsworth in particular, modern poetry has either been helped or hindered by self-consciousness. Eliot sought a synthesis in personal knowledge, a synthesis which involved an awareness of the past in the present, a commitment of faith, and an ongoing process of self-understanding. His search was not without false steps, but it remains the most remarkable poetic journey of the twentieth century. *The Waste Land* expresses a consciousness searching the fragments for a unified vision, but in *Four Quartets* that vision has become incarnate. The poet integrates the tradition within himself and finds the universal in the concrete and the personal experience, the "timeless moment." "History is now and England." The exile has returned home.

Geoffrey Hill: Language as Sacrament

However much T. S. Eliot's poetry has done to "redeem the time," the cultural dissolution and secularization of the West has continued apace. Eliot's *Four Quartets*, his final poetic work, was published before the world knew of Auschwitz, and before the voice of Solzhenitsyn penetrated our apathy with news of the Gulag Archipelago. If I call Geoffrey Hill a postmodern poet, it is not with the intent of reducing his work by affixing to it a convenient label; rather, it is a way of distinguishing his milieu from that of high modernism. For despite the cataclysm of World War I, the high modernists, such as Joyce and Pound, and even someone like Wallace Stevens, with his dream of a "supreme fiction," hoped to create artistic edifices capable of some grand purpose. Hill inhabits a world which has seen the brutality of totalitarianism and the banality of materialism. His generation has set its sights lower, looking to the small moments of lyric inspiration for its subjects.

Geoffrey Hill nonetheless has stood resolutely apart from his poetic contemporaries.[12] For thirty-five years, he has written poetry preoccupied with power and violence in European history, and with religious experience. Hill's baroque, sensual, highly formal verse manifests all the qualities which Eliot believed "difficult" modern poetry must possess—allusions, indirection, and ambiguity abound. Only in the last few years has Hill's stature come to be recognized. It now seems likely that in the future his name will tower over those of Philip Larkin and Ted Hughes, as well as many of his American counterparts.

Hill can be thought of as a Christian poet only in a limited sense. Brought up as an Anglican, Hill has refused in his mature years to identify himself with Christian belief, though he has insisted that he is a theist. He has claimed that his poetry is largely concerned with the inability of someone with a modern consciousness to experience religious faith. Hill's character is in fact very close to that of Simone Weil, who was locked in an anguished dialectic with Christianity and the Catholic Church. Despite the pronouncements of many secular critics who downplay Hill's religious dimension, it remains true that Hill continues to grapple with the tensions of Christian experience, and he has even commented that the poet may communicate grace without possessing it himself. His poetry is of inestimable value because it brings a thoroughly modern sensibility to bear on the experience of faith—and it does so with searing honesty and even, on occasion, humility. His challenge is one that Christians must accept and attend to.

As I indicated earlier, Hill is convinced that we live in a "world growing . . . ever more shameless," in which language, a fallen instrument of fallen man, is implicated in the atrocities of our time. The decay of language is co-extensive with the decay of consciousness; the poet must to the best of his ability write in such a way as to draw the reader into the act of linguistic revitalization. Hill has publicly condemned what he calls the "confessional mode" of poetic utterance, which is a solipsistic indulgence of self, devoid of artistic control and seriousness. But the imaginative process, he has written, takes this form: "From the depths of self we rise to a concurrence with that which is not-self."[13] Even more than Eliot, Hill reaches into the past in order to render judgment as well as to discover sources of order.

Perhaps the best way to glimpse the nature of Hill's vision is through a critical reading of one of his poems. His sequence "Hymns to Our Lady of Chartres" consists of three short poems and provides access to Hill's technique and recurring thematic interests.[14] It is worth noting that the volume Hill published immediately prior to "Hymns" was a single long poem entitled *The Mystery of the Charity of Charles Peguy.* Hill wrote the poem to express his homage to the French religious and political thinker who died in World War I. He is drawn to Peguy's vision of a culture unified from peasant to political leader by Catholic faith and rootedness in the land and folk traditions. Hill unquestionably finds in Peguy much of what he himself holds most dear, and finds himself similarly attracted to, and aloof from, Christian belief. In a note on Peguy appended to his long poem, Hill writes:

[Peguy] remained self-excommunicate but adoring; his devotion most doggedly expressed in those two pilgrimages undertaken on foot, in

June 1912 and July 1913, from Paris to the Cathedral of Notre Dame de Chartres. The purpose of his first journey, as a tablet in the Cathedral duly records, was to entrust his children to Our Lady's care.

Hans Urs von Balthasar has written of Peguy: "In the six great Chartres poems, which must be considered as Peguy's supreme artistic achievement, he appeals from the fallen temporal order to the presence of unfallen time in the holiness of Mary."[15] Perhaps in addition to Peguy, the shadow of Henry Adams, comparing the graceful power of the Virgin to the impersonal mechanism of the Dynamo, is also present.

This background is necessary for a proper understanding of the density and allusiveness of Hill's "Hymns." In these poems he is making the same kind of pilgrimage that Eliot made to Ferrar's Little Gidding: he is going to "kneel where prayer has been valid." The "Hymns" are in fact similar to Eliot's "Ash-Wednesday": both poems constitute a commentary or meditation on that ancient Marian prayer, the Salve Regina. When Eliot concludes a section of his poem with the words "And after this our exile," the explicit sense conveys the speaker's distance from spiritual communion; but the reader, completing the sentence with "show us the blessed fruit of thy womb, Jesus," is drawn toward the hope of redemption. The "Hymns" of Geoffrey Hill work in much the same way.

The first "Hymn" begins:

Eia, with handbells, jews' harps, risible
tuckets of salutation! Otherwise
gnashing and gnawing sound out your praise.
Salve regina! Visible, invisible,

powers, presences, in and beyond the blue
glass, radiantly-occluded Sion, pour
festal light at the feet of the new poor,
scavengers upon grace, and of your true

servant Peguy who cries out from the crowd
where your bienpensants clatter to adore
la Dame du Pilier and her wooden stare.

"Eia"—in this context meaning "Come!"—is a word used in Latin and Greek that can be an expression of joy and urgency, but also of exhortation. Our salutations are often foolish—risible tuckets (i.e., ridiculous trumpet flourishes)—or they are made in pain and reluctance (and yet they also "rise"). The stained glass is seen as "radiantly-occluded Sion;" the glass blocks the light but also captures and transforms it into a vision of the heavenly kingdom. The glass is in this sense sacramental, like the best art: in its density, it mediates transcendent truth. The "new poor" I take to be spiritually impoverished modern men, who may be nouveau riches materially, but who can only scavenge for grace in a church that means little to them. But Peguy is a true servant, a prophetic voice crying out from the crowd. "Bienpensants" is a French word that can mean "right-minded individuals" but is more often used pejoratively in the sense of "self-righteous." Those who "clatter to adore" do not do so with real humility; their very clattering drowns out the still, small voice of God.

The speaker goes on to ask a crucial question: "Through what straits might we come to worship this, / and kneel before you, and be reconciled, / among the flowering lances . . . ?" "Straits" implies both narrow passages as well as distress and desperate circumstances. The path of belief must involve risk and suffering. Thus, the "flowering lances" could simply be candles, but they probably include the lance blossoming in the blood issuing from the side of Christ, and even the flowering of Aaron's rod (Num. 17:8–10), hinting at a new growth of spiritual awareness.

Though the speaker is unsure of his relationship to faith, he begins the second "Hymn" with the words: "Eia ergo," which might be literally rendered as "Come, therefore." In one sense, he asks the reader to contemplate further the mysteries he witnesses in Chartres. But the words "Eia ergo" also come from the Salve Regina; there they are used to ask that Our Lady "turn then" her eyes of mercy upon us. The second hymn begins with a phrase that is both exhortation and plea. The poem continues with a vision of the "great west windows" of the French cathedrals as "full of the sun's holocaust, / the dying blazons of eternity."

Then comes the enigmatic statement: "Love is at odds." A possible interpretation is that love is at odds with our sinfulness, since the speaker continues: "Your beauty has gone out so many times." Our Lady's beauty has been extinguished in men's hearts, but it has also gone out to the devout. Mary is then considered as the "carnal rose that re-enfolds / heaven into earth."

The third "Hymn" returns to the sinful men who need Mary's protection. She is invoked as "Redemptrice of all vows and fealties." Picking up on the feudal connotations of "fealties" the speaker asks that she "Assoil your lordly vassals." "Assoil" is itself a feudal word meaning to absolve sins or to discharge from vows. Our vows—what we pledge ourselves to—are seldom lived up to and must be redeemed; though we are "vassals" to God, we are "lordly," proud. Among those who must be assoiled are "those to whom the kiss of peace is a torment in the midst of mass" and "those who salute you with a raised fist." These I interpret as those hyper-traditionalists who are so upset about the sign of peace that they become irritated in mass, and those hyper-liberals who equate religion with revolutionary politics, the "raised fist." The speaker concludes by asking for Our Lady's prayers for the whole of the Christian community. The gentleness of tone at the conclusion of the hymns, in which the poet sees and accepts our manifold failings in fulfilling our religious aspirations, bespeaks a tone of reconciliation and tenderness not often found in Hill's poetry.

Geoffrey Hill may be "self-excommunicate" but he is one of the few poets now writing who can convey the struggle of a thoroughly modern consciousness with Christian experience. In the drama of Hill's sense of exile and longing, there is reason to believe that Christian culture will continue to find artists willing to undertake the arduous and often painful task of redeeming the time.

8

The End in the Beginning:
The Paradox of Artistic Creativity

Near the beginning of the film *Amadeus*, the reigning court composer of Vienna, Antonio Salieri, wanders through a palace trying
to guess which of the guests at a lavish party is Wolfgang Mozart,
once a famous child prodigy but now a young man acclaimed for his genius
as a composer. Salieri, who has risen from humble origins to his position of
eminence through sheer hard work, is a deeply devout man, having vowed
that he would offer his life and music to God if only God would grant him
artistic genius. Momentarily distracted from his search by a passing tray of
pastries, Salieri enters an empty room. Suddenly a woman bursts into the
room, hotly pursued by a man who proceeds to chase her under a table.
The man's silly giggles and goosings are cut short when he hears a chamber
orchestra begin a piece of surpassing beauty. "My music!" he exclaims, and
tears out of the room to take up the conductor's baton.

Salieri is stunned. How is it possible that such an undignified, scandalous youth could be the creator of music as noble and elevated as that which is
echoing through the palace? In a moment, Salieri's world is undone: instead
of rewarding piety and unremitting labor, God has seen fit to grant a callow
brat a share of divine power.

Even if we acknowledge that Sir Peter Shaffer's *Amadeus* involves a considerable amount of artistic license in embellishing and distorting the historical facts, the dramatic premise of the film (adapted from Shaffer's stage
play) somehow rings true. Creative genius often seems to be ladled out to

those who are manifestly unworthy of it. Indeed, artistic genius has been so frequently bound up with vanity, neurosis, lust, and the rest of the Seven Deadly Sins that it might be considered more of a curse than a blessing. The literature of the West is replete with stories of geniuses whose hubris brings about tragic consequences, from *Oedipus Rex* to *Doctor Faustus* to *Frankenstein* and beyond. Whether in art, science, or politics, creative genius is a form of power, and power, as we all know, corrupts.

As these examples attest, the same capacity we speak of as creativity can also bring about destruction—of personal relationships, social order, and even of human life on a mass scale. We live in a time when human ingenuity has added a series of apocalyptic scenarios to our imaginations. Biological, chemical, and electronic terrors now compete with nuclear weapons in our collective nightmares.

The Poisoner and His Prose

So in what sense might we say that creativity is a virtue? Oscar Wilde, a creative individual if there ever was one, and an artist with his own share of problems, framed the question with his usual wit. "The fact of a man's being a poisoner," he once said, "is nothing against his prose."

If Wilde strikes you as suspect in voicing this opinion, given his own notorious troubles, how about those two paragons of reason and rectitude—Aristotle and St. Thomas Aquinas? They provide a philosophical basis for Wilde's position by distinguishing between two different types of human action: making and doing. Doing involves human choices, the way we exercise our free will. In the realm of doing—or Prudence, as it has been called—the goal is the perfection of the doer. In other words, in our behavior we are seeking to perfect ourselves as moral agents.

But in making—or art, if you will—the end is not the perfection of the artist as a person but the good of the made thing. The moment that art is made subservient to some ethical or political purpose, it ceases to be art and becomes propaganda. Art seems to require an inviolable freedom to seek the good of the artifact, without either overt or covert messages being forced into it. And history demonstrates that it is simply a statement of fact (to paraphrase Aquinas) that rectitude of the appetites is not a prerequisite for the ability to make beautiful objects. Thus, our poisoner with his exquisite prose style. Or Picasso brutalizing the women in his life. Or the legion of artists and scientists who drank or drugged themselves to death.

Of course, many people have condoned—or at least downplayed—the anarchic and damaging behavior of the creative mastermind. One of the enduring legacies of the Romantic era is the cult of genius, which pits the heroic artist, attuned to Nature, against the moral norms of Society, which are seen as artificial and restrictive. A professor of mine once pointed out the enormous cultural divide separating a composer like Franz Josef Haydn, who (like Mozart) worked for a patron and saw himself essentially as a craftsman, and Ludwig von Beethoven, who was the independent genius *par excellence*, the formidable titan with the knitted brow, prepared to bring everyone around him into thrall. The lives of Haydn and Beethoven overlapped for nearly forty years, but the cultural sea change that took place in those two generations was epochal.

It would be wrong, I think, to blame the Aristotelian-Thomist conception of art as tending toward the perfection of the made object for the rise of the Romantic cult of the genius. For one thing, those philosophers were anything but antinomian in their thought; the artist was still subject to the laws of Prudence. Moreover, these thinkers had a broad definition of art, one that did not elevate the genius above the common man—the cobbler and the composer were, in a sense, on the same plane—a fact still alive in Haydn's self-understanding.

The ultimate extension of Romantic ideas about the artist can be found in the thought of Friedrich Nietzsche, for whom the genius was the superman, beyond good and evil. In the composer Richard Wagner, Nietzsche thought he had found an artistic avatar. Wagner's epic operas, with their sense of the ending of the old order of gods, to be followed by a new era of human emancipation, seemed to embody Nietzsche's belief in the superman. But when Wagner composed *Parsifal*, based on the mythology of the Holy Grail, rooted in Christian metaphors, Nietzsche abandoned Wagner, accusing him of "falling at the foot of the cross."

There have been plenty of other creative individuals in the modern era who were quite content to consider themselves beyond good and evil, and their antics have done much to turn vast segments of the population against the arts.

An Invitation to Virtue

So where does this leave us? If creativity seems unequally distributed, can bring about destruction, does not intrinsically aid in the moral perfection of the creative individual, and has been tainted by the Romantic cult of the genius, then the case for calling it a virtue would seem to be a lost cause.

And yet there is something in most of us that accords a high measure of dignity and worth to the creative impulse. Nearly all the world's religions are grounded in a creation story, one that also ennobles human beings as agents who continue the divine act of creation through their own actions, each of which partakes in some measure of the supernatural powers of the creator.

On a personal level, we witness and are enriched by the grandeur of creativity when we see it in art or engineering or statecraft. We sense that creativity lies at the heart of what makes us human, and that without it, our lives would be spiritually and materially impoverished.

I would argue that the truest, most unsentimental thing we can say about creativity is that it is a constant *invitation* to virtue, that if we step back and look for the deeper meanings of the creative urge, and the lessons of the creative process, we will discover myriad opportunities to develop our inner lives, whether we are makers ourselves or are simply responding to the creativity of others. In what follows, I will draw primarily from the realm I know most about, literature. But one could just as easily search for analogies in almost any area of human endeavor.

Flannery O'Connor and the Habitus of Art

In 1950, at the age of twenty-six, Flannery O'Connor was on a roll. She had left her childhood home of Milledgeville, Georgia, behind, along with her unimaginative and sometimes overbearing mother, Regina, and was living in Connecticut with a young literary couple, Sally and Robert Fitzgerald. O'Connor had already received a degree from the prestigious Iowa Writer's Workshop and a literary prize that gave a New York publisher an option on her first novel. A residency at Yaddo, an invitation-only artists' colony, had introduced her to such literary stars as the poet Robert Lowell and the critic Alfred Kazin. She had been to dinner parties with Mary McCarthy and her circle of New York intellectuals.

As a Southerner and a Catholic, O'Connor had many reasons to feel an almost adversarial relationship to New York as a citadel of the American cultural elite. But she was there to take it on, headfirst. She was feeling her oats.

Then, at Christmas, she developed the first symptoms of lupus, the disease that had taken the life of her father when she was just fifteen. Her father had lived for only three years after the onset of symptoms, and so O'Connor assumed that she would have only that amount of time left. Aware that she would become debilitated and could not ask the Fitzgeralds, with their growing family, to care for her, O'Connor made the only decision she could: she packed her bags and returned home to the family farm, Andalusia, and her sometimes querulous mother.

The defeat could not have been more total. Living with her mother and a family of ducks on the farm, she was cut off from any intellectual or cultural stimulus, confined to letter-writing for contact with the outside world. Her fiction, which employed violence and the grotesque, horrified her mother. "Why can't you write something uplifting," Regina would say, "like the folks at *Reader's Digest?*" As O'Connor confided in a letter to a friend: "This always leaves me shaking and speechless, raises my blood pressure 140 degrees, etc. All I can say is, if you have to ask, you'll never know."

Despite the pain and enervation of lupus, and the daily domestic frustrations, O'Connor did not collapse into self-pity and paralysis. A self-described "hillbilly Thomist," she embraced the Aristotelian-Thomist view of art, especially as she found it described by one of her contemporaries, the French Catholic philosopher, Jacques Maritain, in his *Art and Scholasticism*. She was grateful to Maritain for making the distinction between Art and Prudence, because she believed that a Christian writer's "moral sense" and "dramatic sense" ought to coincide with one another. For O'Connor, as for several other important modern Christian writers, including T. S. Eliot and David Jones, Maritain provided a sort of liberation: he helped explain why a religious writer ought to resist the temptation to turn her work into didactic or propagandistic art.

But she also noted Maritain's argument that art did involve what the ancient philosophers called *habitus,* or the virtue of artistic craft and discipline. Every day she sat down at her typewriter for a minimum of two to three hours, however wretched she may have been feeling, physically or emotionally. She was tart and unsentimental about the creative process, belonging to the school of artists who believe that inspiration can only be found by sitting down at 9:00 a.m. each day and meeting it halfway. At public lectures, she was often asked why she wrote. "Because I'm good at it," she invariably replied. And if some in the audience were offended by this remark, others recognized that she was simply being true to her Thomistic understanding of art.

However, for O'Connor writing fiction involved more than the virtue, or habit, of disciplined effort. She believed that creating a convincing, enduring world in a story required the author to achieve a difficult balance: between judgment and mercy, reason and mystery, nature and grace. She saw the model of perfect balance in the Incarnation of Christ, who was both human and divine, infinitely holy and yet infinitely merciful. She would have agreed with J. R. R. Tolkien that the artist (or creative person in general) engages in an act of "subcreation"—not creating out of nothing, as God does, but creating a microcosm in a manner analogous to that of the Creator.

Good storytelling, she held, was grounded in metaphysical concerns. The creative writer tells us about lives where something ultimate is at stake. "Where there is no belief in the soul" and its need of salvation, she once wrote, "there is very little drama."

A Trinitarian View of Creativity

O'Connor's theology of the imagination was close in spirit to that of another twentieth-century Christian writer, Dorothy Sayers. Like O'Connor, Sayers was a tough cookie, choosing Dante and Aquinas as her heroes, rather than the Romantics. Though she is known primarily for her mystery novels, Sayers was an enormously gifted thinker; she was a playwright, a translator of Dante, and something of a theologian. In *The Mind of the Maker*, one of her most profound works, Sayers contends that the creative process in art-making is analogous to the Christian theology of the Trinity—and that the activity illuminates the other. She first made the point at the end of her play *The Zeal of Thy House*, in which one character says:

> For every work [or act] of creation is threefold, an earthly trinity to match the heavenly.
>
> First, [not in time, but merely in order of enumeration] there is the Creative Idea, passionless, timeless, beholding the whole work complete at once, the end in the beginning: and this is the image of the Father.
>
> Second, there is the Creative Energy [or Activity] begotten of that idea, working in time from the beginning to the end, with sweat and passion, being incarnate in the bonds of matter: and this is the image of the Word.
>
> Third, there is the Creative Power, the meaning of the work and its response in the lively soul: and this is the image of the indwelling Spirit.
>
> And these three are one, each equally in itself the whole work, whereof none can exist without the other; and this is the image of the Trinity.

Or, to put it more succinctly, there is the mind of the author, the act of writing, and the experience of reading and comprehending the story.

All this might seem a bit schematic, but Sayers draws out the implications in a variety of arresting ways. The artist makes things out of love, she says, but this does not imply some sort of jealous possession or domination over the work. Rather, the "artist never desires to subdue his work to himself but always to subdue himself to his work. The more genuinely creative he is, the more he will want his work to develop in accordance with its own nature, and to stand independent of himself." For a writer this means giving the characters in the story free will, seeking their good rather than her own. It also means that as readers we can come to know, in some measure, the mind of the Maker.

The imagination works through empathy, which requires the artist to place herself in the experience of an other—and thus lose herself. While the death of the self may appear to be a loss of control and individuality, the paradox of artistic creativity is that only through this openness to the good of the story and the characters who inhabit it can the maker discover meaning and order.

Flannery O'Connor understood this. Though she has sometimes been caricatured as a testy spinster and a hyper-controlling artist with a rather narrow emotional range, anyone who reads her letters, collected in *The Habit of Being*, will see that this is a misreading of her life and work. She was funny, generous, intensely loyal to her friends, and able to see her own foibles and temptations. She frequently turned that unflinching gaze of hers upon herself.

Parables of Pride and Grace

More often than not, the characters in O'Connor's stories who are the most obtuse and the most prideful, are the isolated, would-be intellectuals who believe their genius puts them beyond good and evil. Take the character of Julian, in "Everything That Rises Must Converge." Forced to accompany his tiresome mother, a woman obsessed by distinctions of race and class and sporting an absurdly inflated aristocratic sensibility, Julian believes that his cynical, disillusioned mind can see through everything—until he suddenly experiences loss.

Or what about Joy in "Good Country People"? Stuck in a rural home with a narrow-minded, pragmatic mother, Joy decides to withdraw into her

own arcane studies (which sound a lot like deconstruction theory) taking
the harsh name of "Hulga" to complete her self-reinvention. When a seemingly naïve and gawky young man comes to her door with Bibles for sale,
she thinks she can see through him. But she has another think coming,
something that strikes down her pride. Did the writer, who chose to go by
her unusual middle name rather than her somewhat plain given name, Mary,
see something of herself in the lonely, angry Hulga?

O'Connor's tales are parables of human pride being confronted by the
shock of divine grace—the violence in her stories is caused not by God but
by the stubbornness of our human attempt to live as autonomous agents. By
the same token, the grotesque in her fiction is not an unhealthy obsession
with deformity but a metaphor for what we make of ourselves, the distortion
that takes place when creatures attempt to think of themselves as gods, as
creators of their own world. In the moment of violence that often concludes
her stories, God's judgment and his mercy are one and the same. That is
why the endings of her stories are open-ended: we don't know whether the
protagonists will choose the virtuous path or not, which throws the question
back at us, her readers: What would we do?

In one sense, O'Connor's creative writing gave her the opportunity to
learn and relearn the virtues of self-knowledge and humility: by seeing her
own sinfulness in some of her characters she recognized her own need for
mercy. But O'Connor did not believe that art is merely self-expression—
another problematic legacy of the Romantic era. Rather, she saw herself as
a "Christian realist," and believed that art had to do justice to the world
beyond the self. In one of her letters, O'Connor writes: "Maritain says that to
produce a work of art requires the 'constant attention of the purified mind,'
and the business of the purified mind in this case is to see that those elements of the personality that don't bear on the subject at hand are excluded.
Stories don't lie when left to themselves. Everything has to be subordinated
to a whole which is not you. Any story I reveal myself completely in will be
a bad story."

Since O'Connor's untimely death in 1964 at the age of thirty-nine, one
of the dominant strains in Western thought has held that traditional ideas
about the creative individual are false. A host of postmodern thinkers have
asserted that the very notion of creativity is an illusion. Meaning, they say, is
"constructed," not by an individual who has developed the *habitus* of art, but
by other forces: the "selfish gene," or the unconscious, or the economic means
of production. Postmodern artists and critics have spoken of the exhaustion

of art; awash in the fragments of past cultures, eclectic "quotation" of older artistic works supplants the drive to synthesize the achievements of the past into something fresh and new.

It is no accident that this worldview has no time for the Judeo-Christian understanding of art as subcreation, something analogous to God's creative fiat. The postmodernists reject Samuel Taylor Coleridge's definition of the imagination as the "repetition in the finite mind of the eternal act of creation in the infinite I AM." Like Hulga, these intellectuals think they can see through everything, but they do so at the expense of their own humanity.

The undermining of traditional Western ideas about creativity has brought about a deep cultural impoverishment. Creativity may be only an invitation to virtue—an invitation that is not always accepted—but it exists only in individual souls, souls that must struggle to observe the world, empathize with its inhabitants, and shape an artifact into a form that communicates meaning to others.

Part Three

Six Writers

9

Evelyn Waugh:

Savage Indignation

Both in his own lifetime and in the forty years since his death, Evelyn Waugh (1903–1966) has triggered violent emotional reactions—ranging from adulation to revulsion—in those who encounter his writings. He is in fact one of those rare figures who often manages to evoke positive and negative responses within the same individual. He has been called a Fascist, a snob, a reactionary Catholic, and "one of the three nastiest writers in the twentieth century" (the other two being Wyndham Lewis and Bertolt Brecht). When his diaries were published ten years after his death, the reviewer in the *London Sunday Times* concluded that the books constituted "a portrait of the artist as a bad man." Yet he is commonly acknowledged to be a comic genius and one of the masters of English prose style. All but one or two of his thirty books remain in print, and three recent films made from his novels have appeared to critical acclaim (*Brideshead Revisited*, *Bright Young Things*, and *A Handful of Dust*).

Of course, as you may already suspect, Waugh relished controversy and is undoubtedly looking down on the ruckus which attends his literary reputation with the deepest satisfaction. Waugh's taste for provocation went beyond his outrageously funny satires upon a veritable rogue's gallery of imbecilic aristocrats, petty African dictators, and social climbers. In his later years, he would attend public functions dressed in loudly-checked suits, sporting "a Victorian ear trumpet which he would raise when talking and lower when spoken to," according to one of his recent biographers.[1] He was not averse to making a scene when the mood came upon him.

This same biographer, Martin Stannard, recounts an incident which typifies Waugh's flair for offensiveness. In 1960 the BBC got Waugh to agree to a rare television interview. His interlocutor was a man named John Freeman, whose skills at probing intimate personal matters would easily rival those of Jerry Springer or Geraldo Rivera.

> Soberly dressed, a carnation in his buttonhole, with the inevitable cigar and a quizzical glare of amused condescension, [Waugh] answered all the questions designed to reveal psychological instability with devastating brevity. When pushed for details, he mixed fantasy and truth at just the right pitch of levity to confuse and deflate his inquisitor. At last, somewhat desperate, Freeman managed to pin Waugh to a definite statement. The novelist agreed that the best he could hope for was that people should ignore him. "You like that when it happens, do you?" "Yes." "Why are you appearing on this programme?" "Poverty," came the reply, "We've both been hired to talk in this deliriously happy way."[2]

Pleasant as this story is, there is perhaps another anecdote which cuts closer to the heart of Waugh's personality. In the early 1930s, Waugh—his reputation already established—had the opportunity to meet Hilaire Belloc, the aging, crusty Catholic controversialist. When the meeting took place, Waugh remained uncharacteristically shy and reticent; he was then a recent convert to the Catholic Church and felt awed in Belloc's presence. After Waugh had left, Belloc was asked about his impression of the young man. His answer was not what Waugh's friends had expected. "He is possessed," Belloc said.[3]

What Belloc meant by that mysterious comment was not that Waugh was—literally speaking—a hostage to the Devil. Rather, the old man was paying tribute to Waugh's capacity not so much to outrage others as to be outraged by the sins and follies of his time. In short, Waugh felt himself to be plagued by the demons of the modern world; his writings were to become acts of exorcism that would cast out the things that so thoroughly galled him.

A Personal Debt

As I reflect on my personal debt to Waugh's literary and spiritual vision, I realize that it is this fierce inner struggle that accounts for his greatness and the fascination he holds for me. The figure in literary history to whom he seems closest is Jonathan Swift, the eighteenth-century wit who also blended venom and comic inventiveness into a potent satirical mix. Like Waugh, Swift was accused of snobbery, reactionary politics, and, above all, hatred for his fellow man. But critics have rarely understood that compassion and principle can coexist with stinging ridicule—particularly when they have felt the lash of the satirist's wit themselves.

Perhaps those who place themselves in the role of prophet suffer from the occupational hazard of confusing righteous wrath with wrath, pure and simple. Swift's epitaph, which he composed himself, read: "*Ubi saeva indignatio ulterius cor lacerare nequit*" (Where savage [or fierce] indignation can no longer tear his heart). The prophet and the satirist inevitably appear to be negativists—they are always calling down the thunderbolts of vengeance upon the wicked.

But the most convincing prophets and satirists have never been loose canons firing indiscriminately at whatever happens to irritate them at the moment. In fact, the true satirist is not a pure cynic, but one whose idealism has been wounded by the vision of how far men fall short of their potential. In the crucible of their art, great writers like Swift and Waugh refine away personal grudges and vendettas; their savage indignation, in the end, is the bitter herb which is intended to violently purge the sickness of a world which is truly "fallen." Or, to put it another way, the doctor's knife appears menacing, but it is used to restore health. And without a notion of what constitutes a sound body, there can be no healing.

What I discovered, in time, was that Evelyn Waugh's "possession" was precisely his greatest gift. Yet the more of his fiction I read, the more I was convinced that behind his satirical wit—which was what had attracted and delighted me at first—there also lay a coherent and profound worldview. Waugh's public persona may have been marked by exhibitionism and querulousness, but his fiction spoke to me with the force of prophetic insight.

I began to read Waugh in graduate school, during what proved to be a turning point in my life—between my youth and my mature career as a writer, editor, and teacher. My adolescence had been both rocky and lonely: the experience of living through my parents' separation and divorce deepened a natural tendency toward non-conformism and isolation. Going off to college, I felt not only the normal exhilaration of independence, but also the sense of joining a cause. I had chosen a school that had a national reputation for its ties to the conservative intellectual movement. The late 1970s were bracing times for conservatives, who were advancing toward the political victory of Ronald Reagan's election to the presidency. "Bliss was it in that dawn to be alive, / But to be young was very heaven." Wordsworth's famous lines about his enthusiasm for the fledgling French Revolution perfectly describe my mood at that time. As a budding conservative, I felt, on a deep emotional level, that I belonged to a community. It was a new family.

But even as I progressed through my undergraduate years and the euphoria among conservatives grew in intensity, I became troubled and divided. Many of my professors had introduced me to classic works of history and literature which, far from supporting political triumphalism, spoke of the "tragic sense of life," original sin, and the limitations of partisan politics. The strain of American conservatism embraced by Ronald Reagan, a form of messianism going back to the Puritan conviction that America was the "shining city on a hill" that would lead the world to peace and prosperity, struck me as arrogant, unhistorical, and downright dangerous.

Another set of misgivings soon complemented my intellectual difficulties. As I became more deeply involved with the public institutions of the conservative movement, I found them riddled with hypocrisy, corruption, and greed. At the foundation where I worked immediately after graduating, the phones seemed to be ringing off the hook with conservatives desperate to get high level positions in executive-branch bureaucracies they were committed, in principle, to abolishing. (These same conservatives soon began talking about their departments as "agents for constructive change.") In one sense, of course, my youthful idealism was getting its inevitable battering; I was growing up. But it was no longer possible for me to seek comfort in an ideological family. I went off to Oxford for graduate work in English literature, once again relieved to be away from a painful environment, but no longer so anxious to "belong."

In the long vacations between the grueling eight-week Oxford terms, I read through the entire Waugh canon, starting with the early romps, *Decline and Fall* and *Vile Bodies*, and ending with his much-underrated World War II trilogy, *Sword of Honour*. What these novels gave me—apart from sheer delight, which is, after all, the one prerequisite for good art—was a way to organize my experience. As a Christian in the late twentieth century, I needed to find a way to address the spiritual crisis of the modern West without falling into either apathy or the ready-made answers of ideology. I found it, in part, in Waugh's tragicomic vision. That vision, with all of its stylistic brilliance and complex ironies, was fueled, not by personal malice or childhood trauma, but by an unshakable conviction that civilization could only be held together by religious faith.

The Stiletto in the Ribs

Waugh's novels are excruciatingly funny—in a very literal sense. The essence of Waugh's comic genius is his ability to cause the reader to feel both pleasure and pain. No sooner are you laughing at some bizarre caricature or piece of knockabout farce than Waugh suddenly inserts the stiletto between your ribs. In *Black Mischief*, an early satire of the crumbling British Empire set in an African nation, the young innocent abroad shares a meal with some natives only to find that he has just digested his girlfriend. Rather than an isolated piece of grotesquerie, an episode like this fits into a tautly constructed whole. As Waugh explained:

> [*Black Mischief*] deals with the conflict of civilisation, with all its attendant and deplorable ills, and barbarism. The plan of my book throughout was to keep the darker aspects of barbarism continually and unobtrusively present, a black and mischievous background against which the civilized and semi-civilized characters performed their parts: I wished it to be like the continuous, remote throbbing of those hand drums, constantly audible, never visible, which every traveller in Africa will remember as one of his most haunting impressions.

What he doesn't say here, but worked out in the novel, was the nearly complete reversal between civilization and barbarism—the colonial British are slowly revealed as the true barbarians.

In short, I came to see that Waugh's deft constructions and thematic seriousness set him above the mere humorist and put him in the same class as the two most devastating satirists in our literature: Juvenal and Swift.

The key to Waugh's irony is absence. What is missing from the world he depicts is religious faith, with its attendant stress on moral and cultural standards. There are, to be sure, regular church attendees and even American revivalists in his novels, but religion has become nothing more than a social habit. For Waugh, civilization is a precarious artifact, not a natural condition. Without the inner ordering which a living faith in a transcendent creator entails, he believed, the external ordering of society would become brittle and collapse into fragments.

Interestingly, many of Waugh's early readers were unaware that his novels had any serious "point." In some ways, they can hardly be blamed. There is in his fiction none of the direct castigation of society's ills such as can be found in Juvenal's philippics.

Most readers follow the anarchic whirl of events in these stories in a state of breathless exhilaration. It should be no surprise that Waugh was, by temperament, an anarchist with a heightened sense of the absurd. As Martin Stannard puts it, Waugh's art was "an anarchic defence of order."[4]

Human institutions, like anything under the sun, inexorably decay; as William Butler Yeats put it: "The centre cannot hold." In 1935, before Auschwitz and the Gulag Archipelago, Waugh published a manifesto which contained these lines.

> Civilization has no force of its own beyond what is given it from within. It is under constant assault and it takes most of the energies of civilized man to keep going at all. . . . Barbarism is never finally defeated; given propitious circumstances, men and women who seem quite orderly will commit every conceivable atrocity. The danger does not come merely from habitual hooligans; we are all potential recruits for anarchy.[5]

The greatest danger, Waugh continues, is not anarchy itself, but the establishment of tyranny to fill the vacuum of disorder. "[A]narchy is the nearer to right order, for something that has not developed may reach the right end, while something which has developed wrongly cannot. . . . The disillusioned Marxist becomes a Fascist; the disillusioned anarchist, a Christian."[6]

Waugh was himself a disillusioned anarchist. He had gone about with the Decadents and Aesthetes at Oxford, and later with the riotous young aristocrats in London, known as the Bright Young Things, at the height of the Roaring Twenties. He married quickly and thoughtlessly and was divorced in little over a year. And while his novels unquestionably capture some of the thrill of the anarchic social and moral conditions of the post–World War I years, they all contain the retracted stiletto blade, which eventually springs out to remind us that we are all potential recruits for barbarism.

A Handful of Dust: *The City and the Jungle*

Nowhere is Waugh's irony more lethal than in *A Handful of Dust*, arguably his greatest work and made into a film. Tony and Brenda Last live in a decaying country house called Hetton. The house, though on the site of the ancient family seat, is a Neo-Gothic monstrosity built in the Victorian era.

Tony, as his surname implies, is the last of civilized men. His love for Hetton is genuine, but his weak aesthetics are the clue to his fatal flaw. He is unaware that this vulgar Victorian imitation of the integrated medieval order is not grounded in the vigorous faith of that earlier age. Tony is a romantic in an age of cold, hard calculation and barbarous passions.

Brenda loathes Hetton and pines for the social life of London. She meets John Beaver, an amoral sponger, and soon moves into a London flat in order to carry on an affair with him. Tony, who enjoys pottering about Hetton, playing the role of country gentleman, remains ignorant of the affair. Beaver's mother is an interior decorator much in demand in London high society. When Mrs. Beaver visits Hetton, she concludes that various rooms should be remodeled in chrome and sheepskin. She, like her son, lives parasitically off the rot of the English ruling class. In her barbarism, she would enclose the remnants of Western art in abstract, antiseptic metal.

Tony's Sunday church attendance is nothing more than a social ritual. "Occasionally some arresting phrase in the liturgy would recall him to his surroundings, but for the most part that morning he occupied himself with the question of bathrooms and lavatories, and of how more of them could be introduced without disturbing the character of his house."[7] But the vicar, the Reverend Tendril, isn't really "there" either. An elderly man, he has spent most of his life as a missionary in the far-flung British Empire. He continues to preach as if to a military garrison in Afghanistan or India. His Christmas sermon provides an example: "Instead of the glowing log fire and windows tight shuttered against the drifting snow, we have only the harsh glare of the alien sun. . . . Instead of the placid ox and ass of Bethlehem . . . we have for companions the ravening tiger and the exotic camel, the furtive jackal and the ponderous elephant."[8]

Reverend Tendril's sermon returns us to the theme of the perennial conflict between civilization and barbarism. Waugh makes this explicit in the novel's conclusion. Tony, the last to learn of Brenda's infidelity, emerges from his passivity (too late, of course), deciding to file for divorce as the injured party and thus refuse Brenda any financial settlement. On impulse, he agrees to accompany a crackpot explorer, Dr. Messinger, on an expedition into the South American jungle to find a mythical city, a lost paradise. Dr. Messinger, who utterly fails to comprehend the natives, meets an untimely end, while Tony comes down with a nearly fatal fever. In Tony's delirium, Waugh presents a richly suggestive phantasmagoria. At first Tony thinks he has seen the mythical city; it is a glorified but sentimentalized version of Hetton, all Gothic turrets and banners. Later he thinks he is addressing John Beaver:

> You would hear better and it would be more polite if you stood still when I addressed you instead of walking around in a circle. . . . I know you are friends of my wife and that is why you will not listen to me. But be careful. She will say nothing cruel, she will not raise her voice, there will be no hard words. She hopes you will be great friends afterwards as before. But she will leave you. She will go away quietly during the night. She will take her hammock and her rations of farine. . . . Listen to me. I know I am not clever but that is no reason why we should forget courtesy. Let us kill in the gentlest manner. I will tell you what I have learned in the forest, where time is different. There is no City. Mrs. Beaver has covered it with chromium plating and converted it into flats.[9]

Instead of the City of God, glimpsed through the highest achievements of Western art and civilization, there is only the jungle. But the new jungle in London will be more inhospitable to man than the Amazon for the simple reason that it denies the essence of humanity itself. As Waugh said on more than one occasion, man without God is less than man.

Nowhere in *A Handful of Dust* is there any representative of traditional Christian faith. Waugh requires the reader to follow the lines of his irony back to the missing element in the equation. In this use of absence, Waugh is actually close to the aesthetic techniques of the modernist writers—T. S. Eliot, Ezra Pound, and James Joyce. In works like Eliot's *The Waste Land* and Joyce's *Ulysses*, the reader is set down in a bewildering world where he must make his own way, taking his bearings from the relationship of the parts to an unstated whole. The great advantage of the modern style is that it requires the reader to weigh various interpretations and make his own judgments. Though few readers will be able or willing to engage in this process of discovering meaning, an encounter with modernist literature can be exciting—the opposite of passive reception. Waugh's fiction cunningly allies modernism in technique with a Christian vision of the world.

The Problem of Standards

My realization that Waugh, for all his public stuffiness about modern art, had mastered some of the stylistic achievements of literary modernism, was also important. It had become increasingly clear to me that the Christian writer in the twentieth century could not merely hearken back to happier ages when the faith was publicly endorsed. We cannot "ring the bell backward. . . . Or follow an antique drum," Eliot reminds us in *Four Quartets*.[10] That would be an exercise in sentimentality and irrelevance. No, the modern Christian artist had to speak to his age in the language and forms of his time. With breathtaking artistic genius, Waugh had managed to use the anarchic and frenetic state of modern society to reflect the poverty of a culture severed from its roots in the cult, the Christian faith.

In reading Waugh, I had started where any good reader of fiction should begin: I tried to take in the unique flavor of his style. I had, in short, accustomed myself to the particular kind of aesthetic lens, with its specific tint and magnification, through which the author wanted me to see the world. But two questions soon obtruded themselves. There was, in the first place, the problem of standards; the satirist has to launch his salvos from a fixed position; the only alternative being a thoroughgoing nihilism. What was the source of the norms against which Waugh measured human folly and evil? The second question involved my curiosity about Waugh's theological background. What strand of Christianity did he find the most satisfying?

As it turned out, both questions had the same answer: the Roman Catholic Church, to which Waugh had converted in 1930. These were not academic questions for me, but urgent, burning issues. Like many young Christian writers in the 1970s, I had come from one of the "Low" churches to embrace the Episcopal Church, or what I preferred to call the "Anglican Communion." My literary heroes, C. S. Lewis and T. S. Eliot, had been Anglicans, and my immediate Christian mentors, Thomas Howard and Sheldon Vanauken, were shining beacons along what has been called "the Canterbury trail." I was intoxicated by the language of the King James Version of the Bible and the Book of Common Prayer; Evensong with an Anglican boys' choir was, I was sure, a direct preview of the heavenly consort. Sacraments, ritual, priesthood—all of these elements of "Catholic" Christianity became like richly colored stained glass through which I basked in the light of God's grace.

But there was soon trouble in paradise. When I looked to the Episcopal Church for clear and unambiguous teaching on the crucial moral issues of the day—marriage and divorce, abortion, homosexuality—I found a Babel of conflicting voices. It was impossible for me simply to "transcend" these problems which centered on the family, the one institution that most clearly stood between civilization and anarchy. Nor could I accept that these were private matters, part of a legitimate "pluralism" within the church. So the question of the teaching authority of the church became paramount. As I stood on the steps of a beautiful Neo-Gothic Episcopal church, I gazed across the street to a hideous roller-rink style Catholic church, envying not the aesthetics of its parishioners, but the force and clarity of their church's teachings.

Because my childhood experiences of Christianity had been in what I call the "Transcendentalist" tradition—Christian Science and liberal Congregationalism—I never had the dogmatic frame of mind that relied on elaborate logical and Biblical proofs. For me, the measures of truth were much more concrete and specific, hence my interest in art and morals. In my own search for a home within the Christian community, therefore, works of the imagination, such as novels or paintings, were not only admissible but essential guides. Evelyn Waugh's early novels, such as *A Handful of Dust*, do not confront the experience of faith directly. But his most famous novel, *Brideshead Revisited*, was about the Catholic Church and the way it shaped and affected its communicants.

Brideshead Revisited: *The Operation of Grace*

Brideshead marked a new phase in Waugh's fiction. His conversion in 1930 had been a relatively intellectual affair, primarily an assent to the dogma of the church. But during World War II, Waugh came to believe that in his personal life, and in his art, he ought to make the church an active force. The ambitious goal he set for himself in *Brideshead* was to show "the operation of divine grace on a group of diverse but closely connected characters."[11]

Ironically, the reaction of many readers, including a good number of Catholics, to *Brideshead* can be summarized by a letter received from an American reader soon after its publication: "Your *Brideshead Revisited* is a strange way to show that Catholicism is an answer to anything. Seems more like the kiss of Death."[12] A plot summary would certainly seem to support that contention. The agnostic painter, Charles Ryder, witnesses one member after another of the Catholic, aristocratic Flyte family die or fade away in lives which appear largely futile. Early in the novel, Ryder's intimate friend, Sebastian Flyte, explains:

> So you see we're a mixed family religiously. Brideshead and Cordelia are both fervent Catholics; he's miserable, she's bird-happy; Julia and I are half-heathen; I am happy, I rather think Julia isn't; Mummy is popularly believed to be a saint and Papa is excommunicated—and I wouldn't know which of them was happy. Anyway, however you look at it, happiness doesn't seem to have much to do with it, and that's all I want. . . . I wish I liked Catholics more.[13]

By the end of the novel, Sebastian and Cordelia are also living sad, stunted lives. But, as happens so often in the fiction of Evelyn Waugh, a throw-away phrase contains the core of the novel's meaning: "happiness doesn't seem to have much to do with it."[14]

For Waugh, the notion that the life of faith ought to lead inevitably to worldly prosperity and what the pop psychologists call "wellness" is both unrealistic and dangerous. In a fallen world, afflicted by evil and stupidity, happiness can never be a gauge of fidelity to God—and our own deepest needs. To think otherwise is to confuse happiness, with its bourgeois connotations of comfort and freedom from any burdens, with blessedness, or what Catholics call the "state of grace."

Waugh's depiction of the mysterious presence of grace in suffering and adversity is not unique: I found it in the other major Catholics novelists of the twentieth century: Graham Greene, Francois Mauriac, Georges Bernanos, Flannery O'Connor, and Shusaku Endo.

Catholics, Waugh believed, have always clung to the foot of the cross, profoundly and intuitively aware of what the Spanish philosopher Unamuno called "the tragic sense of life." Though several of my closest Protestant friends had told me that the Catholic preference for the crucifix, rather than the unadorned cross, was morbid and obscured the "triumph of Christ," I never had that problem. When Julia Flyte, one of the "half-heathens," reaches a moment of crisis in *Brideshead Revisited*, it is the unexpected memory of the crucifix on the wall of her nursery that shocks her into a recognition of how far she has drifted from God.

As the characters in *Brideshead* enact their "fierce little human tragedy," it becomes clear that they are all in some fashion struggling against God and his church, symbolized by Brideshead Castle, that magnificent baroque backdrop to the novel's action. Thomas Howard has spoken of the church as the "unseen" character in the novel.[15] Even the fervent adherents to the church, such as Lady Marchmain, can't avoid abusing their faith. Lady Marchmain's spiritual intensity and unthinking manipulation drive both her husband and her son Sebastian to drink and exile. When Charles falls in love with Sebastian's sister Julia, the lovers awaken in each other a passion for life that they felt they had lost. After failed marriages, Charles and Julia seem at last to be on the verge of happiness. But when Lord Marchmain returns home to Brideshead, and to the church, on his deathbed, Julia realizes that in denying the church (by remarrying after divorce) and trying to seek out happiness on her own terms, she is condemning herself and Charles to a life of alienation from God.

I'm convinced that Waugh deliberately intended to make the church look like the "kiss of death"—not out of perversity, but because he understood it to be a "sign of contradiction." The sufferings that it seemingly inflicts, because of its laws and absolute claims, are the bitter herbs through which the disease of sin is purged. On closer inspection, the lives which the characters lead at the end of the novel, while not "happy," are in many ways "blessed." Sebastian is a holy fool, a drunken porter for a monastery in North Africa. When he learns of this, Charles asks Cordelia: "I suppose he doesn't suffer?"

> Oh yes, I think he does. One can have no idea what the suffering might be, to be maimed as he is—no dignity, no power of will. No one is ever holy without suffering. It's taken that form with him. . . . I've seen so much suffering in the last few years; there's so much of it coming for everybody soon. It's the spring of love.[16]

Cordelia, who has worked for an ambulance service in the Spanish Civil War, returns to this work with her sister Julia in World War II. They and their brother Brideshead are all stationed in the Holy Land. Symbolically, they become true aristocrats, who go to the Holy Land, not for the ambiguous aims of a Crusade, but to suffer with and for others and to defend the remnants of Christendom. The novel ends with Charles Ryder's first hesitant steps to embrace the faith he for so long misunderstood.

An Indelible Stamp

One of the key themes in *Brideshead* is that the church has the power to actually form one's identity, to stamp it, in an indelible way. For the Flyte family, the church had impressed its archetypes in childhood, as even the half-heathens, Julia and Sebastian, discover. Indeed, the Flyte family itself, though its members cause each other enormous pain, is intended by Waugh as a metaphor for the church. The church, like the family, is foundational: you can never really leave it, wherever you go. This was a difficult concept for me to fathom, coming from the Protestant tradition, where there is so much shopping in the religious supermarket for the right denomination, church, and set of theological propositions. The very notion of "protest" implies that the association of believers is voluntary, and can be dissolved or divided when members disagree.

At one point in the novel, Lady Marchmain reads from a Father Brown story by G. K. Chesterton, in which the priest detective says of the thief: "I caught him with an unseen hook and an invisible line which is long enough to let him wander to the ends of the world and still to bring him back with a twitch upon the thread."[17] This is a metaphor for the church, which is a family, not a voluntary association; one's relationship to it has nothing to do with the will. Hence its inexorable claims.

While I was studying at Oxford, I soon had an unexpected confirmation of the Catholic Church's ability to form not only the conscience, but the whole person. My English girlfriend (now my wife) had begun to return to Christianity through my influence. (She had been, in her words, a "collapsed Catholic.") She willingly attended Anglican services with me and never once attempted to proselytize for the Church of Rome. But as her faith strengthened, I watched in amazement as her Catholicism emerged naturally and unselfconsciously. Soon she realized that she was outside of her home, that she needed to be reconciled and to get inside where it was warm and where she would be fed. Charles Ryder witnessed the same process in Julia Flyte; for them, however, it meant a tragic parting.

Brideshead Revisited is a work of fiction, not a tract. It is a dramatic rendering of "the operation of divine grace on a group of diverse but closely connected characters." Its cumulative effect on me was to suggest that the Catholic Church, far from being an external, bureaucratic and oppressive structure, is a channel of grace, the living and undivided body of Christ.

Once again, Waugh was forcing his readers to supply the missing answer. If the church appears as an arbitrary and demanding mother, it is because the characters have been wayward and ill-disposed toward their parent. It is the Bride, sullied at times and often unworthy of Christ, its Bridegroom and Head. It is our Mother. At least, this is what Waugh believed and what his novel implies.

I came to agree with him. On the Feast of Corpus Christi, 1983, I was received into the Catholic Church, a family to which I could belong without tensions or regrets. Evelyn Waugh had played a role in that decision. To celebrate the event, we went off to a pub outside of Oxford, situated in a charming Cotswold village. Later I found out that the pub was once a favorite haunt of the outrageous Mr. Waugh.

10

Shusaku Endo:

At the Crossroads between East and West

With the deaths of Graham Greene and Walker Percy in 1991 and 1990 respectively, it seemed to a number of observers that the great tradition of modern Catholic fiction had come to an end. Both Greene and Percy, while highly individual in their imaginative gifts, emerged from a vital tradition of Catholic letters. Greene, a British writer, was a friend of the great Catholic satirist, Evelyn Waugh, while Percy shared many literary and theological preoccupations with his fellow Southern Catholic writer, Flannery O'Connor. All of these writers were, in turn, influenced by the French novelists Georges Bernanos and François Mauriac.

What these writers shared was a powerful vision of how the Catholic faith could speak to the complex and tragic world of the twentieth century. Their novels did not depict Catholicism as a cure-all for all the maladies of the human condition; indeed, the Catholic characters in their books are rarely superior, morally speaking, to their secular counterparts. What these novelists demonstrated is that Catholic understanding of guilt, suffering, penitence, and redemption provides a powerful account of the drama of the soul's progress through the world.

The central literary device of the modern Catholic novelist has been paradox—that in order to live one must first die, that in the weakness of guilt, suffering, and evasion is the seed of conversion, that God is often more present in the lives of the lost and the degraded than in his official churchly representatives. At times, the exploration of paradox and ambiguity in these

Catholic writers led readers to suspect the firmness of their commitment to the church's teachings. In fact, most of these writers were staunch defenders of Catholic orthodoxy. And even in a figure such as Greene, who in later years attacked John Paul II and church teachings on sexuality, it can be said that his *imagination* was more orthodox than his politics and theology.

The passing of Greene and Percy, then, had the appearance of the ending of a cultural era in the church. Though there were certainly a number of Catholic writers who produced excellent work into the 1990s—J. F. Powers, Brian Moore, and Julien Green come to mind—they did not possess the stature of their predecessors. In the mainstream culture the term "Catholic novelist" has not conjured up the names of Mauriac, Waugh, or O'Connor, but writers who celebrate their "liberation" from the repressions of childhood Catholicism. Mary Gordon would be an example of this school of Catholic writer-in-rebellion. The problem with such novelists is not that they suffered at the hands of sadistic nuns or priests, but that their anger and their desire to be welcomed in secular circles has truncated their moral and spiritual sensibilities.

Japan's Graham Greene

But one writer who outlived Greene and Percy deserves to be recognized as a master of the Catholic literary revival with which they were associated. He is still not well known in the West because he was not from the West. He was one of Japan's leading novelists, winner of every major literary award given out in his country. He was the dominant figure in Japan's Catholic intellectual community. He has been called "Japan's Graham Greene," but his vision remained unique among twentieth-century Catholic writers. His name was Shusaku Endo (1923–1996).

During a career spanning four decades, Shusaku Endo published over a dozen novels and story collections which all grappled, in one way or another, with the tensions and conflicts between Christianity and the Japanese worldview. It is only recently that Endo's literary stature has come to be more widely known in the West (thanks, in part, to Martin Scorsese's film of Endo's novel *Silence*). A writer of astonishing diversity, much of Endo's work, including essays, memoirs, and plays, remains untranslated.

Given the increasing importance of the Pacific Rim nations in our "global village," Endo's explorations of the encounter between East and West constitute an invaluable resource for deeper understanding.

But the ultimate importance of Endo's fiction is that it achieves timeless and universal themes. Though Endo wrote about the indifference and hostility of the Japanese toward Christianity, he was also writing about all men and women, to whom the gospel is at times a stumbling block or "foolishness." Like the other great modern Catholic novelists, Endo's vision was tragicomic. The tragedy of the Fall and the mystery of evil are real; they leave scars that never heal fully in this world. But for Endo, the tragedy of man was encompassed by the Cross, which initiates the comic "happy ending" of man's redemption.

How was it that Japan's premier novelist of the late twentieth century was a Roman Catholic, given that the entire Catholic population of Japan is less than one percent of the total population? Because Endo's fiction was so deeply autobiographical, it is worth knowing the basic facts of his life.

Born in 1923, Endo's parents divorced when he was only a child, and soon after, his mother converted to Catholicism. Endo spoke of his baptism as a formality that meant nothing to him throughout his early years. Yet his relationship with his mother, though far from serene, was intense—a relationship that would affect his perception of Catholicism and reverberate through his fiction.

Endo did not fight in the Second World War, but as a college student in those years he was very much a part of the "war generation." Members of this generation have wrestled with guilt, a sense of complicity in the monstrosities of the war, and a preoccupation with the nature of evil. Another crucial dimension of Japanese life that the war emphasized was its insularity and distrust of anything foreign. Endo naturally drew analogies from his wartime experience to the persecution of Catholic missionaries to Japan in the seventeenth century and the subsequent closure of Japan to foreign countries from 1639 to 1859.

In the aftermath of the war, and with the death of his mother, Endo began to find that his Catholic faith had more of a grip on his soul than he had realized. He was among the first Japanese students to go abroad after the war to pursue postgraduate studies. Endo went to Lyons in France and concentrated his literary studies on modern Christian writers, especially French writers such as Bernanos and Mauriac. He freely acknowledged his debt to those novelists.

As a young man, Endo suffered from illnesses that kept him in hospitals for over two years, culminating in a series of operations that removed several of his ribs and one of his lungs. The pain and trauma of these operations would resurface in many of his stories and novels.

The Clash of Cultures

Both his experience as a Japanese student in France and his developing Catholic faith forced Endo to examine the clash between the cultures of East and West. Endo discovered a wrenching dichotomy in his own soul that he did not initially believe could be reconciled.

Beginning in 1955, Endo turned this internal debate into the subject matter of his fiction. He found that in the experience of the early Catholic missionaries he had the perfect paradigm of the divergence between East and West. His two masterpieces, *Silence* (1966) and *The Samurai* (1980), are, on the surface, historical novels, but they are at the same time autobiographical and thus contemporary.

After the initial successes of St. Francis Xavier and his fellow Jesuit missionaries in gaining Japanese converts, the Shoguns (feudal lords) began to persecute Christians. The persecutions were caused by political and cultural factors. Fearful of foreign powers, the Shoguns saw the spreading of Christianity as part of a plan by Spain and Portugal to subdue Japan.

The persecutions began with the burning of Christians at the stake. However, it soon became clear to the Shoguns that martyrdoms were having the opposite effect; the spectacle of martyrs singing hymns as the flames consumed them only kindled the faith of the Christians. Henceforth, the object of the persecutions was not merely execution, but apostasy.

The authorities required Christians to signify their apostasy by trampling upon a small copper bas-relief (called a *fumie*) depicting Christ, Mary, and the apostles. The image of the *fumie* is a central one in Endo's fiction, a pathetic object in which the face of Christ has been worn smooth by the feet of those who have rejected Him.

For those who refused to trample on the *fumie*, a number of ingenious tortures were devised. Perhaps the worst—and the most effective—was known as "The Pit," described by a historian of the period:

> The victim was tightly bound around the body as high as the breast (one hand being left free to give the signal of recantation) and then hung downwards from a gallows into a pit which usually contained excreta and other filth, the top of the pit being level with his knees. In order to give the blood some vent, the forehead was lightly slashed with a knife. Some of the stronger martyrs lived for more than a week in this

position, but the majority did not survive more than a day or two.

The persecutions did achieve thousands of apostasies, and eventually, in 1639, Japan was closed off to the West. Christianity survived only in small "underground" pockets of believers known as *kakure*, who preserved but slowly altered the faith. For the *kakure*, Mary became a figure as great, or greater, than Christ. When Japan was finally opened to the outside world in 1859, the *kakure* generally refused to rejoin the church because the new missionaries did not reflect the vision of Catholicism that had evolved over the two centuries of isolation.

For Endo, the dominant question was why Christianity had encountered such stubborn resistance or indifference on the part of the Japanese, and why he had felt such a sense of division within himself. One of the characters in his play *The Golden Country* describes Japan in this way. "It's a mudswamp much more frightening than what the Christians call hell—this Japan. No matter what shoots one tries to transplant here from another country, they all wither and die, or else bear a flower and a fruit that only resemble the real ones." In *The Samurai*, a Jesuit missionary says: "The Japanese basically lack a sensitivity to anything that is absolute, to anything that transcends the human level, to the existence of anything beyond the realm of Nature: what we would call the supernatural."

It might be said that such a view of the Japanese is itself too absolute and dangerously close to despair. But Endo's fiction does not succumb to despair; rather, it explores the tragic conflicts and misunderstandings between people, and probes the mystery of faith itself. Endo never gave up his Catholic faith or his search for understanding.

Silence: *Martyrdom Redefined*

Silence, a classic that ought to take its place alongside such works as Greene's *The Power and the Glory* and Bernanos's *The Diary of a Country Priest*, reveals the same tragicomic vision that marks the modern Catholic novel. The protagonist of *Silence* is Sebastian Rodrigues, an ardent young Jesuit who embarks on a clandestine missionary effort to Japan just as it is being closed to the West. In many ways, Rodrigues is the flower of Counter-Reformation Catholicism: zealous, confident, willing to endure physical and mental suffering for his mission. There is, without doubt, something heroic and noble about him.

Of course, when Rodrigues arrives in the mudswamp of Japan he quickly finds out that his mission is fraught with more ambiguities than he had imagined possible. He is especially puzzled by a vagabond named Kichijiro, an apostate Christian who nevertheless clings to the priest, running errands for him. A shambling, pathetic figure, Kichijiro is at once obsessed with Christianity and utterly untrustworthy.

At first, Rodrigues thinks of Kichijiro as little more than a Judas. For the Spanish priest, there are only two categories of men: "the strong and the weak, the saints and the commonplace, the heroes and those who respect them." But these categories, which are characteristic of modern Western thought in its most arrogant form, soon break down in the face of the torture and inquisition which Rodrigues himself must face.

The Japanese inquisitor forces Rodrigues to listen to the cries of Christians suffering in the Pit. Suddenly he is confronted with a moral conundrum which he cannot fathom: "He had come to this country to lay down his life for other men, but instead of that the Japanese were laying down their lives one by one for him." The torture of Sebastian Rodrigues is a heartrending experience, yet in the process the pride of Western man is broken. Throughout Rodrigues's suffering Kichijiro is near him, a pathetic figure certainly, but in a mysterious way as tenacious in his equivocal faith as any martyr singing amid the flames.

There are those who would read *Silence* and see it as an exercise in compromise and dilution. But Endo's Catholic imagination is neither heretical nor vague: he does not say that faith is a purely subjective matter that is up to the individual believer. It is precisely because the truth of Christ's love is at the center of his search that he wants to explore the prideful "strength" of the West and the pathetic "weakness" of the East.

Endo believed that the form Christianity had taken in the West was inappropriate for Japan. The Japanese, he wrote, are fearful of the strong patriarchal God of Western Christianity; they are far more drawn to the comforting mother figure. That is why the *kakure* Christians focused so much of their devotion on Mary. Here too it is important to note that Endo did not endorse a facile feminist notion of God as Mother. Rather, he believed that the "feminine" side of Christ, if more fully evoked, would speak directly to the hearts of the Japanese. His book, *A Life of Jesus*, is written to emphasize this dimension of Christ.

"Mothers": The Feminine Side of God

One of Endo's most moving short stories is the autobiographical tale, "Mothers." The story alternates between the present, in which the narrator visits a community of *kakure* on a remote island, and the past, when as a youth he found himself unable to relate to his mother. In journeying to the *kakure* village, the narrator is ultimately looking for some truth about himself. He feels strangely attracted to the *kakure*, with their intense devotion to Mary and their sense of failure. Above all, they remain acutely conscious of the two centuries during which they hid their faith. This is symbolized by their chapels, which are, on the surface, Buddhist shrines, but which conceal rosaries and other devotional objects that can be taken out and reverenced in secret ceremonies.

The narrator of "Mothers" has a recurrent dream. He is in the hospital, hooked up to a variety of life-support machines, heavily drugged. But his mother is with him—not his wife or his doctors, just his mother. Later, he remembers:

> The image of my mother in my school-days—that image within my heart was of a woman abandoned by her husband. She sits like a stone statue on the sofa in that dark room at nightfall in Dairen. As a child I could not bear to see her struggling to endure her grief.

His mother seeks consolation in her Catholic faith with a kind of doggedness that seems "hard" to the narrator. His mother's long years of playing the violin have given her calluses under her chin and "the tips of her fingers, too, were hard to the touch as pebbles. . . ." She is a *pietá*, a "stone statue," whose grief has brought her to a single-minded pursuit of the absolute. Just as she seeks in her violin-playing to find the "one note" of perfection, so in her spiritual life she strives to find the absolute, the "one true faith."

But the narrator, both as a boy and as a man, feels both awe and fear for his mother. If her personality became hard, by virtue of that awful concentration, he, on the other hand, has always been soft and inwardly divided. He recalls his lies to his mother during his school-days about where he had gone and what he had done. He felt the need to escape her. "The more she compelled me to share her faith, the more I fought her oppressive power, the way a drowning child struggles against the pressure of the water." Hence his identification with the *kakure*, whose spirituality was formed in an environment in which a form of lying was necessary. "Sometimes I catch a glimpse of myself in these *kakure*, people who have had to lead lives of duplicity, lying to the world and never revealing their true feelings to anyone."

If works like *Silence* emphasize the tragic dimension of the conflict of differing paths toward truth, then "Mothers" is a tale of acceptance, reconciliation, and hope. For if the narrator can never embrace the hardness of his mother's faith, neither can he abandon that faith. Both "strong" and "weak" models bear witness to the same faith. Over twenty-five years ago, Endo wrote:

> But after all it seems to me that Catholicism is not a solo, but a symphony. . . . If I have trust in Catholicism, it is because I find in it much more possibility than in any other religion for presenting the full symphony of humanity. The other religions have almost no fullness. Only Catholicism can present the full symphony. And unless there is in that symphony a part that corresponds to Japan's mud swamp, it cannot be a true religion. What exactly this part is—that is what I want to find out.

Shusaku Endo never claimed that he had single-handedly found the answer to what the Japanese part in the Catholic symphony is. His method was that of the novelist, not the theologian. But he would not have been surprised that his own vision was reflected in a book written by one of the twentieth-century's greatest theologians, Hans Urs von Balthasar. The title of von Balthasar's book is *Truth is Symphonic: Aspects of Christian Pluralism*. In it he argues that "the purpose of . . . pluralism is this: not to refuse to enter into the unity that lies in God and is imparted by him, but symphonically to get in tune with one another and give allegiance to the transcendent unity."

Endo was a Catholic writer fully committed to the symphony, as were his predecessors in the tradition of the modern Catholic novel. Unlike a number of recent Catholic writers, who seem to believe that everyone can play their own melody line, Endo believed that only within the symphony of the church can the music achieve its full beauty and meaning. But he firmly held to the belief that the Japanese chairs in the orchestra should not be left vacant, or placed somewhere else. In clinging to this conviction, and conveying it in a deeply moving, humane fashion, Endo's fiction poses a challenge to which all readers ought to respond.

11

Geoffrey Hill:
True Sequences of Pain

Already, like a disciplined scholar,
I piece fragments together, past conjecture
Establishing true sequences of pain;

For so it is proper to find value
In a bleak skill, as in the thing restored:
The long-lost words of choice and valediction.
—Geoffrey Hill

For a long time the poetic achievement of Geoffrey Hill was unjustly eclipsed by the cultural dominance of the post-war school of British poetry known as the "Movement" and by its successors. Except for the efforts of a few poets and critics (Donald Hall, William Logan, Christopher Ricks, Harold Bloom), Hill's poetry has had to speak for itself, since he refuses to participate in the often self-serving rituals of the literary establishment. At a time when the Movement fostered a skeptical, agnostic stance characterized by plain diction, "rational structures," and a preoccupation with the present moment, Hill produced a series of modernist lyrics soaked in the blood of violence and sacrifice, burdened by history, often baroque in form and sensuous in language. Hill's poetry has been accused of being cold and difficult, obsessed with religion and the past. But the sheer integrity and depth of his vision, and his genius with language, have kept him in public view.

Indeed, the time may have arrived for Hill to be recognized as one of the few enduring poets of his generation.[1] Born in Bromsgrove, England in 1932, Hill began to make his mark even as an undergraduate at Oxford University in the early 1950s. It quickly became evident that Hill's poetry owed more to modernists like T. S. Eliot and Ezra Pound than to the Movement poets of his own generation.

In many ways, Hill has been the antithesis of Philip Larkin, a key figure in the Movement. The death of Philip Larkin, the preeminent representative of post-war British poetry, elicited many tributes and memoirs celebrating his unique poetic voice and skill, but it also gave rise to a certain amount of literary soul-searching. For Larkin, the agnostic master of irony, found himself unable to write poetry in the last years of his relatively short life. This silence, far from being pregnant, is uncomfortably close to despair. The modern poetic apocalypse of fire and ice has seemingly played itself out: the Confessional Poets burned themselves out in a blaze of unfocused emotion while the Movement poets ended in a frosty entropy.

Such an apocalypse seems the perfect conclusion to Eliot's much-abused "dissociation of sensibility" thesis. Geoffrey Hill has struggled to recover a unified vision, and indeed his poetic career might be seen as an extended debate with Eliot—a debate which does not entail opposition per se, but something more like refinement and distinction. Like Eliot, Hill has sought to "purify the language of the tribe" because the decay of word and spirit is coextensive. Hill has confessed to the "priest" in him: a poem must involve a speaker who submits to an "exemplary ordeal," providing a mimesis for the experience of the rawness and contingency of the world. The poet thus enacts a sacrifice and offers redemption.

But Hill knows that the poet himself stands at one remove from experience: the power of words includes the power to evade or distort reality. Hill has spoken of "the tongue's atrocities." In the epigraph to his aesthetic manifesto, a brilliantly condensed essay entitled "Poetry as 'Menace' and 'Atonement,'" Hill turns to the theologian Karl Barth to find expression for the paradox of the poet's relationship to language: "Thus my noblest capacity becomes my deepest perplexity; my noblest opportunity, my uttermost distress; my noblest gift, my darkest menace."

Though Hill was at Oxford when the Movement poets were coming together, he remained (and continues to remain) aloof from literary groups. The son of a police constable, Hill grew up in Worcestershire. While he cannot be called a regional poet, Hill insists that his native countryside has been one of the most enduring forces in his poetic imagination (this is most evident in *Mercian Hymns*). Right up to his matriculation at Oxford, Hill sang in his church choir; his appreciation of the formal properties of liturgy and his lifelong grappling with religious aspiration undoubtedly grew out of that youthful experience.

Aside from the obvious influence of the great modernists, Eliot and Yeats, Hill is most indebted artistically (significantly enough) to the Fugitive or Agrarian poets, especially Allen Tate and John Crowe Ransom. Hill's poetic career has been carried out in an academic setting, first at the University of Leeds and recently at Cambridge and Boston University. He has also written two dozen dense, but highly rewarding literary essays, many of which are collected in *The Lords of Limit*.

New Disciplines of Form

Hill's early collections all bear characteristic stylistic marks, but each has pursued new disciplines of form. *For the Unfallen* (1959), Hill's first book, is fully mature: in addition to lyric poems using political and religious themes as metaphors, *For the Unfallen* includes longer poetic sequences of a type that recurs in Hill's work. *King Log* (1968)—the title alludes to a fable of Aesop about good and bad rulers—deals more insistently with political themes: tyranny, guilt, and the way the mind evades and distorts truths which are incriminating. Hill's next book, *Mercian Hymns* (1971), defies simple description: it is a series of thirty prose poems centering around Offa, an eighth century king of Mercia (an area in the West Midlands of England, including Hill's own countryside), the first monarch to unify Britain and thus a "founder" of a political and national order. Like Eliot's *Four Quartets*, *Mercian Hymns* is a poem about England refracted through the prism of the poet's own life and family history. *Tenebrae* (1979) returns to lyric forms; the themes are erotic love and spiritual love and the suffering these entail. The metaphors and verse forms derive from the Renaissance (especially Petrarch), and are shot through with the mystical theology of the Spanish Carmelites, St. John of the Cross, and St. Teresa of Avila. Finally, *The Mystery of the Charity of Charles Peguy* (1983), a poem of one hundred quatrains, is an extended homage to the Catholic agrarian socialist and visionary killed at the Battle of the Marne. For Hill, Peguy is an integrated man, not an ideologue; the poem celebrates (and criticizes) the French thinker's attempt to find a myth adequate to provide order for France in the modern era.

Hill, like Wallace Stevens, is a modernist who works primarily within the lyric form, though he has reinvigorated the prose poem in his *Mercian Hymns*. His poems do not surrender the duty of the poet to give form to experience, but they also reflect the disjointed perception of experience of modern consciousness: thus Hill can write sonnets which nonetheless are syntactically contorted and open-ended. The lines quoted at the head of this essay come from "The Songbook of Sebastian Arrurruz," a sequence of short lyrics spoken by a figure who acts as Hill's persona. The "fragments," which the modernist poet connects, are not merely "thrown together" (the root meaning of "conjecture"); they bespeak human suffering and thus to some extent atone for it. The "bleak skill" of the modern artist consists in rescuing "long-lost words." These words are not only "choice" in the sense of "well-chosen," but words involving human choices between good and evil. The use of language is an inescapably moral act.

A Heretic's Dream of Salvation

In a fallen world, the business of poetry is to establish "true sequences of pain," warning men of folly and wickedness and redeeming the time. The ubiquity of theological symbols and ideas in Hill's writings has led some enthusiastic critics to call him a "Christian poet." But Hill has described his poetry as "a heretic's dream of salvation expressed in the images of the orthodoxy from which he is excommunicate." He claims that he is not an agnostic, but his is a thoroughly modern consciousness locked in an anguished dialectic with Christianity. That he has not abandoned belief altogether is a sign of the integrity of his struggle. Though his imagery is Christian, much of Hill's poetry poses sharp challenges to religious piety, hypocrisy, and escapism. If he is not personally able to subscribe to orthodoxy, his refining sensibility has gone a long way toward making a spiritually valid orthodoxy possible in an age when language has become nearly incapable of communicating transcendence. In one sense, "transcendence" is precisely what Hill himself is unwilling to affirm. He writes, in a poetic sequence entitled "Tenebrae":

Veni Redemptor, but not in our time.
Christus Resurgens, quite out of this world.
'Ave' we cry; the echoes are returned.
Amor Carnalis is our dwelling-place.

But to read these lines simply as a rejection of Christian "otherworldli-ness" is to miss the layers of Hill's irony. Such a reading, however, is common among the commentators on Hill's poetry. Henry Hart, author of the first book-length study of Hill, persistently misunderstands Hill's religious sensi-tivity. In "Poetry as 'Menace' and 'Atonement'" Hill quotes Jacques Maritain on the sin of "angelism," which is "the refusal of the creature to submit to or be ruled by any of the exigencies of the natural order." Hart takes the Maritain quote, without indicating its source, implies that the words are Hill's, and equates angelism with "Christian supernaturalism." But angelism is heretical because it is a false transcendence: it is an attempt to throw off the givenness of nature, the world in which man must struggle. Hill equates angelism with modern technocracy, not with Christian belief.

Hill has been quoted as being fascinated by what he calls "the psycho-pathology of the false mystical experience" and the "self-indulgent mystical cults of the present day." A secularized era presents not only the problem of a religious tradition under siege, but a plethora of pseudo-religions providing shallow and dangerous comforts. For Hill, true mysticism is an "exemplary discipline," a way of giving shape and direction to ascetic and spiritual pas-sions. Without claiming to be a mystic himself, Hill finds in the theology of St. John of the Cross and St. Teresa of Avila a language which gives meaning to suffering. "He wounds with ecstasy. All the wounds are his own." Hill demands that religion be true to the human experience of pain and desire, not a sugar-coating of piety.

> O light of light, supreme delight;
> grace on our lips to our disgrace.
> Time roosts on all such golden wrists;
> our leanness is our luxury.
> Our love is what we love to have;
> our faith is in our festivals.

In this and the other sections of *Tenebrae* Hill uses the traditional analo-gies between erotic and divine love to interpenetrate each other, revealing the tensions between sacrifice and possession.

A Political Dimension

Not all of Hill's poetry is quite so mystical in bent; most of it, in fact, extends from the personal to the social realm, giving his art a historical and political dimension that has yet to be properly expounded. Like his modernist predecessors, Hill has an intense awareness of the past in the present, of the relationship between word and deed and between the order of the soul and the order of the commonwealth. Much of Hill's poetry has been written in response to the attitude taken by the Marxist critic, Theodor Adorno, who said: "No poetry after Auschwitz." Hill has wrestled with the inadequacy of language to comprehend atrocity, but he has not surrendered the poet's atoning work, nor has he escaped into artifice and wit in order to avoid harsh realities. The epigraph to his second volume of poetry, *King Log*, comes from Bacon's *Advancement of Learning*: "From moral virtue let us pass on to matter of power and commandment." The dichotomy between power and morality implicit in Bacon's words becomes Hill's subject.

Unlike so many modern poets, Hill refuses to be drawn into partisan enthusiasms. His whole oeuvre enacts a drive toward objectivity and balance. Yet his "political" poetry is not a dry affair of weights and measures, but a passionate commitment to right order and the disciplines, moral and institutional, that restrain violence and rapacity. Hill's political dimension cannot be separated from his historical consciousness: the past is not only a book of moral exempla, but alive in the present, whether recognized or not. The tangle of human deceit, sloth, hypocrisy, and lust for power changes little over time. Hill finds his political subjects in the War of the Roses, the two world wars (especially the Holocaust), British imperial conquests, even the American Civil War.

The power of Hill's vision of social disorder arises not out of its originality, but in its balance of irony, satire, and compassion, its deft linking of personal and social spheres, and its metaphoric subtlety. Hill's political understanding has been influenced primarily by Eliot and the Southern Agrarians. Though he refuses to sentimentalize bygone golden ages, he holds that a traditional, organic order guided by a common good has been supplanted by technocratic empires of capitalist or totalitarian varieties. His only political heroes are the Radical Tories of the nineteenth century—men who would be echoed by Charles Peguy. Another epigraph from a volume by Hill—this time *Mercian Hymns*—indicates his awareness of the crucial differences between a society oriented to transcendent principles of order and the leviathan state merely manipulating the "interests" of certain groups. The epigraph, worth quoting in full, is from the English poet C. H. Sisson, another important but sorely neglected post-war literary figure.

> The conduct of government rests upon the same foundation and encounters the same difficulties as the conduct of private persons: that is, as to its object and justification, for as to its methods, or technical part, there is all the difference which separates the person from the group, the man acting on behalf of himself from the man acting on behalf of the many. The technical part, in government as in private conduct, is now the only one which is publicly or at any rate generally recognised, as if by this evasion the more difficult part of the subject, which relates to ends, could be avoided. Upon 'the law of nature and the law of revelation,' Blackstone said, 'depend all human laws.' This quaint language, which would at once be derided if it were introduced now into public discussion, conceals a difficulty which is no less ours than it was our ancestors'.

Mercian Hymns focuses on the figure of Offa as Shakespeare focuses on Bolingbroke in the history plays: the king is ruler, but also an individual soul, the meeting point of the public and private realms.

Against the Gnostics

In "Locust Songs," three short poems on American history, Hill evokes the tortured and self-destructive dialectic unleashed by America's Puritan settlers. The gnosticism of the Puritans, which posited nature as an evil, hostile force, is set alongside their belief in the New World as the New Jerusalem. The first poem is called "The Emblem," an appropriate title in light of the seventeenth-century poetic tradition as practiced in America by the Puritan Edward Taylor.

> So with sweet oaths converting the salt earth
> To yield, our fathers verged on Paradise:
> Each to his own portion of Paradise,
> Stung by the innocent venoms of the earth.

Because nature ("salt earth") is seen as evil, it must be subdued; rather than cooperating with our fathers, nature must "yield" and be dominated in order to yield its harvest. The poem is divided in half: the first two lines set up the image of the Puritans as touching the Promised Land (they only "verge" on it, however); but the final lines contradict that vision: to divide Paradise by attempting to selfishly possess it is to bring on discord and struggle. By putting evil in the natural sphere, the Puritans miss the evil in themselves and set up a moral confusion that will plague American history.

The theme is continued in "Good Husbandry," but finds a more panoramic expression in the concluding poem, "Shiloh Church, 1862: Twenty-Three Thousand." The poem is not about the Civil War battle, but Shiloh stands as an image of the civil strife initiated by the Puritans erupting into bloody conflict.

> O stamping-ground of the shod Word! So hard
> On the heels of the damned red-man we came,
> Geneva's tribe, outlandish and abhorred—
> Bland vistas milky with Jehovah's calm—   ʹ
>
> Who fell to feasting Nature, the glare
> Of buzzards circling; cried to the grim sun
> 'Jehovah punish us!'; who went too far;
> In deserts dropped the odd white turds of bone;
>
> Whose passion was to find out God in this
> His natural filth, voyeur of sacrifice, a slow
> Bloody unearthing of the God-in-us.
> But with what blood, and to what end, Shiloh?

The Puritans make America the special "stamping-ground" of Christ, damning the Indians and setting up their bland vistas of paradise. Yet there was a "fall": both to the plunder of nature and to nature's revenge. Ironically, the false transcendence of the "God-in-us" leads to a surrender to the cruelty of natural forces. Given the divine mandate for "dominion," the Americans are driven westward in their desire to possess the earth; but they "went too far." At the mercy of a fiendish dialectic, Americans have lost sight of ends in their struggle for domination over nature. It is a parable with continuing relevance.

It is difficult in the space of an introductory essay to convey what I consider to be the achievement of a difficult but masterful modernist poet. The work of Geoffrey Hill deserves, and will repay, a vast amount of critical attention. His early critics have done much to bring sources to light and prepare paraphrases, but his poetry is already being treated by secular, politically unsophisticated writers in such a way as to constrict the scope of his vision. In my opinion Hill follows Eliot's path—the path of history, religious struggle, and the purification of language—in the modernist tradition. The other modernists—Pound, Joyce, Olson, Williams, et al—have erected great epics of the self, but in the end their art founders upon the very limitation of their selfhood. Eliot and Hill begin with the self but move outwards. As Hill has written, "From the depths of the self we rise to a concurrence with that which is not-self." That "rise" is accompanied by suffering and atonement, artistic mastery and an acknowledgment of the limits of art. The poetry of Geoffrey Hill traces this movement.

12

Andrew Lytle:
Myth and Memory

The past isn't dead; it isn't even past.
—William Faulkner

O f the many distinguished essays which comprise *I'll Take My Stand,*[1] the now classic defense by "Twelve Southerners" of the South's traditional agrarian culture (published in 1930), only one attempted a sustained description of the actual texture of life on the small family farm. That essay, with a title whose comic irony was to become the author's trademark, was "The Hind Tit," by Andrew Nelson Lytle (1902–1995). To be sure, the contributors to this volume conferred beforehand to determine who would write on specific approaches to the South's dilemma: art, religion, economics, the "race" problem, and so forth. But Lytle's assignment was not derived accidentally: from this first published essay onward, his concern for preserving the memory of the first three centuries of Southern society made itself known in books, essays, reviews, and, for those who have heard him in the classroom or on his porch, in a steady stream of anecdotes and stories.

Andrew Lytle's first book was a biography of the Confederate cavalry general, Nathan Bedford Forrest[2]; his latest, *A Wake for the Living,*[3] was a chronicle of the generations of his family in America. Though a comic irony may have been typical of Lytle's public persona (and a religious faith which allowed him to put man's folly in perspective), his historical and cultural writings have sought to recall to success-minded Americans their nation's heritage of brutal internal conflicts. *A Wake for the Living*, for example, describes the conquest of the American Indians, the internecine struggles between Whig and Tory during the American Revolution, the Civil War and Reconstruction, and the rapid industrialization of the South. Lytle's desire to know the truth of the past is motivated by a belief he shares with T. S. Eliot: "human kind cannot bear very much reality."

Between Lytle's first and last books, however, lies the body of his true work: fiction. For all his interest in historical and religious truth, Andrew Lytle always approached his material with the eyes of an artist. Lytle jealously guarded this distinction, for as he acutely pointed out in his literary essays, art cannot be reduced to the abstraction of ideas (if it can, it is not art but propaganda). Even his nonfiction bore the marks of the artist's active imagination, fusing concrete experience with the form appropriate to disclosing the meaning of that experience. The editors of a book containing the papers delivered at the semi-centennial of *I'll Take My Stand*, in describing Lytle's contribution to a panel discussion, put it this way: "Lytle, who remains the storyteller par excellence, develops his themes as parables that pique the imagination and turn from near absurdity into subtly finished moral truths."[4] This method applies particularly to *A Wake for the Living*, a work that can be called tragicomic in vision.

Allen Tate, in his preface to a collection of Lytle's literary essays, makes a striking, and at first glance puzzling, assertion. "Lytle's problem as novelist has been to discover in his native milieu typical actions (he calls them mythical or archetypal) that permit him to write, not historical novels but novels as history. . . . The action takes shape out of a vast and turbulent cloud of events, as the funnel of a tornado suddenly forms and descends."[5]

Novels as History

Tate's phrase, "novels as history," would seem to conflate the spheres that Lytle believes should remain separate. But if taken as a metaphoric exaggeration, this packed expression of Tate's may become clearer. Tate is drawing attention to Lytle's convincing illusion of "felt life" which is combined with an ability to focus the larger historical action into the specific conflict between central characters. Lytle himself employed terms which help to make this clear. A formally conceived fiction operates on two levels: the "enveloping action," or the moving pattern of events (one might almost say "history") which lies behind the "action proper," or the specific conflict of the "story." The resolution of the fiction should unite the action proper and the enveloping action.

In a discussion of the novel "whose subject lies in the past," Lytle acknowledged the parallel methods of historical novelist and professional historian.[6] Both must research the full range of customs, manners, religious beliefs, and institutions of a past culture in order to bring the past to life. Lytle believed that history and fiction diverge because history as a "science" seeks "principles and causes" whereas fiction seeks "people." In this instance, though Lytle earlier protested that "it seems to me highly arbitrary to place the historian among the social sciences," he limited the scope of historical inquiry by thinking of it as a "science." But to those who are not under the thrall of positivistic science, the purpose and goals of historical study are in fact closer to historical fiction. As Stephen J. Tonsor has written:

> The ancillary sciences [such as demography and geography], however important they are for the study of history, will not yield history, for the historical lies precisely in the realm of value, in the realm of morals, in the realm of choice. As we study the past we come more and more to realize that we study it not as a science but as one would study a great piece of literature. We think in terms not of scientific formulations and predictions but of alternatives, the baffling interplay of fate and freedom, of great and surprising actions and mean and disappointing motives. The creative and innovating action, the power of love and self-sacrifice, and the tragedy of misspent lives and wasted opportunities are the great concern of historical study. "Social science" yields up the actuaries' tables and the law of diminishing returns and, of course, these are helpful in the study of history. History yields us tragedy and great literature.[7]

Tonsor goes on to argue that since history is a collective effort at self-understanding, the study of the symbols by which men have ordered and understood their existence is the historian's point of departure. Since these symbols include manners, rituals, customs, and art itself, the parallel with the historical novel is perhaps closer than Lytle once thought. Certainly historical fiction, which not only uses symbols but orders them in a highly imaginative fashion, is also a mode of historical "understanding."

The other condition for historical inquiry which Lytle said holds for writers of fiction is the necessity for seeing men in the "institutional restraints" of society. There is no such thing as the "natural man," Lytle declared; man is defined by, and derives his identity from, those institutions created by man, the social animal.[8] That is why the "sociological novel," is gnostic (or Puritan, to use Lytle's term), because it places evil in social structures and not in man. Not only heretical in philosophical terms, this placing of evil in the object is an artistic failure: it makes "action" impossible since there can be no conflict between naturally good beings. The "sociological novel" is not the same as a novel that depicts modern man as uprooted from place and lacking identity. Works of this latter kind can be great art, as in the fiction of Flannery O'Connor and Walker Percy.

Though Lytle would deny that he has any "aesthetics" or critical theory, he does possess critical principles by which he evaluates the literary (and moral) value of literature, as in his censure of the "sociological novel." Much of modern fiction, he wrote, suffers from the unbridled egotism of authors who turn their fictions into expressions of their own personalities, rather than a crafted work of art the purpose of which is to reveal meaning.[9] The anarchy of the unbridled self reflects a deeper cultural malaise, but one from which the American South has been largely protected, at least until recent decades.

The Southern Literary Renaissance

Andrew Lytle's fiction and critical insight must be seen in the context of that flowering of Southern poetry and fiction during the first half of the twentieth century, often known as the Southern Literary Renaissance. The fiction of William Faulkner is a towering presence in the Renaissance, but a host of major artists have been part of it, including, in the realm of fiction, Robert Penn Warren, Allen Tate, Eudora Welty, Caroline Gordon, Thomas Wolfe, Katherine Anne Porter, and Andrew Lytle. Above all, this flowering of narrative fiction is characterized by its unflinching recovery of Southern history. The specific literary approach of each artist is unique, of course: Robert Penn Warren has been termed a writer of "novels of ideas" while Faulkner's characters are rarely props for intellectual abstractions.

The nature and causes of this remarkable outpouring of historical fiction have been analyzed by several outstanding critics.[10] For a proper appreciation of the background to Andrew Lytle's fiction, an outline (based largely on the seminal work of Lewis P. Simpson) is sufficient.[11] Simpson holds that the antebellum South developed as a reactionary society based on chattel slavery, a social arrangement that separated it from the modern, industrial North. The very newness of the chattel slave society required a defense from literary men that was necessarily political and rhetorical, though that defense caused Southern men of letters to grow more and more alienated from modernity. The attempt to depict the South as a pastoral society ran into the obstacle of the non-pastoral innovation of slavery, hence the growing sense of alienation.

The antebellum justification of the slave society continued after the Civil War, and in some respects became far less political and far more romantic and sentimental. At root it demanded a withdrawal from memory and history. But it was the experience of defeat and the harsh and imposed confrontation with modernity brought about by Reconstruction and, later, the American entry into World War I, that caused the Southern literary mind to develop a self-consciousness that would lead to a recovery of memory and history. There is a famous passage by the historian Arnold Toynbee which recounts his feelings as a boy during the Diamond Jubilee of Queen Victoria. Toynbee felt that England was on top of the world, that "history" was something that happened to "other" people, a feeling he later believed the confident commercial inhabitants of New York in 1897 also would have possessed. He continues: "Of course, if I had been a small boy in 1897 in the Southern part of the United States, I should not have felt the same; I should then have known from my parents that history had happened to my people in my part of the world."[12]

Allen Tate found an analogy for the recovery of history by Southern writers in an epigram of the Irish poet, W. B. Yeats: "Out of the quarrel with others we make rhetoric; out of the quarrel with ourselves, poetry." For Tate, this applied to the "shift from melodramatic rhetoric" (the sentimental, political Yankee-bashing literature of the South prior to World War I) to "the dialectic of tragedy" (the Southern Literary Renaissance).[13] Lytle took up the modern Southern writer's self-consciousness in an essay on Faulkner's *Intruder in the Dust*:

> There is for any Southern writer of imagination an inescapable preoccupation with his native scene and especially with its historic predicament. He can no more escape it than a Renaissance painter could escape painting Her Ladyship the Virgin and the Court of Angels. He has been made to feel too sharply his uniqueness and the uniqueness of his society in the modern world. His self-consciousness does for him what blindness did for Homer. He has been forced to achieve aesthetic distance.[14]

That "aesthetic distance" made possible the full tragic vision of Southern history. Ironically, for all the invective directed against the defenders of the South by Yankees like H. L. Mencken, the artists of the Southern "Renaissance" have delivered the most telling critiques of their region. As we shall see, Andrew Lytle's fiction reveals tragic flaws in many of the institutions that grew up in the South, such as the family, even though he upholds the family as indispensable for civilized life.

The Self's Internalization of History

In an essay on *I'll Take My Stand*, Lewis Simpson adds another dimension to the analysis of the Southern writer's recovery of history. He describes there the nature of modernity as secular man's taking history into his own hands. By removing the anointed ruler of society from his role as God's agent, and hence subject to God's law, modern man became his own judge. Starting with the Renaissance, Simpson argues, great artists have been engaged in a critique of "the drama of the self's internalization of history." Simpson speaks of the modern poets' intimacy between self and history, poets who "know not only an isolation of the self in history but an isolation of history in the self."[15] For this reason, it should not be surprising that the central authors of *I'll Take My Stand* were artists. Ransom, Tate, Davidson, Warren, and Lytle were not painting a rosy picture of a past that never was, but were bent on placing the South's traditional society in the context of the classical-Christian European inheritance as distinct from the secular liberalism that dominated the North's progressivist industrialism. In their fiction and poetry, these Southerners took up the quarrel with their own historical past. Their recovery of history was founded on a tragic sense of life.

Andrew Lytle's historical sensibility accords with Simpson's description. In several places, Lytle spoke of "the second fall of man, the fall into history." The fall he defined as "man judging man as final truth."[16] In the secular dispensation, the medieval "God's wealth" (prior to the modern "commonwealth") is replaced by a world of "endless discretion." The "new testament" for this world, according to Lytle, is Machiavelli's *The Prince*.[17] In Lytle's usage, "history" is essentially profane history, the complete replacement of "sacred" history, or man's openness to God, the mysterious Lord of time. Though he does not use these terms systematically, Lytle's reference to "history" is often in its "profane" sense, and the "past" is given a positive connotation. Lytle assailed the notion that one can learn "lessons" from history,

since looking to "man for the judgment of mankind" is a warped and errone-
ous measure.[18]

Unlike "history," which to Lytle betokens the secular deification of the
human will, the "past" is a more neutral term, involving the race's collective
memory. The end of remembering is not specific knowledge of facts, but a
constant awareness of human frailty and propensity to evil. Without memory,
men are unhinged, prey to the passions and abstract schemes which assume
that human nature is malleable. In his "family chronicle," Lytle wrote:

> If we dismiss the past as dead and not as a country of the living which
> our eyes are unable to see, as we cannot see a foreign country but know
> it is there, then we are likely to become servile. Living as we will be in
> a lesser sense of ourselves, lacking that fuller knowledge which only the
> living past can give, it will be so easy to submit to pressure and receive
> what is already ours as a boon from authority.[19]

Lytle's own efforts at conveying the "living past" always stemmed from
his concrete experiences of family and region. In a sense, he was a practitioner of what John Lukacs has called "personal history," that individual
consciousness of a shared past. As a Southerner, Lytle believed that historical consciousness is inseparable from attachment to place and to the family,
"the large connections of kin amplifying the individual unit." For Lytle, the
essence of Christendom is the family: it provides us with identity and schools
us in love and self-sacrifice. Modernity, on the other hand, is characterized by
the desire for power, a lust which leads man to wander, alone, separated from
the community in the monstrosity of his ego. Technology without limits, the
secular welfare state, the arts dominated by pornography and neurosis—all
these are the effects of power without love, the individual without community. These interlocking themes are the constant in Lytle's fiction, as in his
historical and social criticism.

A Double Meaning

In conveying a sense of the past in the present and the present in the past,
Lytle's fiction is almost unrivaled in the twentieth century. In the historical
novel, Lytle wrote, "you have not only the illusion of the present, but the
past permeates the immediacy of this illusion; the fictive personalities take
on a certain clairvoyance; the action a double meaning, as if the actors while

performing disclose the essential meaning of their time, even of all time." In the crucible of art, past and present are fused, the concrete merges with the universal, myth and history meet. Lytle's historical fiction is remarkably successful in the primary duty of creating the illusion of "felt life," but it also is a mirror for our age because it centers around the peculiar qualities of the "second fall of man" into secular "history," the modern version of the first, archetypal loss of innocence.

Lytle's fictional output was small, but each work is unique in form and style, revealing a writer of versatility and vision. All four of his novels are "historical" in one way or another. *A Name for Evil*, which takes place during the Second World War, is not just about the solipsistic fantasies of a writer, but about the attempt to "restore" history directly, without realizing that the past cannot be recreated by an act of will. *At the Moon's Inn*, by centering on the founding of the New World by a modern, materialist search for gold, has a profound resonance for the present. In this novel Lytle achieves a symbolic richness and complexity of striking proportions. Lytle's last, and finest, novel, *The Velvet Horn*, while it has been analyzed in terms of myth and archetypes, is actually a forceful depiction of the Cumberland hill country in the latter half of the nineteenth century. The experiments with narrative technique, and the invention of Jack Cropleigh, a "hovering bard" who interprets the action like a Greek chorus, justify Caroline Gordon's contention that this novel is "a landmark in American fiction."

But for the purposes of this essay I want to provide a critique of Lytle's first novel, *The Long Night*, partly because it has been unjustly neglected and neatly labeled as a "Civil War novel" (which it isn't), and partly because its "enveloping action," the historical movement of events in the South, is brilliantly interlaced with the "action proper."

The Long Night is the story of Pleasant McIvor, whose father is murdered when he learns too much about a large slave-stealing operation. Pleasant's gradual revenge upon his father's murderers, and its eventual cessation in the swirling events of the Civil War, form the action of the conflict. The war, with its pressure to leave private needs for the larger public need, brings Pleasant out of himself and he forms a friendship with Roswell Ellis. When his guilt at not pursuing his revenge against the remaining murderers (who are now in the Confederate army) causes him to delay giving intelligence of the enemy's positions, Ellis is killed, and in remorse, Pleasant deserts not only the army, but the whole human community, by isolating himself in the hills of Winston County.

Much has been made of the shift in narrative voice which takes place early in the novel: from Pleasant McIvor's first person to the omniscient third person. While this does involve some awkwardness, the preoccupation with the narrative shift has distracted attention from the way the story is framed. Pleasant's narrative is actually mediated by his nephew Lawrence. While on his way home from Arkansas, where he had finished a college degree, Lawrence receives a message from Pleasant, asking him to stay with him. Since Pleasant had disappeared during the Civil War many years earlier, his sudden request is like "a communication from the other world." Lawrence is the next of kin, since his father and uncles, except Pleasant, are dead. Thus Pleasant's desire to pass on his tale is both a cathartic sharing of his isolation with a member of the family, and the handing on of the family's history. Pleasant's story is indeed searing; during its telling, Pleasant's grey eyes "spitted" Lawrence to his chair.

The Revenger's Tragedy

But the situation is more complex and replete with ironies than an Ancient Mariner detaining an unsuspecting wedding guest, though this only becomes clear as the novel's action unfolds. Only then does the significance of the introductory scene shock the reader into a recognition of the fiction's full significance. Lawrence is the son of the eldest McIvor, William, whom we discover was "a quiet man and something of a scholar." Even his build, tall and spare, with sensitive eyes, is unlike the square toughness of the McIvors. A good horseman, William doesn't like hunting. Early on, Pleasant describes his older brother:

> He had the curious notion that no animal ought to be trapped and killed unless there was need of the meat. He must have picked that out of some book. He didn't believe in settling disputes of honor with firearms either, said that nothing was ever settled that way. Don't misunderstand me—he was not a coward, and he was not a weakling. He just warn't a McIvor.[20]

When his father is murdered, William quietly rejects the call to vengeance, which the large group of McIvor kin gather to pursue, preferring to seek a legal remedy. The law, however, is hopelessly ineffective, since the courts and sheriff are in the pay of the slave stealers. This reticence outrages the kin, who hunger for immediate justice, but an inner group decides to allow William his way while planning secret vengeance, the only method effective against such a widespread and powerful gang. One of the wisest men, Armistead McIvor, turns to William and says: "Son, I understand how you feel in this matter. You're a fine Christian boy, and we are going to support you." He tells William of a younger brother who believed "the niggers would be better off free," an opinion Armistead "respected."[21]

Though not directly patronizing, Armistead's ironic forbearance toward William reveals a split in Southern culture. William's meekness and preference for ineffective law over direct action is equated with being a "Christian" and an abolitionist. William cannot perceive sharply the power and threat of evil as Armistead and Pleasant can: they think they can deal with it directly, using guile and force, somewhat "unchristian" talents. Cameron McIvor, the murdered father, embodies this split within himself. An old Indian fighter with the reputation for physical prowess, he settles down to a life of cultivating the land. A man of honor, he can respond with devastating force to outright attacks upon himself and his property.

Cameron's ability to achieve immediate justice, through the decisiveness of his personality, leads him to kill a young man and his penalty is exile from the community. This initial uprooting is the "complication" (Lytle's literary term) which begins the "conflicts" of the story. It is when they settle in to raise a crop that Cameron runs into the slave stealers, under the powerful control of Tyson Lovell. These "pirates" are symbolic of the endemic, institutional evil permeating the whole of the human community, and they cannot be countered by a single man. Lovell's men are, in a way, a wicked parody of the extended kin comprising the McIvor clan, but their evil cannot be separated out from the community, and it is the false belief that it can (like the abolitionists' belief that eliminating slavery will bring about utopia) that provides the motivating power to Pleasant's revenge.

Lytle enacts this tragic split in the larger culture and in the person of Pleasant ("enveloping action" and "action proper") on several different levels. Pleasant became his father's "favorite," and in teaching his son the arts of tracking and living in the wilderness, the son came to see his father more and more as a "brother." Yet such an attitude offends the proper hierarchy of the family. Pleasant inherits his father's qualities as an Indian fighter, the side of his personality which knows the wilderness intimately. Here, as in all of Lytle's fiction, the wilderness exerts a powerful attraction: it beckons as a place of simplicity and unity beyond the myriad conflicts of good and evil in the world. In historical terms, the wilderness or backwoods was never far from the surface of Southern society, much as Shakespeare's England always felt the potential chaos (such as erupted in the War of the Roses) lying beneath the surface of civilization.

Vengeance and Providence

Pleasant withdraws to the dark and anonymous world of night and unseen places, where he becomes a seeing eye. He identifies his vengeance with God's Providence, and indeed his watchful vigils over his victims reveal the multifarious forms of evil. Like an artist, Pleasant gives his victims poetic justice: for example, the sheriff who descends to animality in his immoderate passion for breaking horses (he once brings a horse into the bedroom, a travesty with sexual overtones) is trampled to death by his favorite horse through Pleasant's devising.

God, of course, is the first artist, and Pleasant's taking upon himself the role of Death to his victims is a form of blasphemy. It is the same role which Tyson Lovell claims for himself. Lovell manipulates the lives of those around him by working on their weaknesses, as the story of Judge Wilton reveals. When Pleasant secretly comes to kill Lovell, they meet in the dark—the element to which they both belong—and Lovell tells him that the Civil War has begun. Lovell realizes that the war thwarts his dream of a slave empire, but Pleasant doesn't perceive that the war means the end of his vengeance as well. Lovell, in response to Pleasant's rough request that he make his peace with God, says: "Come, come, my young savage. Let us behave like gentlemen. One may be brutal but never rude before the dark portal. I, who have sent too many through it, should know the amenities."[22] Pleasant vows to return for a final reckoning with Lovell, once he combs the army for the other murderers, but it never comes about.

Pleasant and Lovell are isolated men, governed totally by their wills. They can manipulate the lives of others, but they cannot share their lives with others. In one of the stories within the story, Lytle sets Pleasant against a young man named Damon Harrison, the son of an aristocratic planter who has gambled his inheritance away over a game of marbles. Now a general-store proprietor, Damon's father watches his son mingle with the hill people, the inhabitants of a different world. Damon's rite of passage into the hill society is his successful breaking of a mule, and when he falls in love with Ruth Weaver, he comes even closer to union with the plain people. The death of two members of the community at the hands of Pleasant and his kin brings the community together for the wake. Pleasant remains on the outside looking in, like a ghost (one man who sees him believes it to be a "hant"). Damon, whose love for Ruth bespeaks a regeneration of society and the continuity of life, takes her out for a walk in the woods. In his elation he comes upon Pleasant and hurls at him the lie that Lovell's men have spread about Cameron McIvor, that he was "an old son-of-a-bitching nigger stealer." Pleasant, enraged, wounds Damon mortally.

Pleasant's murder of Damon marks a turning point in the novel. Though it is left ambiguous, my reading is that Damon was not part of the gang that killed Cameron, hence Pleasant murders someone not directly guilty. Damon has become part of the community, but by repeating the lie about Cameron which the community has accepted, he shows that he too is infected with the evil all men are heir to. Pleasant symbolically attempts to kill a member of the community not for his guilt but for his very humanity. The tragedy is that both youths are divided, and that they have within themselves the virtues needed to restore unity to man in his creaturely nature. Damon's love for Ruth would redeem his squandered aristocratic inheritance while gaining the vigor and realism of the plain people who live according to the rhythms of the land. The story of Damon is not a historical exemplum, but a vividly realized conflict uniting with the enveloping action of Southern history.[23]

Civil Wars

The novel's shift to the large canvas of the Civil War has also been criticized as a break in the narrative flow which involves a whole new set of actions. But this section in fact follows inevitably from Lytle's thematic development. Though this part has been praised for its masterful battle scenes, Lytle does not include them as inert patches of "color"; they, and all the war scenes, advance the novel's unfolding meaning. The central action is continually reiterated in different forms. Here the problem of the claims of the public and the private realms, so central to Lytle's work, comes to the foreground.

When Pleasant comes upon his uncle Armistead McIvor, who is commanding a regiment, he sees a leader who has knit his men together and lifted their morale by his noblesse oblige, his willingness to suffer with his men while exercising his authority. Armistead tells Pleasant to forget his vengeance because it is "every Southern man's duty to put away his private life now." The private realm is not seen as less intrinsically important for it is

precisely what the public conflict seeks to protect. Lytle establishes the goodness of the private world of the South in a few deft strokes. For many of the
Confederates, their private activities are experienced so keenly that public
duty is difficult to comprehend. One man "deserts" because he tries to visit
his sick mother. Some Mississippi privates on outpost duty "romped around
shooting squirrels," and when arrested they are indignant. Perhaps the most
powerful of these scenes is the tale of a famous race between a Kentucky
horse and a South Carolina horse. The love of thoroughbred horses, whose
blood lines are known for generations, and whose racing is a form of play (as
all sport ultimately is) for its own sake, is linked to the regional loyalties. The
great race itself is a ritual enactment of all these private loves, and the lovers
of horseflesh listen to the story in that time of satiation and reflection after a
good meal. Though the race itself might be called a public act, it arises out of
each man's loyalties and enjoyments.

Pleasant finds himself in a firm and rewarding friendship with Roswell
Ellis, an attachment that takes him out of himself. His commitment is
not complete, however, and periodically Pleasant places a ring of coldness
between himself and the lieutenant. The Battle of Shiloh provides the novel's
climax, for here Pleasant is stripped of his desire for revenge.

Lytle's depiction of the commanders, Albert Sydney Johnston and P. T. G.
Beauregard, is not an attempt at reportage, but an imaginative recreation of
their personalities from what is known of their behavior. Lytle sees Johnston's
offer to step aside as commander in favor of Beauregard as a magnanimous
gesture, given Johnston's previous failures. Though Beauregard declines the
offer, he is portrayed as yet another creature of the will.[24] Johnston's quiet
deliberation, his utter reserve, is set against Beauregard's impetuous and furious activity. Johnston remains self-contained while Beauregard deteriorates
into a pallid fraction of a man.

In *The Long Night* the contrast between these two men is another itera-
tion of the theme. Johnston refuses to turn back when Beauregard is convinced that they have been heard by the Union forces because he knows he
must turn his civilian force into an army. During the battle he leaves the
proper safety of a commander and rides to the front, stopping the men from
looting and encouraging them to fight. Johnston leads his men to the noble
death in a war fought for a just cause. At a crucial point in the battle, he ral-
lies his men, and is described by the narrative voice: "He was inviting men
to death. As they saw the light in his gray eyes, his splendid presence full of
the joy of combat, life became suddenly unreal, a mean and ignoble thing."[25]

Johnston is the opposite of Pleasant and Lovell: he leads his men to the dark portals in an epiphany of self-sacrifice for the private realm, which alone gives meaning to our individual lives. His death is an outcome of placing himself in peril, but his actions have redeemed the battle.

Pleasant acts as a scout, for which his knowledge of the long night qualifies him, and the day before the battle he remains alone in the Shiloh forest while Ellis returns to camp. In his consciousness, the forest takes on a sinister character, containing the evil of the enemy. "Anything was better than wandering in this torture of sound beating down the ravines. It was no noise that man could make. He knew what it was. It was this forest turning loose all its sullen vicious strength on the men who had come to trample its rank and twisted ground."[26] This transformation of his attitude toward the "wilderness" is one sign of his inability to maintain his inhuman assertion of will in isolation. When the battle arrives, once again he is alone, a seeing eye. But before long his fear grows and during heavy fighting he sees the sun glinting off the bayonets of Confederate reinforcements. "His people had come at last!" The army is now "his" people, not merely the collection of individuals containing the remaining murderers to be killed. The community he could not enter before is here, at least briefly, affirmed.

The Fractured View

The novel ends with Pleasant's final attempt to exact private revenge, the result of which is the death of Roswell Ellis. Whereas the death of Johnston at Shiloh had been redemptive, Ellis's death is meaningless and unnecessary. The news of Ellis's death undoes Pleasant, and he chooses to opt out of community by deserting and hiding in the hills.

The conclusion brings the reader back to the introduction, where Pleasant is seen as an older man. His life has the appearance of order and plenitude; he has an understanding wife, several children, and well-worked land. His wife, in fact, is the woman Ellis loved and he had made Pleasant promise to see her if he died. His marriage to her, his family and farm, are mitigating factors for his isolation, but his eyes betray his loneliness, his knowledge of a truth he cannot wholly confront. To a limited extent, Pleasant is like the artist: possessed of a vision which tortures him but which he must communicate, even if his audience cannot or will not understand him. But unlike the repentant Ancient Mariner, Pleasant cannot expiate his guilt by telling his tale to any passerby. It must be handed down if the experience of the McIvor family is to have meaning.

Which finally brings us back to nephew Lawrence, Pleasant's audience and the mediator of the story. Lawrence is William McIvor's son, and like his father he has become "something of a scholar," as his Arkansas college degree indicates. Lawrence's immaturity is evident in his florid language and tired platitudes. Both forms of language place reality at a distance, hidden in meaningless verbiage. On leaving college, Lawrence says, "I had paid my debts and with tender remonstrances of lasting affection bade farewell to friends and acquaintances."[27] When describing his arduous walk to Pleasant's hill home, he comments: "A good sweat will do wonders for a man."[28] When he receives Pleasant's summons, Lawrence is on his way to a waiting bride and the responsibilities of heading a household, but his impatience while staying with his uncle indicates his innocence before the world's complexities. These fatuous comments would not mean much if they were uttered by a young man, but in apologizing for mixing his own research in with Pleasant's narrative, Lawrence says: "Of course you must understand that, at this late date, I cannot tell which words are his and which are mine." Lawrence is telling the tale well after he had heard it, and his lack of understanding is that of a grown man. The wrenching irony is that Pleasant's story has done nothing for Lawrence.

Lawrence, as William's son, is the "good Christian boy" who retains certain civilized values but fails to understand the tragic reality of evil and corruption. Pleasant, a McIvor to the end, is trapped inside himself, and even his attempt to express his knowledge falls on Lawrence's untutored ears. The old man and his nephew are still the tragically divided representatives of Christendom in the new world. Lytle wrote that the South lacked a deep religious faith and sense of a unified community in a single church. The South, he said, was the inheritor of Christendom, and remained on the defensive against the Faustian spirit of modernity, which was materialist. "But it is the fractured view of this Christian drama, the loss of its inner meaning, which has confused Southern institutions and required of the family more meaning than it can sustain."[29]

Lytle, though he was an adamant defender of the family, believed that in the South's experience the family existed outside its proper context. In *The Long Night*, Pleasant is a Southern representative of modern man. He is too close to the temptations of the wilderness, and in his attempt to escape from the necessity of accepting the duality of a world of good and evil he becomes a disembodied will, divorced from humanity. The South's "fractured view" of its Christian inheritance was its tragic flaw. The nearness in time of Lawrence's telling of the story makes clear the sense of the past in the present, for we still live in that fractured world, and it is up to us to forgive our enemies and join the fallen human community as an equal member. This is the truth which Andrew Lytle's historical fiction calls us to affirm.

13

Wendell Berry:

Marriage to a Place

Throughout the series of interconnected novels and stories that make up Wendell Berry's fictional world of Port William, Kentucky, one of the central characters is a wayward soul known as Burley Coulter. In a community made up primarily of married farmers, Burley is an anomaly—a confirmed bachelor who would just as soon go squirrel hunting as milk a cow or bale hay. He owns no land of his own. That he fathered a child with a single woman named Kate Helen Branch is more or less an open secret in the neighborhood. While he quietly finds ways to support his son, he never acts like a father to him. He's also a prankster and a teller of tall tales. Burley delights his nephews by making up stories about being a teamster for Barnum and Bailey Circus, wrangling the horses on which scantily clad, beautiful women ride with ostrich plumes in their hair. His zingers include the story of the man who bored a hole in the bottom of his boat to let the water out and the one about the man who woke up dead.

Then there's the story of his courting a lady one evening while parked in a buggy in the midst of a pasture. Burley backs the buggy up and manages to roll over a sleeping cow, who promptly gets up and overturns the buggy. When one of his hearers asks why he was courting a lady in a buggy in the midst of a pasture, Burley retorts: "Now you're wanting to know facts."

Though Burley Coulter may appear to contradict all the values that his neighbors in Port William hold dear—values which, the reader suspects, Wendell Berry also espouses—the truth is that he is an essential, if eccentric, member of the community. He is a link between the absolute wildness of untamed nature—symbolized by the woods and the rivers, where he spends as much of his time as possible—and the domesticated world of agriculture and human civilization, the world of farms and churches and towns.

Burley plays about on the margin of the settled community, but he never leaves it. When a crop needs to be taken in, he is there to do the back-breaking labor with everyone else. When his sister-in-law dies young, he stops hunting on the weekends to help raise his nephews.

In a sense, Burley is a fictional descendant of another great character from early American literature—Natty Bumppo, the hero of James Fenimore Cooper's *Leatherstocking Tales*. A tracker and woodsman, Natty lives between the Native American community, with their closeness to, and reverence for, nature, and the white community, which is given to wasteful, rapacious treatment of the land. Like Natty, Burley sometimes seems an extremist, someone who can hardly serve as a model for others. You could be forgiven for asking of these figures: who can actually live on berries and nuts and squirrels?

The Gadfly and the Lover

But looked at another way, these half-wild men can be seen as prophets. In biblical terms, a prophet is someone both on the margin of society and yet passionately engaged with it. The prophet is both gadfly and lover of the community. By reminding human beings of the fundamental order of the universe that exists prior to the exercise of will and power, the prophet calls his people back to reverence and humility. And while the prophet is traditionally seen as thoroughly wayward—think hair shirts, locusts, scraggly beards, and bulging eyes—he is, in fact, the castigator of waywardness in others.

With this paradox in mind, it is possible to read even Burley Coulter's tendency toward irreverence in religious matters as ultimately more spiritual than the conventional pieties of those around him. When his family and friends are working in the barn or the fields, he enjoys standing before them as a mock preacher, mimicking the intonations of itinerant evangelizers. One day Burley gets up and intones, like a backwoods St. Paul:

> Oh, yes, brothers and sisters, we are members one of another. The difference, beloved, ain't in who is and who's not, but in who knows it and who don't. Oh, my friends, there ain't no nonmembers, living nor dead

nor yet to come. Do you know it? Or do you don't? A man is a member of a woman and a worm. A woman is a member of a man and a mole. Oh, beloved, it's all one piece of work.

For all the bad grammar and deliberate cheekiness of this pseudo-sermon, truer words are never spoken in the hundreds of pages that make up the collective saga of Port William. For the belief that humans are part of a cosmic membership of love and responsibility that includes all living things— past, present, and future—is as close to a credo as anyone in that community ever utters.

And you can be sure that it is a credo that Wendell Berry—who in his puckish moments bears a distinct resemblance to Burley Coulter—believes with every fiber of his being.

The One-Handed Farmer

Who, then, is this irreverent prophet of reverence? Who is this spinner of tales about the nearly timeless world of a small rural community, a writer whose output is so out of touch with the postmodern irony that dominates the twenty-first century literary scene?

The first thing to say about Wendell Berry is that he is one of those writers who has been given the gift of deep roots in a particular place, a connection that is so powerful and primal that it has determined his entire *oeuvre*. Berry knows and loves Henry County, Kentucky, the way Charles Dickens knew and loved London.

Born in 1934, he is the eldest of four children born to John and Virginia Berry. His father's family has farmed in the county for five generations and his mother's family for six. In addition to being a farmer, Berry's father was also a lawyer, someone for whom the law was also cultivation—the careful management of the ties between the land and the people who worked that land. In the fictional Port William, the father and son duo of Wheeler and Andy Catlett correspond to Berry and his father.

In short, Berry grew up in a home that had both a firm anchoring in the soil and in the life of the mind. While he attended secondary school at Millersburg Military Institute, and then pursued Bachelor's and Master's degrees in English at the University of Kentucky at Lexington, the young Berry was not averse to going out to see the world. In 1958, Berry received a Wallace Stegner Fellowship, which enabled him to attend Stanford

University's creative writing program. There he studied under Stegner in a seminar that included several other future writers, including Larry McMurtry, Edward Abbey, and Ken Kesey. Other scholarships and awards, including a Fulbright Fellowship, took him and his wife Tanya Amyx, to Italy, France, and New York City.

But the pull of home was inexorable. In 1964 he and his wife purchased a rundown farm close to where he grew up. The next year they moved onto the land, where they have grown tobacco, corn, and small grains, as well as raising sheep. Part of their 125-acre farm adjoins the Kentucky River, near the place where it flows into the Ohio.

After a stint as a professor at the University of Kentucky, Berry left teaching to devote himself fully to writing and farming. While he has admitted that he is a "one-handed farmer," Berry's devotion to the land is not half-hearted. In addition to his crops and livestock, Berry and his family have always kept a vegetable garden, dairy cows, and hogs, striving for the ideal of subsistence farming. Among his more radical choices has been to do without a tractor as much as possible, which he sees as representing the tyranny of technology. What horses and mules can do on the farm, they do for Wendell Berry.

With a wonderful—and perhaps terrifying—consistency, even Berry's writing habits conform to the organic realities of life on the farm. He writes only during the daytime in natural light.

> I write in longhand, with a pencil, and make many changes and erasures as I go along. Every morning, before I begin, I read over and correct the work of the morning before. When I have finished a chapter or a story or essay, I read it aloud to Tanya, my wife, and make the corrections that this reading suggests to her and to me. Before she types it, I read it again and make further changes. Between typescript and publication many more changes may be made.

It should come as no surprise then that Berry once wrote an essay entitled, "Why I am Not Going to Buy a Computer."

Unsettled America

Though a soft-spoken Kentucky gentleman, Berry is a man of adamantine principle and a practitioner of such uncompromising consistency that he stirs up equal amounts of devotion and controversy. He is America's leading agrarian, meaning that he is the most articulate defender of the old Jeffersonian idea of the yeoman farmer, the citizen who is literally invested in land, region, family, and community. Berry believes that the modern cult of technology and innovation has come close to destroying the environment, caused vast numbers of people around the world to be uprooted from their native places and scattered into sprawling, anonymous cities, and torn at the very fabric of marriage, child-rearing, and local institutions that provide identity and ensure good stewardship of the world's resources.

It is not so much that Berry contests the success of capitalism; rather, he laments its results—a mobile but restless and rudderless society, addicted to instant gratification and the junk food and junk culture that feed such an appetite; a hyper-individualism that celebrates competition instead of cooperation; a mentality based on rights and entitlement rather than one grounded in lifelong commitments and reciprocity.

In a steady series of essays, collected in such volumes as *The Unsettling of America, The Gift of Good Land, What Are People For?*, and *Sex, Economy, Freedom, & Community,* Berry has dared to question what most of us refuse to consider: that the costs of our vaunted progress and prosperity have taken far too heavy a human toll. This is undoubtedly one reason he is so controversial: he calls attention to the secret most of us would like to sweep under the carpet. Most of us, when confronted by the litany of woes that Berry cites, tend to shrug our collective shoulders, assuring ourselves that there is little or nothing we can do to slow down the juggernaut of modern life.

But Berry insists that we all *can* do something, and that makes us uncomfortable. He takes great pains to set out practical steps to promote what he calls the "local economy," a vision of regional agriculture and production that avoids the mass-produced, chemically-enhanced materials of daily life, from tomatoes that taste like plastic to goods made by prisoners in China. Berry is not an advocate of state socialism, but he is a harsh critic of multinational corporations, which he sees as place-less entities, without real ties to living communities, whatever their corporate philanthropy might give back in dollar terms to the places where they operate.

Pinning down Berry politically is a difficult, if not impossible, thing to do. He has supporters and detractors on both the Left and the Right. His writings have done much to fuel the environmental movement around the world, and yet he shares little in common with the typical Sierra Club member. His defense of marriage, family, and local community, and his ongoing debt to the Christian worldview are a source of embarrassment for many of his "green" friends. And while he has fervent supporters among those who call themselves "traditionalist" conservatives, Berry would be regarded by most readers of the *Wall Street Journal* as little more than a crackpot.

Add to all this that he is an absolute or near-absolute pacifist and you can see why he causes blood pressures to rise. Since 9/11 he has written widely about America's foreign policy in an era of terrorism, denouncing the use of military force around the globe. His essay, "Thoughts in the Presence of Fear," contains a sequence of measured but tough pronouncements, including this statement: "What leads to peace is not violence but peaceableness, which is not passivity, but an alert, informed, practiced, and active state of being. We should recognize that while we have extravagantly subsidized the means of war, we have almost totally neglected the ways of peaceableness." For Berry, these ways are based on the ideal of local self-sufficiency, modest consumption, and good stewardship of our natural environment. We go wrong, he believes, by imposing our politics and economics on the rest of the world.

To those who sneeringly comment that this is all very well, but that few people would be willing to give up the conveniences and pleasures of a global economy, Berry has a maddeningly forthright answer. Yes, he says, changing over to a local economy would require suffering and sacrifice, but such a change would be worth it.

And the one thing his critics have to admit is that Wendell Berry practices what he preaches.

The Port William Membership

To the extent that Berry's essays make him a controversial figure, some may be tempted to ignore his fiction and poetry, or to assume that they are little more than thinly veiled position statements.

That would be a grave injustice to the work of a consummate artist. True, Berry's literary works revolve around his central concerns—the land and our relationship to it—but they till the soil of language as meticulously as a farmer tills the earth. Berry is a craftsman who respects the reader's imagination. In fact, it might be argued that his nonfiction writing is something of a necessary evil—a manifestation of his anxiety about the state of our culture—and that his true calling lies in the realm of fiction and poetry.

For the purposes of this essay, I will look briefly at Berry's novel *Hannah*

Coulter. This book is a part of a larger whole—the spreading roots and branches of what Berry (and some of his characters) call the "Port William Membership."

Through seven novels and several dozen short stories, Berry has faithfully elaborated a single fictional setting. The combined works have been compared to William Faulkner's Yoknapatwapha County for the color and richness of the social, cultural, and personal tapestry they weave. Certainly both writers created richly detailed Southern landscapes, full of three-dimensional human relationships, but the comparison is problematic because the two writers possess vastly different sensibilities. Faulkner was a tragic writer whose protagonists achieve an almost heroic stature. One need only think of his classic novella *The Bear* to recall the way Isaac McCaslin's epic hunt for the ancient, scarred beast rises to the level of myth.

Berry, on the other hand, renders Port William on a less heroic scale. Whereas Faulkner's Yoknapatwpha was grounded in a tragic act of violence and betrayal against the native peoples, Port William simply grows organically out of the landscape. In the short story "The Hurt Man," we read:

> The town was the product of its own becoming, which, if not accidental exactly, had also been unplanned. It had no formal government or formal history. It was without pretense or ambition, for it was the sort of place that pretentious or ambitious people were inclined to leave. It had never declared an aspiration to become anything that it was not. It did not thrive so much as it merely lived, doing the things it needed to do to stay alive. This tracked and rubbed little settlement had been built in a place of great natural abundance and beauty, which it had never valued highly enough, had damaged, and yet had not destroyed. The town's several buildings, shaped less by art than by need and use, had suffered tellingly and even becomingly a hundred years of wear.

But if Berry's cast of farmers and shopkeepers are not drawn in operatic fashion, it does not imply that they don't suffer loss or hardship, or that their lives are merely mundane. The land is abundant, but it is demanding; only those willing to master the virtues of good stewardship can make it fruitful. Unremitting labor, thrift, humility, and a vivid awareness of the fragile link between the generations are required.

In Berry's imagination, the business of marrying and raising children is the spiritual and psychological equivalent of cultivating the soil. The land calls forth the disciplines of mind and heart needed to do it justice, but human beings are free to avoid that call. Berry's first novel, *Nathan Coulter* (1960), recounts the fraught relationship between Nathan's father and his older brother, Tom. As Tom grows into manhood, his father pushes him relentlessly, creating a primal struggle between the generations. The result is that Tom leaves the farm. A few years later he is killed in World War II. Nathan witnesses this breakdown between the generations, which he is powerless to change but from which he learns.

A Story Begun Long Ago

Hannah Coulter picks up the story where that first novel leaves off. The narrative reads more like a memoir than a conventionally plotted work of fiction. Told in Hannah's voice, the story accumulates slowly; it has the force of testimony and of wisdom.

Born a couple years apart in the early 1920s, Hannah and Nathan live through the rest of the twentieth century, witnessing huge social and cultural changes. Hannah's first husband, Virgil Feltner, is another casualty of the Second World War, after only a few months of marriage. Finding herself both a widow and a new mother, Hannah struggles to find her place in Port William. She feels profoundly indebted to the Feltner family, but she is a young, beautiful woman with most of her life before her.

When Hannah becomes aware of Nathan Coulter's love for her, she does not simply fall for him, though he is described as a "beautiful" man. Here we begin to see the way that Berry's vision differs from the prevailing ethos of our culture. That Hannah would restrain her feelings because of her sense of obligation to, and love for, the Feltners, whose grandchild she has borne, may seem almost medieval to postmodern minds. But then Wendell Berry doesn't subscribe to the idea that romantic love trumps all other relationships, including those of the extended family and the community as a whole. Only when Virgil's parents recognize Nathan's love and release her from her crisis of conscience does she feel free to marry him.

Their marriage is not the product of merely "falling" for one another. As Hannah puts it, her relationship to Nathan is grounded in a "knowing love." A part of that "knowing" stems from the fact that she was married before, but another part of it comes from the way that Nathan woos her. Rather than basing the relationship on chemistry or charisma, Nathan reveals to Hannah what sort of life he wants to live—the kind of farmer, and man, he wants to become. "I know you're afraid," he says to Hannah on the property he hopes to own and farm, "But can you see a life here?"

It is because she can imagine that life that Hannah marries Nathan. The same attitude had shaped her marriage to Virgil. As she puts it:

> Like maybe any young woman of that time, I had thought of marriage as promises to be kept until death, as having a house, living together, working together, sleeping together, raising a family. But Virgil's and my marriage was going to have to be more than that. It was going to have to be a part of a place already decided for it, and part of a story begun long ago and going on.

One might call this the communitarian view of marriage, as opposed to the individualistic one. For some contemporaries, this view undoubtedly would call forth remarks about returning to the old days of arranged marriages, but the more profound question would be: what have we lost in abstracting marriage from family, community, and history? Throughout much of Western history, marriage was considered not only a private reality but a *public* one as well—part of the larger web of obligations that hold the community together, a hard-won victory over the temptations of the restless human heart.

Needless to say, fidelity in marriage is another given among the older generations of Port William. It is not something that the characters articulate, as if it were a theory; fidelity is simply a concomitant of the natural order, the virtue needed to do justice to the land. Love is not a passing emotion but a fundamental commitment, a rootedness in being; its shape and meaning can only be known on the scale of a lifetime. To bind oneself to a spouse is the same as binding oneself to a place. As Hannah says,

> Most people now are looking for "a better place," which means that a lot of them will end up in a worse one. . . . There is no "better place" than this, not in *this* world. And it is by the place we've got, and our love for it and our keeping of it, that this world is joined to Heaven.

The citizens of Port William are anchored to the land and to their common history, but they are also formed by their biblical faith. Aside from the occasional traveling preacher or mentally disturbed eccentric, the people of this community are fairly reticent about their religious convictions. They rarely make points by citing biblical proof texts. But their hearts and minds are molded by the stories and wisdom of the Bible. Some, like Burley Coulter, can be "wayward," but when they are tested, they will acknowledge—or at least act—according to the moral truths they have inherited. In the end, actions speak louder than words in Port William. Hannah reflects this when she says:

> You can't give yourself over to love for somebody without giving yourself over to suffering. . . . It is this body of our suffering that Christ was born into, to suffer it Himself and to fill it with light, so that beyond the suffering we may imagine Easter morning and the peace of God on little earthly homelands.

Wendell Berry has leveled hard words at what he sees as the collaboration of institutional Christianity in America with many of the ills he decries. Like his characters he, too, can be reticent about his relationship to creeds and denominations. But there can be little doubt about where he turns for moral authority or the spiritual resources he believes are needed to fulfill our purpose on this earth. In this he is a lot like Burley Coulter, whose irreverence is intended to stir people out of complacency and see that we are all members of one another: man, woman, worm, and mole. Because "it's all one piece of work."

14

Larry Woiwode:
The Overwhelming Question

In a special issue of the *New Criterion* dedicated to surveying the arts in America since World War II, the journal's literary editor, Bruce Bawer, contributed an essay on the novel entitled *Diminishing Fictions*. As the title indicates, Bawer believes that contemporary American novelists have retreated from the broad and open territory of the human heart into little hermetically-sealed empires of art. The essay is vigorously argued, but the most vivid part of it is a critique of the new literary minimalism. The minimalists are known for their flat descriptions of the lives of punishingly ordinary, obscure people. Much of this description, according to Bawer, consists of catalogues of the brand names of products used in the home, along with the names of television shows and ads which drone on in the background—punctuated by the insipid staccato dialogue of nearly moronic characters.

Like most critics of the American literary establishment, however, Bawer is better at marshaling empirical evidence than at diagnosing the root causes of our cultural malaise. Neoconservative critics of the arts rightly point to a crucial loss of confidence among artists, affecting the scope and form of their art, but this crisis of confidence is understood primarily in political terms, as a rejection of bourgeois democracy by disaffected radicals.

There are two crippling problems with this kind of argument. First, by confining themselves largely to the political plane, the neoconservatives leave themselves open to the charge that their positions are also politically motivated. The pages of the *New Criterion* and *Nation* (to pick a couple obvious antagonists) are filled with this circular type of name-calling.

The second, and most important, weakness in the neoconservative critique is that it does not go far enough. The self-doubt of our novelists does not stem from a petulant refusal to support the bourgeois order (though it often includes this), but from a more radical doubt about the intelligibility of the world. In short, the crisis of confidence in the West has theological and philosophical roots.

The belief that our knowledge of the world is either relative or mere delusion has had an inevitable impact on narrative fiction. From the huge, expansive novels of the nineteenth century, with their affirmations and "realism," we have moved to works which self-consciously call attention to their fictional machinery. If the novelist cannot provide a window into reality, then he must ultimately write about himself; and his technique, or politics, or personal problems come to the forefront of his work. Like the postmodernist Pompidou Center in Paris, with all its pipes, wires, and elevators on the outside, the postmodern novel refuses the "hidden" artistry of the realistic tradition in order to flaunt its bag of tricks. The minimalists may appear to be more objective, but their world is so enervated that their "affirmations" are almost nonexistent. With the minimalists, less is . . . less.

An Undiminished World

In what may be one of the most perceptive tributes to Larry Woiwode's fiction, the novelist and critic John Gardner suggested that the value of Woiwode's work lies precisely in its rejection of the diminished world of the self-conscious writer in favor of an expansive exploration of the human heart. Unlike the modern Prufrockian writers, who prefer to avoid the Overwhelming Question about the mystery of our existence, Woiwode has always faced up to the problems of love and death, memory and desire, faith and doubt. The publication of Woiwode's novel, *Born Brothers*, coming nearly twenty years after that of his first novel, provides an opportunity to examine the work of a writer who has been widely admired, but perhaps only fitfully understood.

Woiwode's literary career began when his first story was published by the *New Yorker*; he was just twenty-three. His first novel, *What I'm Going to Do, I Think*—a dark tale of a newly married couple living in a cabin in the Michigan wilderness—won the William Faulkner award for the best first novel of the year. In 1975, Woiwode gained a wide readership with the publication of *Beyond the Bedroom Wall*, the opening novel in what would become a series of novels centering on the Neumiller family of North Dakota. Subtitled "A Family Album," this 600-page story traces four generations of the Neumiller family through snapshots arranged in a roughly chronological order.

Born Brothers returns to the Neumillers, but it is told almost entirely through the controlling consciousness of Charles Neumiller, whom we have met as the second son of Martin and Alpha in *Beyond the Bedroom Wall*. In between these two volumes about the Neumillers, Woiwode published a volume of poems, *Even Tide* (1977) and a short, controversial novel, *Poppa John* (1981).

Despite the fact that he lived for a time in New York City, and that his long relationship with the *New Yorker* remains unchanged, Woiwode has remained aloof from the American literary establishment and its seats of power; he is not a frequenter of PEN conferences, or a regular reviewer for the *New York Review of Books*. After his sojourn in the East, Woiwode and his family returned to his native North Dakota, where he has worked a farm. For him, as for Charles Neumiller in *Born Brothers*, it is possible to go home and find meaning in the exploration and renewal of personal roots.

What one English reviewer said of Woiwode's first novel applies to nearly all of his fiction: "This is a world where marriage, kinship and religious faith are taken seriously; so are shooting, carpentry and the baling of hay." Woiwode's respect for the deeply conservative—almost medieval—mores and manners of the northern Midwest has remained a constant in his work, though the limitations of that world are also present and keep his fiction from descending into sentimentality.

In his love for the land Woiwode shows his affinity to the great Southern writers, such as Allen Tate and William Faulkner. For the Southern Agrarians, as for Woiwode, the landscape has a sacramental quality; it seems to mediate a reality beyond itself. The land reminds man of his limitations and requires him to enter into its mysterious rhythms like a lover. In *Born Brothers*, Charles reflects:

I know now why academic technicians, out of a sacred kind of fear, resort to programs and chemicals to slap the land into shape; it has the power to undo anyone who depends on it in a single turn. Beyond control. Stewardship is another story. The original covenant commanded not only dominion but fruitfulness, multiplication, replenishment, fill-

ing out—all of which imply a relationship. Down on your knees like
the most dedicated gardener.

The relation of a technician to nature is one of power and manipulation;
it is abstract, incapable of the strange, seemingly reciprocal love between the
gardener and his garden. It is not without significance that the gardener is
usually on his knees. Throughout Woiwode's fiction, city and suburb are
ultimately measured against the values fostered by the land.

The analogy of Woiwode's work with that of the Southern Agrarians
should not give the impression that his fiction is programmatic and political.
Though he roundly criticizes the "empty liberal pieties" of recent years in the
interview published in the September 1988 issue of the *World & I*, Woiwode
also cautions against any reliance on politics for the crucial task of preserving
civilization.

The Neumillers: A Preference for Concreteness

Woiwode's characteristic style reflects his preference for concreteness over
abstraction: his ability to convey the texture of daily life, with its small but
significant rituals, losses, and joys puts him at the opposite pole from those
who write for a cause. In the Neumiller books in particular he demonstrates a
masterful ability to reveal the archetypal essences implicit in the commonest
activities. Though the lack of obvious drama at times seems almost minimal-
ist, Woiwode "less" quietly suggests to the reader that the ordinary is actually
replete with mystery.

Nowhere does he do this better than in his descriptions of the Neumiller
children: in their early sexual adventures; in their quasi-religious, thoroughly hierarchical clubs; in their experiences of love and of injustice at
their parents' hands. In short, Woiwode owes far more to Henry James's
belief that fiction should possess "solidity of specification" in the service
of creating the sense of "felt life," than he does to minimalists or literary
magicians.

The density of Woiwode's fictional world, like the landscape itself, is
a means by which we may apprehend the identity of the characters—and
of ourselves in those characters. The theme evoked in the passage quoted
above—the struggle between human restlessness, the desire to control and
possess the world, and the need to come to terms with loss and limitation—
constitutes the Overwhelming Question that lies at the center of Woiwode's

imagination. The drama in the lives of his characters, and of our own, arises from the persistent human effort to avoid the Question.

It should, therefore, be no surprise that Woiwode has little sympathy for the modern effort to reject the limits and moral structure of human nature—whether in matters of sexuality or the environment. Woiwode's characters possess consciences that register their agonized distance from their true identities. The "Me Generation," by contrast, dances around the Question in a mad whirl in order to pretend it doesn't exist.

Woiwode's depiction of the family and the conflicts between the generations—especially between fathers, sons, and grandfathers—is omnipresent in his fiction and may constitute his enduring literary achievement. Unlike most modern novelists and intellectuals, who have seen the family as a restrictive and outworn institution that stifles freedom and individuality, Woiwode clearly sees it as inherent to the human condition, and for this very reason he treats it with more subtlety and compassion than those who would reduce it to a mass of Oedipal complexes and shuck it off. Here too the theme of love and acceptance versus power and autonomy suffuses the texture of his stories.

Woiwode's unflinching eye captures all the violence and injustice and love which simultaneously bind the family together and maintain a mysterious distance between its members. One of the reasons he treats the experience of children so intimately, as he suggests in an interview, is his sense "of the grief children feel at the inconsistencies of adults." Alpha Neumiller's fierce love for her children often leads her to be too harsh with them—something she recognizes with tears of remorse. But she remains the true Alpha, the beginning from which they proceed into the world, and when she dies at an early age from uremia the family is scarred in such a way that it never fully recovers.

Just as the family and the land remain potent forces that profoundly shape Woiwode's characters, so too is the presence of religious belief a vital, if imperfectly attained, reality. The Neumillers are Catholic, and the rituals and moral categories of the church affect the manner in which they interpret their experience. Alpha is a convert to Catholicism, but the process of instruction she undergoes reflects her independence of mind; when she accepts the church, it is a decisive and irrevocable choice. Alpha, an earthy and sensual woman, does not adopt any of the mannerisms of piety. But when the priest calls her a "saint" at her funeral, the reader is willing to accord this word a vibrant meaning: Alpha's sanctity emerges in her suffering and in the demanding love she has for husband and children. She is not a porcelain saint, but a living, breathing woman whose goodness is hard-earned.

Poppa John: *Rendering Conversion*

Not surprisingly, Woiwode's reviewers have been ambivalent toward his perception of Christian faith. In his first two novels, the reviewers accepted religion as part of the social order Woiwode portrayed so convincingly. But with the publication of *Poppa John*, a short novel hinging on the protagonist's conversion experience, a chorus of indignation arose from the book sections of the leading journals.

Most of the reviewers objected to the lushness of the novel's language and to its brevity; this change, they contended, was an abandonment of Woiwode's artistic genius. But given the fact that 200-page novels, poetic language, and artistic innovation are regularly praised by the selfsame critics, the offensive element of *Poppa John* was in reality the directness of its portrayal of the possibility of conversion. The tone struck by his secular critics was largely condescending and admonitory. Jonathan Yardley began, "Writing this review is a painful obligation," and ended, "So let's hope that *Poppa John* has gotten the preaching out of Woiwode's system." Anne Tyler, writing in the *New Republic*, did not once allude to the religious dimension of the novel—a curious omission—but concluded: "That he does know how [to write subtly about the human condition], in fact, is the reason for the truculence of this review . . . I believe I'll . . . wait with undiminished hope for his next novel."

It is true, of course, that the change which accompanies a discovery or rediscovery of religious faith is difficult to make convincing in a fictional setting, yet conversion is a central and recurring human experience. *Poppa John*, though a flawed work, is nonetheless a bold and admirable attempt to understand the lostness of late twentieth-century America and to depict an individual's brush with madness and subsequent spiritual reorientation.

Ned Daley is an aging actor who has become a national success on a soap opera for his portrayal of a wise, Bible-quoting, grandfather figure. Known for his characteristic wave, Poppa John, as his television persona is called, dominates the show. However, the producers decide that Poppa John represents old-fashioned values that are giving way to the young and the restless, and so he is killed off. The process of dying increases the show's ratings, but eventually Poppa John "dies" and must confront his own inner loneliness and unresolved psychic problems.

Poppa John takes place on Friday, December 23, as Ned and his wife Celia go Christmas shopping. In the course of a one-day Joycean ramble through New York, Ned is confronted, figuratively speaking, by his father's ghost, and by the memory of the grandfather on whom the character of Poppa John is modeled. Ned, like many of Woiwode's other characters, must come to terms with the meaning of fatherhood and the inevitability of death; in so doing, he comes to understand the divine Fatherhood. At the end of the day, Ned experiences what the psychiatrists would call a nervous breakdown, but which is actually an intense conviction of his insecurity and of the fact that he need not be his own savior. This day of reckoning is a recollection of Good Friday. On Sunday, Ned experiences both Christmas and Easter.

The television character of Poppa John gives Ned a kind of control over his fears, but only in defenselessness does Ned find his true identity. Thus, *Poppa John* also raises another central theme of Woiwode's, namely the destructive effect on our culture of the media and of television in particular.

As a media figure, Poppa John is a twentieth-century priest; appearing in the tabernacle of the television tube, he dispenses clichés to salve the anxieties of modern men. He is, as Celia says, a "double being," but for Ned the disjuncture of self and image is the opposite of the incarnate unity of the dual natures of Christ. In *Born Brothers*, we see Charles Neumiller as a popular radio-show host. But Charles ends up inventing and impersonating all the personalities on his "talk show." Despite the fact that radio is less offensive than television because it gives some scope to the imagination, Charles involves himself in the ultimate abstraction: he records his show in the isolation of his soundproof room, and he becomes the god of his invented world. This picture is a powerful insight into the solipsism which is the end result of radical doubt; in these circumstances the artist, like Charles, becomes the god of a closed world. To be sure, this is the temptation all artists must confront, but the true artist, unlike Charles, does not close himself off from experience.

Woiwode's brief against television is not, as some of his critics have insinuated, a prudish condemnation of "sex and violence." Rather Woiwode sees television as the enemy of the imagination: it provides a false, lulling sense of continuity in a world where change and decay are constants. This "continuity" is nothing but an ephemeral present that provides no true links with the past.

For Woiwode, as for Nabokov, imagination is memory. Imagination is rooted in the real; it is at the furthest remove from fantasy. Like Coleridge,

Woiwode sees imagination as a creative force which takes its meaning from the Creator who is called "I AM." The human act of subcreation can only fulfill itself when it catches the mystery at the heart of being itself. This is what Charles says in *Born Brothers*: "There's no possibility of engaging reality in the endlessness to which it corresponds without understanding the life at the center of it, for its own glory."

It is in Woiwode's concept of the imagination that his Christian vision and his understanding of the conflict between power and love come together. Contrary to the critics, Woiwode does not feel that Christianity is a facile grasping at certainty. With Flannery O'Connor, he holds that Christianity is true because it recognizes the mystery of being. The imagination leads ultimately not to human certainties but to an intuition of the glory within the complex mystery of the world. It is precisely in the twin errors of over-confident scientism and of radical doubt that man seeks power over being. Of course, Woiwode does not equate imagination with faith. But it is possible for art to bring man into the precincts of the Overwhelming Question. As Woiwode says in the interview in the *World & I*, "Fiction is a continuing spiritual exercise that any reader may join in on."

Part Four

Three Artists

15

Fred Folsom:

Grace à Go-Go

It's two thirty in the morning at the Shepherd Park Go-Go Club in Silver Spring, Maryland. The lights have just come up, signaling last call. But just in this moment, this flashbulb slice of time, you're aware that everything is still in full swing. There are at least a hundred people jammed into this place. Music throbs through the speakers; neon crackles in half a dozen beer signs on the walls. A haze of blue smoke drifts up to the klieg lights that are pointed at a raised platform in the center of the room.

A stripper on that stage is nearly through with her routine. She's the center of attention, the intersection of grinning leers and vacant stares. You notice that her figure is classical, voluptuous, her expression distant, inward, pained. She presents a mystery, this Venus de Milo in a strip joint. You promise yourself that you will confront her mystery later, but for now your eye is eager to look into the faces and gestures of those who encircle her.

Over at the bar, a full-bodied woman kneeling on the counter has just flung off her bra. It's not clear whether she's being paid for this—a secondary striptease act—or whether she's merely frolicking with her friends. You suspect that she's a regular.

On the large TV screen over the bar you can see the words: "ABC NEWS SPECIAL REPORT." But nobody is looking at the news.

The Shepherd Park's a pretty rough place. Machismo is the theme of this gathering. The enormous hulk of a bartender bulges out of a T-shirt that reads: "FUCK OFF." A broken hacksaw blade on a table in front of one drinker hints at an occupation on the wrong side of the law. But the clientele is not restricted to thugs and lowlifes. There are a couple of military men who've come to the club on their way home from the Walter Reed Army Hospital. Bureaucrats and businessmen in rumpled suits also nurse their beers and take in the show.

Near the entrance a handsome young middle-class couple seems out of place; they are lost and need directions. The husband is using the pay phone, holding up a scrap of paper with a phone number on it. Actually, he is looking past the paper to the stripper, a grin forming on his face. The pretty wife, heavily pregnant, stands with her back to the club in protest; she can't wait to get out.

As your eye circles around this spectacle, it tends to come back to a figure in your immediate foreground. He is slouched in his chair, young but already potbellied, rather drunk but entirely harmless. There's a round bulge of chewing tobacco in his cheek; he's a stupefied chipmunk. The medical tape on his nose and the splint on one of his fingers indicate that's he's been in a fight. As he gestures with one hand, the beer bottle in his other hand moves into a horizontal position, spilling beer onto his lap.

You look at this greasy young Bacchus partly because he is looking back at you. Though you're not inclined to take him very seriously, he does seem to be pointing to his right, as if he wants to send your eye on another trip across the room. You are helped along by another figure who is twisting in his chair, looking in the same direction. A policeman directs a flashlight into this far corner. But all you can see at the edge of your vision is a hand holding a glass of wine; whoever is holding it is almost completely out of sight. There's a wound on the hand, partially covered with a Band-Aid. Nothing more.

Hearing the Call—or Not

Fred Folsom's *Last Call (at the Shepherd Park Go-Go Club)* took four years to paint. It consists of three panels, each measuring 6½ x 6½ feet, the total area adding up to 127 square feet. To view it properly you have to walk back and forth across the width of the painting, as if you were pushing through the crowded bar itself. Each of its more than ninety characters is a portrait. The majority of these characters are people whom Folsom knows well—local artists, art critics, policemen, auto mechanics.

Last Call is a masterful depiction of a particular place, certainly, but it is not merely a work of sociological reportage. The casual critic who might

Last Call (at the Shepherd Park Go-Go Club)

dismiss *Last Call* as little more than the work of a clever illustrator would be wide of the mark. Folsom is more than a Norman Rockwell in reverse, a mere recorder of the dark underbelly of American society. There is an expressive intensity and a subtle imagination at work in this painting. A closer inspection reveals discontinuities in the realism of *Last Call*. Among the contemporary revelers are figures from history—the scientist and theologian Blaise Pascal and the American legend Davy Crockett. A plump girl from Manet's painting *The Plum* sits at a table. Allegorical symbols proliferate. And there is the central incongruity of the stripper herself, a Hellenic beauty in a bump-and-grind joint.

As in all of Folsom's paintings, *Last Call* draws the viewer into a complex and paradoxical relationship with the world that is depicted. We are both attracted to and repelled by the teeming, raucous life of the Shepherd Park. The impulse to condemn its patrons is almost instinctive. It would not take long to pick out representatives of each of the Seven Deadly Sins in this painting.

At the same time the very individuality of these figures mitigates our desire to judge them. This is not some faceless group of damned souls, but a ragtag collection of humanity, utterly diverse in their sufferings, evasions, hungers. We seem to know these people; their faces contain stories that they might tell us if they were in the mood and we were willing to listen. Of course, a few of them look as if they would just as soon slit your throat, but even the hardest of these thugs might yet hear the "call." In contemplating the crowd at the Shepherd Park, the words of an old cartoon strip character come to mind: "We have met the enemy, and he is us."

Just as novelists claim that they love *all* of their characters, even the evil ones, so Fred Folsom loves the patrons of the Shepherd Park. Only a special kind of love can induce a man to spend four years laboring on one painting.

Folsom is primarily a realist, but this does not mean that his paintings are photographic reproductions that can be viewed passively. Nearly all of his works contain submerged allegories, obscure symbols, surrealistic images from the regions above and below our rational minds. They are dynamic rather than static; they demand that the viewer participate in a process of discernment and interpretation. Folsom's paintings are constantly provoking us to reveal our innermost selves, to peel back the layers of pride and prejudice that isolate us from others.

Folsom faces his own form of isolation. As a serious Christian artist in late twentieth-century America, his work will either be ignored by, or offensive to, the majority of his fellow believers. Some secular critics, on the other hand, admire his artistry without recognizing the theological dimensions of his imagination.

But Fred Folsom is not filled with angst by this paradoxical isolation from church and art establishments. He is so grateful that he is no longer the greasy young Bacchus of the Shepherd Park that worries about his place in religious or cultural circles seem trivial. Looking at him today, it's hard to believe that this trim, nattily dressed man was the pathetic figure in the foreground of *Last Call*. Fred Folsom continues to wonder—both personally and through the medium of paint—about the mystery of his rescue from that world, about those who are still there, and about all those proper people who pass by the Shepherd Parks of the world with a shudder.

Your Project Is You

Fred Folsom's life would have followed an entirely different course if he had grown up with the ability to read well—or so he says. In a letter to the man who commissioned his *Grisaille in an Ice Storm*, Folsom wrote: "If I could read well, I would be an electrical engineer, anthropologist or scholar, not a painter. A perceptual and memory problem makes reading difficult except when I *really* concentrate, when it becomes impossible. This poltergeist randomly changes, fragments and erases information, names and sequences. Obvious matters become abstruse. For thirty-five years I thought I was stupid. It was a great comfort when the problem was diagnosed as dyslexia."

As a child, Folsom did not have the benefit of that belated comfort. Born in Washington, D.C. in 1945, Folsom the dyslexic grew up in an extremely literate household. His father was the chief of the criminal tax division at the Department of Justice for twenty-six years. His mother was a proofreader at *US News & World Report*. "People who could read scared me," he says. "It was as if they were in on a private joke. . . . It was as if I was living in enemy territory."

His experience at school was agonizing. He took psychological tests to explain his poor performance, and the results claimed that it was his own fault, that he was being rebellious and vindictive. He turned to drawing to compensate. He tried to deflect his teachers' attention to his poor writing by adding beautiful illustrations to his book reports. "I had to cheat with written stuff; I had to go and interview good students to sneak by. I didn't feel like a thief when I was painting."

His earliest efforts in drawing involved attempts to emulate the style of Jack Davis's cartoons in *Mad* magazine—a fact that sheds some light on his sense of humor. Later, an art teacher in high school, Mrs. Michaelson, encouraged him to pursue art as a vocation. She would meet with him before class to go over his work.

Folsom's nameless handicap led him to feel that he was not a "normal" person. Once when his parents took him into downtown Washington, they lost him, only to come upon him talking to a wino. This incident, which bears an uncanny likeness to the Gospel story of the finding of the child Jesus in the temple, speaks volumes about Folsom's identification with the losers and outcasts of society. This child of a respectable middle-class family felt more attracted to thugs and bums than to anyone else. "I felt more comfortable in life-threatening situations than I did with proper, normal people who meant me well."

After graduating from high school, Folsom went to the Pratt Institute in Brooklyn, New York. One of his classmates was Robert Mapplethorpe. Another was Robert Wilson, who went on to become an avant-garde playwright and set designer, best known for his collaborations with composer Philip Glass (including *Einstein on the Beach*). Folsom remembers little about Mapplethorpe, but he drew inspiration from Wilson's intense work ethic, his willingness to throw himself completely into the creative act.

The time at Pratt was immensely rewarding, but also tense. Unlike medical school, where the student's project is "on the table," in art school, Folsom recalls, "your project is you." The enormous psychic pressures on the students at Pratt often took their toll. "People were jumping off buildings."

Though the reigning orthodoxy in New York at that time might have been Abstract Expressionism, Folsom had at least one teacher who emphasized traditional, figurative painting from live models. Martha Erlebacher told Folsom that the "nude is everything." That remark stayed with him; nearly all of his paintings today contain at least one nude.

When he was at Pratt, Folsom painted wet, splashy abstractions that he calls "expressionistic landscapes." They usually had a vague horizon line in them. Little figurative gestures would emerge—possibly a tree, a sun. Gradually the representational elements gained more substance and form. Folsom claims that his turn toward realism was aided considerably when he found that he needed glasses. There might be some truth to this, although it sounds a little like *Mad* magazine humor creeping in to his autobiography.

Time of Troubles

It was after he left Pratt that Folsom entered his time of troubles. His style inchoate, his skills undeveloped, failed to produce work that was competitive enough to get into the galleries. He got a job as a bullpen artist for Washington's leading advertising agency—an eminently proper job for a perfectly normal person. He couldn't handle it; within a few months he quit. He became a dishwasher at a honky-tonk in Maryland, not far from the Shepherd Park. "I got fired three times as a dishwasher, but they kept hiring me back. I was always there, hanging around."

He concentrated his efforts, as he puts it, in "turning cold yellow liquid into warm yellow liquid." So he gradually devolved into the good-old-boy of *Last Call*. He was hanging around with people he understood and genuinely liked, the sort he had always felt most comfortable with. His art, of course, was going nowhere. "I was trying to paint on inspiration, which meant that I was properly drunk and that the booze would tell me that it's time to be a great artist. I held on to the bohemian notion that all of your successes can be claimed as genius, while all of your failures you can blame on 'them.' The truth was that I was playing around with booze until it began to play around with me."

Like so many people in Folsom's situation, his decision to seek help and break out of his self-destructive habits was sudden and drastic. But the will to change had been growing in him for some time. He realized that the price of a beer was roughly equivalent to that of a brick. He began to think of what he could build with all those bricks. And then, suddenly, the decision was made; he had traded the beers for bricks.

The change had nothing to do with religion, nor was it an effort to rejoin the world of proper middle-class Takoma Park, Maryland. In fact, the people who provided him with the best support were reformed drug addicts and alcoholics who had created a network of informal counselors. Folsom would go on to become a part of this network himself; over the years, it has kept him close to those who have felt the same pain and despair and manic hilarity that he found in places like the Shepherd Park.

With his life in order, Folsom's art began to take shape. He discovered that he could no longer paint landscapes; they were simply "not enough." He wanted to paint portraits of his friends; he needed to do pictorial justice to the losers and outsiders he understood so well. Few of his early efforts, which include drawings and paintings of winos, tramps, and the urban poor, achieve more than a documentary value; some are merely sentimental. It would take time for him to find settings, such as the go-go bars, that would give complexity and the hard edge of experience to his vision. He also came to appreciate the wisdom of Professor Erlebacher's belief that the human figure, the nude, is "everything."

Folsom's conversion to Christianity came several years after he had begun painting seriously. "I wasn't in desperate trouble at that point," he notes. "I did not 'come to Christ'; it was the other way around. I was running away from Him, running as hard as I could."

In childhood, Folsom's only experience with the Christian faith had been a "passing connection" with the Methodist Church. His struggle with the faith was thus an intensely private matter. He questioned God about what he thought of as the "Christ thing." The answer was neither direct nor immediate. But one night, driving south on Route 522 from Winchester to Front Royal, Virginia, under a full moon, he realized that he believed in the divinity of Christ. He decided that he should be baptized, so he went to a Baptist church; it seemed the right place to go. Because the dyslexia made reading impossible, Folsom bought the New Testament on audio tape, listening to it repeatedly.

In Christianity, Folsom found the pattern and the meaning of his own story. Christ's love for the outsiders, the prostitutes and publicans, marked by shame and failure; his scorn for the "proper" Pharisees; the redemptive failure of the Cross itself—these Gospel themes made sense of his own experiences.

But Folsom's belief that the Christian story tells the ultimate truth about man has not led him to black-and-white simplifications. His paintings depict a world in which the wheat and tares are intimately entwined. The apocalypse is always imminent in this world because the drama of the soul is played out with each choice that we make. But Folsom leaves the story open-ended, mysterious. He recalls writing in a grant application that he was hoping to show, in the dozens of faces of *Last Call*, "the reflection of the face of our cruel and merciful God. And I realized that I can't do that. But perhaps I can show some of God's love for us and acceptance of us and hopes for us."

Though he feels uncomfortable with theological concepts and sectarian disputes, Folsom has found himself at last on a pilgrimage toward a particular communion. His wife, Rose, a convert to Catholicism, has been an important influence in this journey. He followed her into the church a few years later.

Rorschachs for the Soul

Fred Folsom has both benefited and suffered from the anarchic condition of the art world in the last two decades. To hardened proponents of modernism, many of whom are entrenched as museum curators and gallery owners, his paintings are quaint anachronisms, illustrations rather than works that explore the formal properties of paint and canvas. But for those who appreciate the phenomenon of postmodernism, with its return to representation and its interest in maintaining a dialogue with the past, Folsom's works are more intriguing.

Unlike most of the artists assembled in Charles Jencks' survey, *Post-Modernism: The New Classicism in Art and Architecture*, Folsom has not sought inspiration in the classical art of Greece and Rome, except perhaps for his nudes. Rather, he has turned to the great Dutch and Flemish painters of the seventeenth century. He shares an affinity with artists such as Jan Steen, who combined wit, moralism, and narrative enthusiasm in their depictions of the bourgeois life of their time. Steen typically portrays a crowded scene of merry-making, either in a domestic setting or in a tavern, with plenty of drinking, dancing, and smoking. The boisterous fun of these people immediately engages the viewer's sympathy. But diffused throughout the scene, in symbols, allegories, and gestures, are moral judgments that undermine the seemingly innocent festivity. Running throughout the paintings of Steen and his contemporaries is the *vanitas* theme: the vanity and irresponsibility of men and women who forgot that the things of this world were ultimately frail and evanescent.

Folsom's go-go bar paintings appropriate many of the conventions employed by Steen, but their tragic, compassionate spirit is alien to the comic moralism of the seventeenth century. However, Folsom has painted a large number of works that are best understood in terms of the *vanitas* genre: they are among the most ingenious and disturbing things he has done. He has called these paintings "wide-open Rorschachs" and "raw material for prejudice." In one sense the analogy is apt, because Folsom's Rorschachs are so enigmatic and unsettling that they force the viewer to reveal his or her emotional reactions to various forms of ugliness, violence, and squalor. Of course the analogy is limited because Folsom's paintings are not the amorphous splats of ink used in a psychological test, but highly realistic depictions.

Dining with Mr. Eccleston is a representative example of Folsom's Rorschach paintings. The title immediately creates a mood of irony and black humor. The raucous thugs in this picture have nothing to do with the Anglo-Saxon decorum of the phrase *Dining with Mr. Eccleston.* We witness a moment of hilarity that is infectious; we want to know what the joke is. But as we take in the character of these men and their surroundings, our sympathy ebbs away quickly. The gap-toothed fellow in the center, with his tattoo, greasy hair, and leather jacket is repulsive; a socio-economic embarrassment. His leather vest is covered with medals, including patriotic symbols and the iron cross of Germany. The cross around his neck swings as his body convulses with laughter; the cross itself is upside down. He holds a gun in one hand; it is pointed toward him. Is this the source of the joke, the lucky aftermath of a game of Russian roulette?

If the viewer is able to get over his temptation to turn away from the scene, he will become intrigued by the puzzle-like details in the painting. The black man on our left is less repellent in physical characteristics, but his clerical shirt and collar are utterly out of character. The three watches on his forearm hint that this "preacher" is a con man, ready to sell you stolen wares. What is it, exactly, that he is looking at with that smile on his face? He looks in the direction of a completely nude woman who is largely outside the picture. We see her hand flicking the ash of a cigarette into an ashtray; the rest of her appears in a mirror hung on the cinder block wall. A closer look reveals that the ashtray in the mirror is different than the one on the table. What is illusion and what is reality?

The sexuality of the woman in the mirror and the pornographic pictures stuck onto both mirrors are highly ambiguous. Neither classically beautiful nor horrifically ugly, these women make themselves available to us. The woman who appears to be in the room is presumably there to be used as a sexual object by these men. And yet she, like the stripper in *Last Call,* seems to be detached from the foulness of her environment. There is a touch of grace in her body; her hair is piled on her head like some bather out of a Degas painting. But the red streaks on the mirror (lipstick?) that rake over her legs evoke a feeling of latent, bloody violence.

The table is littered with cigarette butts, beer cans, and empty plates; the "meal" seems to have consisted of nothing but Budweiser and Pabst Blue Ribbon. Here the symbols are less ambiguous. A lottery ticket, with its connotations of gambling and the urge to acquire wealth without effort, reinforces the themes suggested by the Russian roulette game. These people have placed themselves under the sway of Chance or Fortune. A glass eye sits on the table, signaling a loss of moral vision. The eye has been plucked out, but not because it offends its owner. Visible in the mirror on the right is Fred Folsom himself, slumped on the table in a drunken stupor. His head is on a platter, but he is clearly no John the Baptist.

Dining with Mr. Eccleston is a Rorschach test; it demands that you look at something ugly and yet terribly human; it asks you to judge the characters and at the same time it forces you to examine the disinterestedness and humanity of your judgments. Its blend of realism and surrealism requires that we reconsider the very act of seeing itself. It is close, in spirit and technique, to a Jan Steen painting, which employs an elusive and subtle form of irony to convey its moral concerns.

Folsom is aware that his Rorschachs are frequently misunderstood. Feminists have attacked them as being exploitative of women, even though male lust and violence are among Folsom's central themes. He also knows that few of his Christian brethren will recognize the spiritual dimensions of his paintings. "I get a lot of this: 'Why can't you do something pretty, like a vase of flowers or some happy dancers?' I've never had artists tell me that. But daisies in a jar don't mean anything to me. Other 'juicers' and people who've been on the outside of what we consider to be society have a perfect idea of what my paintings are about. I like that."

Saint Danny of Takoma

If Folsom generally avoids sentimental uplift, he has, nonetheless, created a number of paintings that celebrate people he has known and loved. *Danny Robson, or Saint Danny of Takoma, Maryland* may appear on the surface to be another grim encounter with despair and alienation, but it is really a parable of hope. In a note on this painting, Folsom writes:

> Big Danny was a Captain in the U.S. Marine Corps, later a mercenary, a boxer (under the name of Fontanini), a gangster, "bagman," back alley brawler and "enforcer"—a violent, unscrupulous man. By any definition he was a very evil man. In 1958 Danny was sentenced to St. Elizabeth's, finally convicted of a double murder. In this hospital for the criminally insane he experienced a revelation and was released, a completely changed man.

After his release, Danny spent the next twenty-three years working as a "no-frills therapist," counseling drug addicts and alcoholics. He ran

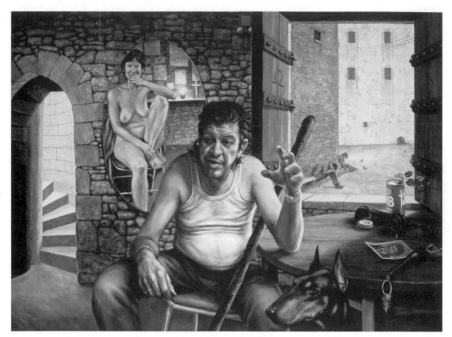

Saint Danny of Takoma

a halfway house that helped people make the transition from hospital or prison back into the world. Throughout this time, Danny himself lived in almost monastic poverty. "Big Danny's own," Folsom continues, "were the hopeless ones, the incorrigibles that nobody could or would help. At St. Elizabeth's they call themselves 'The Lost Battalion.'" He was extraordinarily successful.

Danny's therapeutic method was extremely simple: like a drill sergeant, he would marshal his troops and harangue them with insults and commands. According to Folsom, Danny was given to colorful expressions of moral advice. He would turn to his troops and say: "You've been sitting on your brains; you'd do a lot better on your knees." "Knowing Big Danny was like knowing Long John Silver, Alley Oop, and Mother Teresa in one," Folsom has written. He got to know Danny after he had passed through his own time of troubles. "Danny always called me Paul."

In *St. Danny of Takoma*, the potbellied Danny dominates an austere room that looks as if it were part of a medieval castle. To his right a window opens out into the courtyard of a mental institution similar to St. Elizabeth's. A number of forlorn inmates sit in the courtyard, knees drawn up and heads bowed in an attitude of despair. The high-barred windows of the hospital extend the metaphor of castle-hospital-prison. The heavy wooden shutters of Danny's window bear the Christian signs of Alpha and Omega, the divine beginning and ending. Our lives, whether "normal" or badly mangled, are all pilgrimages between the mystery of our creation and ultimate destiny.

To the left of the painting, an arched passage leads to a spiral staircase. The stairs leading up are bathed in light, while the stairs going down are dark. The staircase is also a traditional symbol of moral choice. He who is not going up is likely to go back down. Danny's therapy is not about "self-esteem" and "self-acceptance," but about the burden of responsibility. His own shattered life has reduced him to the essentials: prayer and moral choice.

The rest of the painting provides us with the clues to what made Big Danny tick. He leans forward, his left arm raised in some gesture of emphasis; Danny is the talking, not the listening, type. A huge stick leans on the table next to him, a phallic symbol unmistakable in its proportions. The stick is echoed by the key chain on the table, made out of a billy club. To complete this array of machismo talismans, a doberman pinscher sits by Danny, its expression alert and its ears erect.

Danny's interlocutor appears to be a nude woman sitting on a folding chair. We see her only in an oval mirror. She is amused by whatever he's saying: Danny's a charmer. Their relationship cannot be called erotic, except in the most general sense. In the mirror we can see behind her a sort of mantelpiece with a small votive candle burning, a simple cross, and what look like holy cards with saints' images on them. Hanging on the wall are a clutter of mottoes and epigrams, along with the famous Dürer drawing of hands in the attitude of prayer.

St. Danny of Takoma lacks the shock value of Folsom's Rorschach paintings, but it harbors its own riddles. Danny's conversion has brought him to God; he may not understand much about the intimacy of love, but he knows that obeying the law is the path toward salvation. He is a changed man, in that he is no longer a criminal, but he is still a tough guy, a drill sergeant in God's army. His machismo is not the threatening force that pulses through *Last Call* and *Dining with Mr. Eccleston*. Rather, there is something akin to veneration in the impromptu shrine visible in the mirror. The mirror's oval is shaped like the old mandorla, or full-body halo, that enclosed images of Mary and the saints in the Middle Ages.

Folsom's note on this painting provides an important gloss. "Perhaps a man born 800 years too late, [Danny] would have made a great feudal war lord." Big Danny, his noble hunting dog by his side, is the master of his castle and its domain. We see him, as we would see a feudal baron: powerful, accustomed to the use of force, and yet somehow on the side of justice. His spiritual transformation has not altered his essential character. To use the language of Catholic theology, God's grace operates through nature. Danny may be a limited or narrow specimen of humanity, but God can use even the shabbiest of materials to his own ends. Of Danny Robson, Folsom has said: "The Body of Christ has some really bizarre representatives."

Self-Portrait of a Vocation

Over the years, Fred Folsom has wondered about his own escape from the prison of despair that Danny Robson knew so well. Why was he called out, when so many others have not? For what purpose was he spared? These questions are of course inseparable from the mystery of one's vocation. When Folsom received a commission recently to paint a self-portrait, he took the opportunity to explore his sense of vocation. The result is a painting with the self-effacing title, *Grisaille in an Ice Storm*.

Folsom's studio in the foothills of the Blue Ridge Mountains is often subject to winter ice storms that knock out his electricity. This happened one day while he was at work on *Last Call*. He stoked up the stove and was soon able to get back to work. He picked up the mirror he was using to paint the portrait of his former self, the greasy young Bacchus, and looked at his reflection. Without the use of his floodlight, or the audio cassettes he listens to while working, Folsom realized that he was painting in the same conditions that his Dutch and Flemish heroes had experienced. Looking at the mirror, he saw himself bundled up in jacket and scarf, with a cowboy hat perched on his head, and chuckled to himself. He took a snapshot of the scene. Five years later, when a collector commissioned a self-portrait, Folsom returned to the moment captured in that snapshot.

In *Grisaille in an Ice Storm*, the original light-hearted episode is given a more serious treatment. The pose is traditional: the artist is at his work. The grisaille is, for Folsom, the second step in a painting. First he draws the major figures and outlines directly onto the canvas. Second, he creates the underpainting (historically known as the grisaille or cartoon), a monochrome layer of acrylic paint (either burnt sienna or cool blue). Working with a grisaille offers a number of benefits. Too many layers of oil paint tend to creep or peel in relation to the canvas. Oil adheres well to the acrylic, and it also helps in the definition of contrasts between light and dark tones. The final step is the glazing of the oil paint in transparent layers over the grisaille.

Well into his four-year labor on *Last Call*, Folsom looks into a mirror in his left hand, while his right hand leans on a mahlstick (a device used by painters on which to rest the hand). Behind him the glow of the stove emerges out of deep shadows. At his feet is a machine incorporating a filter and a rubber hose: it is an "art respirator" that Folsom developed and patented to limit an artist's exposure to turpentine.

The dynamism of this picture derives from the interplay among the three Fred Folsoms, each of whom is separated from the other by time and perspective. One of the key structural elements of the painting is the triangle formed by the mirror and the two portraits. The most obvious relationship is between the mature Folsom, confident in his skills and experience, and his earlier self, stupefied by alcohol to deaden the fear of failure. The painting of *Last Call* is the mature Folsom's attempt to understand and to forgive his younger self. The portrait in *Last Call* is unsparing in its realism and its sensitivity to pain and suffering, and yet it also possesses a comic spirit. The Shepherd Park Folsom administers a false baptism to himself, as his beer bottle spills over his leg; later, he will be given the grace to recognize the need for true baptism.

But the most important interaction is between the two selves depicted in the painting and the unseen artist reflecting on them. The creator of *Grisaille in an Ice Storm* focuses his attention on the burden of his vocation, both as an artist and as a Christian. The symbol of his craft, the paintbrush, intersects with the mahlstick to form a cross. If the vertical part of the cross draws a line that separates the two selves, the paintbrush is the horizontal instrument that serves as a bridge between them. According to scholars, it is likely that when Christ made his way to Calvary he carried only the crossbeam, not the entire cross. Thus the crossbeam, which Christ bore on the Via Dolorosa, and upon which his arms were stretched, is invested with the pain and redemptive suffering of the crucifixion. As an artist who is also a Christian, Folsom feels that his paintbrush must be a conduit both for the pain of fallen humanity and the reconciling vision of faith.

Lest anyone accuse Folsom of indulging in the Romantic cult of the artist as savior, the *Grisaille* presents a humbling metaphor: on either side of the cross in this painting there are two thieves. The mature painter is perhaps the Good Thief. But like his biblical counterpart, Folsom believes that as a fallen man he does not deserve to get off scot-free.

As usual, Folsom leaves a number of symbols scattered throughout the painting, but the most interesting and suggestive of these is the yin-yang symbol on the back of the mirror. For Folsom the yin-yang signifies an inclusive vision of the world. The interlocking of these shapes, and the spots of the opposite color in each half, suggest an acceptance of paradox, an awareness that "either-or" statements do not always adequately account for the ambiguities of the world. Folsom is troubled by the way many Christians seek to define their faith in sharp opposition to everything else in the world: Christianity versus other religions, Christianity versus science, sect vs. sect. Yet he does not subscribe to a vague relativism that negates the truth claims of the creed. If you look carefully, you can see on the back of the mirror that the vertical shaft bisects a portion of the yin-yang. The shadow of the cross falls on everything.

In his letter to the gentleman who commissioned *Grisaille*, Folsom notes that the canvas is mounted on a 125-year-old stretcher that previously supported the likeness of a Civil War general. The ancient stretcher stimulated Folsom to make an analogy: "*Grisaille's* stretcher is out of date. Oil painting is out of date, just as old gingerbread buildings are. They require too much time and too much thought and care; too much of one's life—they simply cost everything. They're the last bargain in town."

True Religion: Greatness and Misery

Fred Folsom pays this extravagant price in order to pursue his vocation. He labors under conditions that are as lonely and isolated as a mountain cabin in an ice storm. Most of those entrenched in the art establishment would dismiss his work as quaintly illustrative. Even among the champions of postmodernism there are few who are able to appreciate the tragic and spiritual dimensions of his art. So much of what goes under the banner of postmodernism today is vitiated by a puerile sort of irony. Postmodern irony can be cute and, on occasion, cleverly satirical, but it is often trivial. Folsom's irony has the power to arrest our attention and challenge our souls because it is not merely a free-floating attitude. His irony is tragic because it proceeds from a worldview anchored in a profound understanding of human nature. Like the paintbrush held between the two thieves in *Grisaille*, it measures the distance between good and evil. More often than not, Folsom's irony is at the expense of the viewer, not the characters he presents. In the end, his irony is tempered by a compassion that affirms the possibility of redemption.

Last Call is a painting that offers us a metaphor both for the "news" of God's offer of redemption and the finality of the Last Judgment. Since no one is paying attention to the "special report" that is being broadcast to them, it seems unlikely that they will fare well in the apocalypse that awaits them. And yet, for the alert viewer, it is possible to see the presence of grace in this eleventh-hour world.

Last Call is Folsom's summa, an epic work that by its size, virtuosity, and profound Christian humanism reveals the price that the artist is willing to pay in his search for meaning. Here, as in the best of Fred Folsom's paintings, is a vision that moves beyond social commentary and political protest to achieve the radical personalism of the Gospels. In taking us into the world of "publicans and sinners," Folsom maintains a tension between judgment and compassion, between the reality of evil and the mystery of grace.

Last Call has been likened to novels by Dickens and Balzac because it teems with individuals from all walks of life and expresses a passionate interest

Last Call (at the Shepherd Park Go Go Club)
center panel

in telling their stories. A better comparison would be the Christian humanism of such modern Catholic novelists as Leon Bloy, Georges Bernanos,
François Mauriac, and Graham Greene. Folsom shares with these writers an
understanding of the paradoxical ways in which grace interacts with nature,
and an awareness that our restlessness and longings are manifestations of our
hunger for God.

One of the presiding spirits in *Last Call* is the French precursor of
these twentieth-century writers, Blaise Pascal, who has been called the first
Christian existentialist. He leans on the red-and-white-checked tablecloth at
the lower left of the painting. The paradoxical vision expressed in Pascal's
Pensées is very close to the spirit of *Last Call*. "The true religion," Pascal
writes, "must teach greatness and misery; must lead to the esteem and con-
tempt of self, to love and to hate." Also: "The knowledge of God without that
of man's misery leads to pride. The knowledge of man's misery without that
of God causes despair. The knowledge of Jesus Christ constitutes the middle
course, because in Him we find both God and our misery."

The portrait of Pascal forms one corner of the huge triangle that gives
structural coherence and meaning to *Last Call*. The apex of the triangle is,
of course, the stripper. Folsom has described her as "philosophic, Hellenic, a
centerpiece on an altar. . . . The expression on her face and her gestures are
infinitely complex." She seems to be simultaneously detached from the world
of the Shepherd Park and suffering all of its pain and confusion. Her hair
rises above her head in a circular tangle that glows like a halo. The Hellenic
perfection of her figure bespeaks the greatness of man, but she is treated
instead as an object of lust. Her arms are in the process of lifting up to an
outstretched position, an implicit crucifixion.

If we follow the lines created by her arms we find the sides of the triangle that shapes the painting. In the lower left corner sits Pascal. Moving
across the baseline we come to Folsom himself, almost directly underneath
the stripper. Following his pointing hand we come to the lower right corner
of *Last Call*, which presents us with the wounded hand holding a glass of
wine. It is this hand that contains the secret of the painting, and of Folsom's
imaginative vision. It is the hand of the one who said: "But I say unto you, I
will not drink henceforth of this fruit of the vine, until that day when I drink
it with you in my Father's kingdom." It is the hand of the one who issues
the "last call" to all of us. But if he is the source of the call and its insistent
demand, a demand we find it difficult to hear or respond to, he also sits with
us, perpetually ready to raise his glass.

16

Mary McCleary:
Constructing Paradox

One of the ideas emerging out of postmodernism that has most deeply penetrated our cultural consciousness is the notion that our views of the world are "constructed" on the basis of the building blocks of our personal identity—race, class, gender, ethnicity, and so on. While there are those who have criticized this postmodern concept as overly subjective or relative, a wide spectrum of thinkers have welcomed this insight as a healthy corrective to simplistic thinking, a reminder that truth and meaning cannot be trapped and held in large abstract systems of ideas, but are rooted in the particularity of an individual's journey through life. Along the path of that journey we pick up the building materials with which to construct a vision of the world.

The theme of construction is also central to the artistic achievement of Mary McCleary. As a collage artist, McCleary works in a medium that emphasizes the slow, meticulous accumulation of materials and forms. At the same time, by placing the technique of collage in the service of painterly illusionism, she complicates our response: on the one hand, we are drawn to the dazzling variety of textures and individual components of the work (from painted sticks to gum-ball-machine plastic spiders), while on the other we take pleasure in the loving realism of the persons and places depicted therein.

Each of her pieces is both an assemblage of brightly colored bits and a naturalistic rendering of the world around us. Is the truth to be found in the fragments or the whole, the materials or the narrative content, the ancient

religious and cultural subjects she draws upon or the familiar immediacy of
the contemporary men and women she portrays?

I would suggest that the enduring power, mystery, and depth of
McCleary's art stem from this tension between the contingency of human
structures and our persistent hope for a transcendent truth that somehow
undergirds and validates our efforts. Perhaps the ultimate symbol for this
tension is the grid of toy eyes that appears in many of her mature paintings.

Screen and Gateway

The presence of the grid, which conjures up the conventions of Renaissance
perspective, is the most palpable reminder McCleary gives us that, despite the
naturalism of rendering in the painting, we are looking at an artifact, a made
thing. Yet the eyes also intimate that there may be an unseen presence—an
order of grace and truth—hidden in the very fabric of being. Those eyes may
be interpreted as full of judgment, especially when the subject of the painting
is sin and folly, but they can also be interpreted as symbolic of an ordered
love that transcends our fallen world and encompasses it. The grid is both
screen and gateway.

McCleary dares us to wonder if our human constructions can in some
fashion reach out and touch—or be touched by—the deeper structures of
creation itself. In this sense she works within the two-thousand-year-old
Christian sacramental tradition. As the artist-poet David Jones once pointed
out, the sacrament of the Eucharist is not composed of wheat and grapes;
rather, it begins with bread and wine, both of which have been transformed
by human craft. Only after that initial transformation can the ultimate
transformation—from bread and wine to the body and blood of Christ—
take place. The sacraments, in turn, are grounded in the Christian belief in
the Incarnation: the descent of the divine into human form, almighty God
becoming one with a babe in the manger. McCleary has made no secret of
her conversion, as a mature woman, to faith in this Incarnation.

Of course, some critics would argue that an incarnational perspective,
and all the religious baggage that tends to come with it, might weaken or
diminish the fertile tensions and paradoxes in her work. But for McCleary
the Christian story is *all about* paradox, that magnetic tension between the
poles of flesh and spirit, faith and doubt, sin and grace, judgment and mercy.
Without that fundamental tension, how do we explain that odd combination
in her paintings of dark or tragic subject matter (Cain and Abel, the Tower of

Babel, fires, drownings) and exuberant, comic treatment (from plastic spiders and skulls to gum wrappers and erasers)? How else to account for her reverence not only for the topoi of high art but for the tackiness of pop culture?

The Moral Sense and the Dramatic Sense

Of equal importance is the balance McCleary maintains between what Flannery O'Connor called "the moral sense and the dramatic sense." Though her themes are intense and profoundly religious in nature—the vanity of human wishes, the danger of trying to deny our mortality, the Seven Deadly Sins—the tone of her work is never didactic or preachy. On the contrary, McCleary's approach is dramatic. The viewer who encounters these works does not have the impression that the artist is placing herself above us, looking down, but that she and the viewer are both implicated in the mystery of evil.

Part of this is due to McCleary's use of contemporary people to inhabit the ancient roles of Adam and Eve, Nimrod, Potiphar's wife, and the Good Samaritan. These figures are not remote and exotic; they are recognizable as our neighbors, colleagues, family members. Moreover, McCleary's rendering of these iconic subjects is not moralistic but suggestive and ambiguous. In *David & Bathsheba*, we see a man in the act of either removing—or replacing—a jacket from a woman's shoulders. Is this the moment before or after King David has committed adultery with the wife of his general? *Mrs. Potiphar* presents us not with a cartoonish harridan panting after the biblical Joseph, but an attractive, middle-aged woman staring pensively at her reflection in a mirror. McCleary treats the incident not in terms of mere lust, but in a larger psychological and spiritual context of loneliness and fear of death.

There has been a subtle, but significant, evolution of McCleary's vision in recent years. She has demonstrated a willingness to move beyond the biblical subjects that dominated her work for years to classical mythology (*Icarus*). More intriguing still, she has felt the freedom to create her own symbolic narratives (*Sentinel, Death of Michael Rockefeller, I Fled Him Down the Days & Down the Nights*)—narratives that do not rely on overtly religious texts.

These recent works, while allegorical in nature, do not yield tidy moral summaries. They have too much respect for mystery for that. *To Be Redeemed From Fire by Fire* is based on a famous photograph of the Hartford circus fire of 1944 in which 167 people died and nearly 500 were injured. It is an apocalyptic vision, the end of the world in fire and smoke. A grotesque clown with a skull-like face holds his head in his hands, reminding us of our mortality.

David and Bathsheba

To Be Redeemed From Fire by Fire

But as the title suggests, fire not only destroys but purifies. (The surface is studded with hundreds of pencils, their erasers alluding to the possibility of redemption, the cleansing away of sin and error.)

The title of this painting comes from T. S. Eliot's *Four Quartets* and suggests that the fires of hell can be purged by the fires of heaven, if only we are willing to open ourselves to that terrible refining power. One of the fleeing figures in the painting wears a ferocious-looking tiger mask—reminiscent of another phrase from Eliot: the image of "Christ the Tiger" as a wild, untamable beast who devours us in order to give us new life.

Harrowing and playful, virtuosic and yet humble, the art of Mary McCleary revels in paradox. The worlds she constructs impinge on our private worlds, disturbing our peace and yet rewarding us with moments of pleasure and recognition. The constructions of Mary McCleary help us to feel that somehow our different journeys may ultimately meet in a single place—that from the loneliness of our individual selves we may yet find a place of communion and joy.

17

Makoto Fujimura:
Refiner's Fire

The only hope, or else despair
Lies in the choice of pyre or pyre—
To be redeemed from fire by fire.
—T. S. Eliot, "Little Gidding" from *Four Quartets*

To immerse oneself in the sequence of works by Makoto Fujimura known as "Water Flames" is to undertake a journey toward the mystery and beauty of paradox. As with the record of any journey, the viewer of these works has a choice: you can merely glance with pleasure at the passing sights, or you can imaginatively enter the path of the artist.

If you choose to become a fellow traveler, you are likely to discover that you not only travel alongside the artist, but also in the company of those who have gone before him. "Water Flames" derives its initial aesthetic inspiration from the poetry of T. S. Eliot, and in particular from the late work, *Four Quartets,* written during and immediately after the cataclysm of World War II. Eliot's experience of the war was direct and immediate: he remained in London throughout the conflict, serving as a fire warden, walking the streets each night after the air-raid sirens had blown the all-clear signal, searching for fire and survivors.

That Fujimura should find such a powerful resonance with *Four Quartets* in the months and years following 9/11 should come as no surprise. Like Eliot, he struggled to come to terms with the reality of evil and of suffering on a massive scale. For the artist, the challenge is how to remain totally honest about the darkness and yet find hope—a hope that itself must shun any hint of sentimentality.

The more Fujimura delved into the richness of Eliot's late masterpiece, the more he came to realize that Eliot himself drew upon his own artistic guide: Dante Alighieri, the greatest poet of the Middle Ages. Dante, who had known both war and exile, had, in turn, relied on the Roman poet Virgil, whose epic, *The Aeneid,* dealt with the moral and emotional conflicts within a budding empire.

Of course, in detailing the historical precedents that inform the "Water Flames" series, one cannot ignore the centrality of the Nihonga tradition of Japanese art, which has characterized all of Fujimura's mature work. Nihonga involves the use of crushed mineral pigments and precious material such as silver and gold leaf.

Tongued with Fire

To speak of all these strata of aesthetic influence may seem overly precious, but for the artist engaged in a high-risk attempt to make sense of pain and grief, companionship on the journey is a necessity, not a luxury. The need to reach out and find kindred spirits across the ages is a universal phenomenon. As Eliot puts it in *Four Quartets:* "the communication of the dead is tongued with fire beyond the language of the living."

In the spirit of Dante and Eliot, "Water Flames" traces a journey—one might almost say a pilgrimage. As the work of each of these artists attests, the inner and outer landscapes that appear along the way belong to the realm of paradox. To call a collection of paintings "Water Flames" is to boldly invoke paradox.

But what do we really mean by the word? For some people, it merely signifies mystification—mumbo-jumbo without substance. But for others paradox is the only language we humans have to approach the precincts of mystery.

There are various mathematical and scientific paradoxes that are baffling to the mind, but the deeper, more emotionally compelling sense of paradox is that of an apparent contradiction that somehow manages to embody a larger truth. The best paradoxes always makes sense, at least at the level of our intuition. The language of love—whether human or divine—is full of paradox. We speak of love so powerful that it hurts, of darkness that illuminates, of dying in order to live.

Golden Fire

So, too, with the paintings of "Water Flames." Here we have water creating fire, as Fujimura pours his pigments and awaits their ignition upon heavy Kumohada paper. The mineral elements of earth are crushed and ground only to be reborn in the airy lightness of translucent color.

Fire destroys but it also purges impurities, clears away choking brush in order to allow for more fruitful growth. As Fujimura has stated, he resonates most with the section of Dante's *Divine Comedy* known as the *Purgatorio,* where the souls experience suffering not as punishment, but as the "refiner's fire," a paradoxically painful and joyous experience. For Dante, sin and evil are not blithely turned into mere stepping stones; they retain their power to haunt and wound. But even a wound can break something open so as to reveal another beauty beneath the surface.

In his artist's talk on "Water Flames," Fujimura quotes Eliot:

Dante, because he could do everything else, is for that reason the greatest 'religious' poet, though to call him [merely] a 'religious poet' would be to abate his universality. *The Divine Comedy* expresses everything in the way of emotion, between depravity's despair and the beatific vision, that man is capable of experiencing.[1]

While Fujimura would never compare himself to Dante, it is safe to say that he, too, strives for universality in these works—a language that can speak to people across the diversity of human experience.

The One in the Many

Nor should we be surprised that Fujimura's exploration of fire have taken him in the direction of monochromatic works. Nothing can be more paradoxical than to penetrate the heart of something that seems so singular only to find that within that unity is a hidden multiplicity, a richness that a broader palette would have obscured.

That the culminating work of this sequence should be a monumental piece entitled *Golden Fire* has a sort of epic inevitability about it. Gold is the quintessential element requiring the refiner's fire. It is a heavy substance that somehow lifts into what the writer Milan Kundera has called "the unbearable lightness of being." This element, found deep within the earth and created through the turbulent processes of change, becomes something that symbolizes the eternal and unchanging. Gold is the possession of kings, and yet we often speak of the common person as having a heart full of it.

In the terrible fires of Hiroshima and 9/11, as well as in the daily ordeals we all face, the gold within the human heart may yet be glimpsed. It is the special role of gifted artists like Makoto Fujimura to remind us of this paradoxical truth.

Part Five

Four Men of Letters

18

Russell Kirk:
Politics and the Imagination

Imagination rules the world.
—Napoleon Bonaparte

Russell Kirk (1918–1994), known for decades as the "father" of modern American conservatism, has not been in fashion among the majority of those calling themselves conservative for quite some time. He is respected, of course, and occasionally invoked to bolster an argument or otherwise lend legitimacy to a cause. But the younger conservative crowd hasn't heard of him, much less read his books (which are not published by the major New York houses but by small, relatively obscure presses). The thinker who helped to found what has been called "traditionalism" has few contemporary disciples to carry on the tradition.

Even on the level of ideas, Kirk's relationship to conservatism today is faint and ambiguous. At the risk of some simplification, one might say that the three most energetic factions within conservatism are the libertarians, the neoconservatives, and the populists. It is well known that the libertarians and the neoconservatives have never had much sympathy for Kirk. The populists have been more cordial to him, in part because they share certain principles and predilections, including a sympathy for localism and regionalism. But Kirk was never comfortable with the nationalist and nativist strains that dominate the populists' agenda.

In short, Russell Kirk may be the father of modern conservatism, but many of his children have either disowned him, or cannot recognize his paternity. That is a grievous loss. There is a remarkable amplitude and hospitality to Russell Kirk's conservatism that stands in marked contrast to the narrowing tendencies of these other factions. Compared to the breadth of Kirk's worldview, other conservatives tend toward ideology and the utopian rhetoric of contemporary political partisanship. Like heretics, they take a part of the truth, wrench it from its larger context, and thus distort it.

I would contend that what each of these factions lack—and what Kirk had in abundance—is imagination. By imagination I do not mean mere inventiveness or tactical brilliance, but the faculty of perception that Burke and Coleridge first defined, and Kirk, throughout his writings, deepened and refined.

Russell Kirk has received his share of tributes, but most of these have been exercises in the rhetoric of piety. The best tribute that I can pay to my teacher is to take a frank look at the criticisms that have been leveled against him and determine whether they strike home.

When conservatives gained access to power in the presidential elections of 1980, their movement underwent a transformation. Prior to 1980, conservatives were preoccupied with questions of first principles, of theory. They were, after all, out of power, and had the leisure to consider what the ideal polity should be. There was, in fact, furious conservative political activity— the kind of activism that led to the victory of 1980—but the psychic weight of the movement remained on the side of principle rather than pragmatism. After 1980 the reverse became true. It was suddenly necessary to find conservatives who could play the political game within the bureaucracy, the media, and the cultural power centers. Conservatives had to look good in front of the cameras, as well as in the committee rooms and cloakrooms.

A Rhetoric of Reflection

Russell Kirk's rhetorical style, as well as his subject matter, were more suited to the reading chair than to the spotlight. Since Kirk's conservatism was based on deep skepticism about modernity, he deliberately cultivated a mannered prose, full of archaic diction and leisurely rhythms. Like another conservative, Walter Scott, who built himself a medieval country estate, Kirk built a Victorian villa, and filled it with furniture salvaged from old hotels and churches that were being demolished. He always identified with the nineteenth-century men of letters: the Orestes Brownsons and Walter Bagehots who wrote for the quarterly reviews. He was, further, a distinguished practitioner of that most Victorian of literary forms, the Gothic tale or ghost story.

Depending on your tastes and your sensitivities, you will find this Victorianism either charming or irritating. But the harshest criticism of Russell Kirk has come from those who point out that his retreat from the modern world into this nineteenth-century pose is precisely what vitiates his intellectual contribution. They see the antiquarian tone of Kirk's prose and worldview as a retreat into fantasy.

Kirk stands accused of not "facing up to modernity," to quote the title of a book by Peter Berger. In particular, the neoconservatives consider the notion that America was founded on Burkean principles to be a product of Kirk's overactive imagination. The neoconservatives believe that the American political order is essentially an expression of modernity, a creation of the Enlightenment.

Of course, the debate over the character of the American Founding is an offshoot of the larger debate over the legacy of the Enlightenment. An essay in *The Wilson Quarterly* by Mark Lilla puts the neoconservative perspective on this conflict clearly and simply:

> Modern thought carries within itself two tendencies moving in opposite directions, and . . . one must choose between them. Either one resigns oneself to living within the broad Enlightenment tradition that values reason, skepticism, and freedom, or one sets off with the Counter-Enlightenment thinkers who abandoned those principles in the pursuit of order, authority, and certainty. The modern world offers no third alternative.

A more lurid formulation of this dichotomy pits democracy, capitalism, and freedom against an Ultramontane theocracy, a clear-eyed acceptance of uncertainty against a craven retreat under the skirts of religious authority.

The Third Alternative: Imagination

There are many thinkers more qualified than I am to argue both the philosophical issues and the thorny questions surrounding the nature of the American political order. But I am prepared to say that Russell Kirk cannot be conveniently dismissed as a quaint, but deluded irrationalist. It is true, as Gerhart Niemeyer once noted, that Kirk is not a philosopher. But he has, in the course of his many books, developed what amounts to a major philosophical insight. Kirk was one of the few political thinkers of our time who saw the importance of what Edmund Burke called the "moral imagination."

It would be difficult to overestimate the value and relevance of Kirk's understanding of the imagination. The imagination constitutes the "third alternative" that Mark Lilla believes does not exist. It is precisely the faculty which can mediate between the poles of order and freedom, skepticism and faith, the individual and the community.

There is no more pressing need in the moral and spiritual crisis of our time than the need to recover the imagination. We live in an era that is dominated by hollow economic rationalism wrapped in the rhetoric of rights. The political parties pursue big government or big business—the twin abstractions that are bureaucracy and the transnational corporation. Both neglect the ancient principle of subsidiarity—the idea that human problems should be worked out at the more intimate levels where they are more capable of being addressed. Subsidiarity is the principle that fostered the human-scale local and regional cultures that were the heart of the American republic.

Russell Kirk's conception of the imagination is rich and nuanced; it is not merely an aesthetic concept but an essential component of a durable political philosophy. For Kirk, the imagination is not opposed to reason, but the necessary complement to it. The modern concept of reason is deracinated, a narrower and more constricted version of reason as understood by the great pre-Enlightenment thinkers such as Aristotle, Augustine, and Aquinas.

To the ancients, reason found its highest expression in the contemplation of being—the order of the cosmos. One of Kirk's intellectual heroes, Josef Pieper, described the medieval understanding of human thought. According to the scholastics, Pieper writes, the *ratio*, or discursive, logical faculty is paralleled by the *intellectus*, the intuitive perception of reality. "The mode of discursive thought is accompanied and impregnated by an effortless awareness, the contemplative vision of the *intellectus*, which is not active but passive, or rather receptive, the activity of the soul in which it conceives that which it sees" (*Leisure: The Basis of Culture*).

But the advent of modernity caused a shift in the understanding of human thought. The nominalists, and later, Descartes, denied the reality of the *intellectus* and elevated the *ratio* to preeminent status. The moderns begin in doubt, or skepticism, to use Lilla's word, about reality, and proceed to treat reason (*ratio*) itself as the ground of being. Instead of Man the Knower, we have Man the Thinker.

The modern concept of reason is, at root, ideological. Reason, instead of the faculty by which we achieve connatural knowledge of reality, becomes the means by which we construct systems that are imposed on reality. Modern reason had its apotheosis during the French Revolution, when it was symbolized by a beautiful woman who was paraded through the streets as a deity. These same streets would be running with the blood demanded by the goddess Reason, the price reality had to pay for not conforming to ideological visions of perfection.

In its more moderate Anglo-American incarnation, modern rationalism has brought us the managerial state and the mega-corporation. Political parties favor one or the other, despite the growing body of evidence that both are responsible for the economic, military, and environmental catastrophes that have befallen us.

Prudential Politicians, Philosophical Poets

Modern conservatism dates from Edmund Burke's reaction to the French Revolution, as Russell Kirk made clear over half a century ago in his seminal book *The Conservative Mind*. Burke, though he lived at the end of the Age of Reason, was really a precursor to the Romantics, who sought to recover the affective and intuitive pathways to reality. Burke's first major book was an inquiry into "the sublime and the beautiful," two terms that would mean so much to the Romantics. Kirk's own thought can be traced back to the Romantic revolt against the Enlightenment.

The tragedy of romanticism is that it lacked the proper metaphysical equipment to achieve a new synthesis. The Romantics suffered from what T. S. Eliot, another of Kirk's heroes, called the "dissociation of sensibility"— the separation of *ratio* and *intellectus* that has afflicted modern man. The older and wiser Romantics, Wordsworth and Coleridge, came to revere Burke. In the face of industrialization and utilitarianism, the Romantics looked to the past to find an organic society untainted by the dissociation of sensibility.

The danger inherent in this enterprise was and is nostalgia and sentimentality. Certainly the Continental, Ultramontane thinkers such as De Maistre veered dangerously close to a desire to return to a unitary, feudal political order. This is the irrationalism which Lilla and his ilk rightly decry as a dark, reactionary movement toward "order, authority, and certainty."

But *The Conservative Mind* is a history of conservatism that steers clear of Ultramontanism. This was a clear statement of Kirk's political sensibility, but many have ignored it. Kirk signaled his preference for common sense, prudence, and subsidiarity as opposed to mere appeals to authority, whether that authority be ecclesiastical or aristocratic. Indeed, for Kirk, true authority came both from the deposits of common law, the accumulated wisdom of the great thinkers and saints, and the "mediating institutions" of family, church, and local associations that are the basis of civil society.

In *The Conservative Mind* there are two kinds of thinkers who fascinate Kirk. The first group are those who advocate a "politics of prudence." What Kirk admires about such conservatives—including Burke, John Adams, Calhoun, and Tocqueville—is their ability to balance the terms that Lilla insists are irreconcilable. Relying on the lamp of experience and the accumulated wisdom of traditional institutions (reason grounded in history), these conservatives retain a commitment to order and authority while allowing for the maximum amount of freedom and skepticism. Their writings often have a philosophical flavor, but their minds were essentially historical.

But Kirk also singles out thinkers of a more philosophical bent— Coleridge, Hawthorne, Newman, and Eliot prominent among them. Each of these individuals strove to reintegrate classical and Judeo-Christian wisdom in a new synthesis appropriate to the conditions of modernity. They understood that liberalism brought some benefits, but had the effect of slowly dissolving the social and moral bonds that hold communities together. The key to liberalism, they knew, was its secular rationalism, its reduction of man to self-interested consumer. (Kirk understood well how "liberalism" could fork into socialism on the left and libertarianism on the right.)

What these two groups—the prudential politicians and the philosophical poets—have in common is the moral imagination. What, then, constitutes the moral imagination? Burke believed that it involved the ability to see the ordinary in the context of a moral, historical, and spiritual significance. The moral imagination stood against the reductionist mindset of the "sophisters, calculators, and economists," who viewed man as nothing more than an acquisitive animal. To Burke, the "pleasing illusions" that invest our social relationships with meaning are more true than the modernist calculus, derived from Machiavelli and Hobbes, that claims to know the cold, hard facts of life.

There are at least three major dimensions of the moral imagination in Kirk's thought: the presence of the past, the tragic sense of life, and a sacramental vision.

The Presence of the Past

In the face of the ideological abstractions emerging out of the French Revolution, Burke upheld the political genius of traditional institutions. The two central concepts in Burke's thought, singled out by Kirk in *The Conservative Mind*, are "prescription" and "prejudice." As Gerhart Niemeyer has noted, these terms achieve the status of symbols in Kirk's thought. Prescription, the wisdom of institutions tested by time, is reflected in prejudice, the habits of judgment and discernment within the individual. Both of these terms signify the heightened intuitive awareness of the imagination, whether in the collective memory of the community or in the experience of the individual.

Kirk believed that an awareness of the continuing reality of the past is a vital part of the moral imagination. That is why he has championed the thought of John Lukacs, whose writings delve into the nature of historical consciousness. Kirk once singled out this passage from Lukacs's *Historical Consciousness* for special attention:

> Self-knowledge, and the existing potentiality of past-knowledge, are involved intimately with the imagination—a word which suggests a colorful mental construction on the one hand, and an inward tendency on the other. . . . The part played by the imagination, as Collingwood rightly puts it, 'is properly not ornamental but structural'; and the meaning of this truth goes beyond our interest in history. If, for example, imagination is more than a superstructure of perception, the term 'extrasensory perception' is, strictly speaking, misleading, for *all* human perception is, to some extent, extrasensory.

There is no shortage of examples of how a lack of historical imagination can cause grief in the present. As a scholar with a high level of historical consciousness, Kirk knows how fatuous it is to proclaim "the end of history." Moreover, Kirk had nothing but scorn for the notion of "global democracy," the exporting of American institutions, and in particular something known as "democratic capitalism," to the ends of the earth. This is another example of political rationalism devoid of imaginative sensitivity. As Kirk once wrote in an essay entitled "Prospects for Conservatives":

If by the word 'democratic' is meant the complex of republican political institutions that has grown up in the United States, over more than two centuries—why, the new paper constitutions now being discussed in eastern Europe cannot magically reproduce American history. If by 'capitalism' is meant the massive and centralized corporate structures of North America—why, massive and centralized state capitalism is precisely what the self-liberated peoples of eastern Europe are endeavoring to escape. The differing nations of our time must find their own several ways to order and justice and freedom. We Americans were not appointed their keepers.

An imaginative awareness of history teaches us about human nature, and particularly about human limitations. Hence the next facet of the moral imagination.

The Tragic Sense of Life

Kirk often referred to this phrase, taken from the Catholic philosopher Miguel de Unamuno. The tragedy to which Unamuno refers is original sin, the fallen nature of mankind. The tragic sensibility recognizes the nobility of man, but it also acknowledges his fragile position amidst the contingent forces at work in the world.

The tragic sense of life is opposed to ideology, which posits a belief in the malleability of human nature. But it would be wrong to suppose that the only real application of this tragic sense is to the shattered utopian schemes of fascism and socialism. There is a messianic strain in American history, which infects the liberalisms of both left and right. Kirk had little time not only for the messianism of "global democracy," but also for some libertarians' mystical effusions about the technological wonders of a capitalist future.

Kirk believed that any form of political thought which reduces the complexity of human nature to simple abstractions is a dangerous departure from the truth of our tragic condition. He criticized some of the policy proposals made by libertarians and neoconservatives because they are based on the assumption that man is essentially *homo economicus*. To narrow the range of human motivation to mere self-interest downplays the virtues of sacrifice, strong local and regional communities, and solicitude for the common good. Kirk believed that economic "progress" at the expense of the social fabric was no real advance.

Again, Kirk's tragic sense led him to be deeply skeptical about the role of the United States in attempting to remake the social fabric of other nations, whether through war or high-stakes diplomatic pressure. He not only had little time for the notion of global democracy but also thought the rhetoric of "human rights" dangerously abstract. (In that sense, Kirk was a foreign policy realist.) In the end, Kirk didn't see a tragic vision as a recipe for despair or a prescription for passivity, but rather a check on political arrogance—especially when international adventurism had less to do with the larger world and more to do with exorcising home-grown demons.

A Sacramental Vision

The source of Russell Kirk's thought was his sacramental vision, his vivid sense of the createdness of the world. Unlike the moderns, to whom life is a matter of process, of constant activity and "becoming," Kirk held, with the ancients, that man's highest calling is contemplating *what is*. Being precedes becoming; contemplation is prior to action. Kirk viewed this world *sub specie aeternitatis*.

This accounts for the enormous energy and "joy of being" (to quote Gerhart Niemeyer again) that emanated from Kirk. With figures like Dr. Johnson, Chesterton, and C. S. Lewis, Kirk shared a robust delight in the goodness and sacramentality of simple things, from food to fireplaces. Kirk's definition of grace is where time and the timeless meet, where the natural is touched by the supernatural.

It is impossible to separate Kirk's sense of transcendence from his love of particular people, places, and things. I learned this firsthand when I was assigned the job of driving Kirk from Hillsdale College, where he was teaching as a visiting professor, to his home three hours to the north. These trips were always leisurely, made on back roads, all of which Kirk knew intimately. As we drove through the Michigan countryside, Kirk introduced me to the particular delights of each small town along the way. In Homer, he took me to a dinner theater where I tasted the Greek wine *retsina* for the first time. We always looked out for the black squirrels in Albion, as well as the sale table at the Albion College library. We never failed to stop at the ice cream parlor in Charlotte, which had once been the town's railroad depot. And in Ionia we visited the orchard, with its endless supply of apples, cider, honey, preserves, and the aromatic products of the bakery on the premises. Kirk knew the streets where the best examples of neoclassical architecture could be found, not to mention the best diners.

Walter Bagehot, another of the thinkers in Kirk's pantheon, once wrote:

> The essence of Toryism is enjoyment. Talk of the ways of spreading a
> wholesome Conservatism throughout this country: give painful lec-
> tures, distribute weary tracts . . . ; but as far as communicating and
> establishing your creed are concerned—try a little pleasure. The way to
> keep up old customs is, to enjoy old customs.

There is an authenticity, a sense of felt experience, to Kirk's thought,
precisely because his life is continuous with his ideas. One can carp at the
nineteenth-century language, customs, and architecture with which he sur-
rounded himself, but for many of those who visited Piety Hill in Mecosta,
there was a delight in these "pleasing illusions."

The one contradiction in Kirk's sensibility that always distressed me was
his attitude toward modern art and literature—the problem of the artistic
imagination in the present moment, as it were. Early in his career, Kirk followed his instincts and befriended some of the best writers living in England:
T. S. Eliot, Wyndham Lewis, and Roy Campbell among them. He understood that these writers were employing highly innovative literary techniques
to defend ancient Western traditions. But aside from his book on *Eliot and
His Age*, Kirk dismissed nearly all of modern art and literature (with the
exception of a few fantasy writers).

This is a shame, because it encourages the belief on the part of his readers that the best art is behind us. The truly conservative approach requires us
to be alert to the best art and literature of the present, not to relegate them
to the museum. Kirk missed an important opportunity to challenge the phi-
listines in the conservative movement. On the other hand, this is relatively
speaking a peccadillo when seen against the enormous range of sympathies
this man of letters possessed.

There is another problem associated with Russell Kirk's writings, though
it was not of his doing. The clarity and lucidity of Kirk's prose, his ability to convey complex ideas and historical events in ways that can be easily
understood, places him in the same category as a writer like C. S. Lewis. But
those who read Lewis and Kirk often make the mistake of believing that
their books are a substitute for engaging the original works and ideas. These
readers forget that Lewis and Kirk are calling them to undertake the same
disciplines and intellectual adventures they themselves undertook.

The very real danger, both now and in the future, is that Kirk's thought will be treated as a quaint Tory aesthetic, rather than a substantial intellectual synthesis. This process began in his lifetime. He was often asked to speak for certain organizations and think tanks whose day-to-day policy papers contradicted much of what he stood for. Having Kirk in as a guest lecturer thus became a form of guilt money, a nod in the direction of the humanistic tradition on the part of those who had lost sight of that tradition in their own mental and emotional lives.

Unless conservatives regain the moral imagination, and thus the humanism, represented by the writings of Russell Kirk, they will become irrelevant, as recent events have demonstrated. Kirk's greatness did not stem from any originality on his part; in this sense, he was one of the most humble intellectuals on the planet. Rather, Kirk was great because he held one of the truest and most inclusive visions of our spiritual and cultural inheritance. He was a *pontifex maximus*, a bridge builder to the classics of our culture. If we do not cross the bridges built by the likes of Russell Kirk, we will remain stranded on our own islands of ignorance.

19

Gerhart Niemeyer:
Discerning the Spirits

Beginning in the 1970s, there is a noticeable shift in focus and subject matter in the writings of Gerhart Niemeyer (1907–1997). It was in that decade that he began to concentrate less on the intellectual and geopolitical threat of Communism and more on the cultural and spiritual condition of the West. Of course, there are no clear demarcations here: Niemeyer continued to write about Communism through its demise in the Soviet Union, and matters of culture and spirit had been central to his thought for decades. But the shift is unmistakable. It should be remembered that Niemeyer had produced an extensive body of work about the totalitarian ideologies of the modern era, especially Communism, by the 1970s, by which time it was beginning to become clear to most observers that the struggle with Communism around the globe would be a protracted conflict, rather than one likely to lead to apocalyptic violence. The ultimate battleground, Niemeyer concluded, would be in the hearts and minds of those in both the East and West who could bring about renewal through an openness to transcendent truth and the wisdom of the past. In particular, Niemeyer's deepening faith impelled him to find concrete ways to embody the Christian vision in the "public square." And so the essays of his last two decades turn increasingly to matters of culture, literature, the arts, and education in the West.

It may be a truism that the published writings of most great thinkers represent only the tip of the iceberg when compared to the depth of knowledge

215

that never makes it into print. But I would argue that this is especially true of Gerhart Niemeyer. He was a meticulous scholar with a strict code of ethics; even into his eighties he could publish an essay with the cautionary footnote: "The remarks made in this essay do not represent scholarly research. They are intended as topical stimulations for conversation among intelligent and informed people."[1] Though he was a man of enormous learning—in history, philosophy, theology, and literature, among other disciplines—he felt that he needed to speak out of his primary discipline, that of political theory. For example, he had strong convictions about modern developments in literature and the arts, but he rarely addressed such topics directly; his comments on them are found primarily as lines of inquiry within essays devoted to political concerns. Even his last book, the collection of essays entitled *Within and Above Ourselves*, bears the subtitle "Essays in Political Analysis," despite the interdisciplinary breadth of wisdom permeating nearly the entire volume. As a man who became, late in his life, both an ordained priest in the Episcopal Church and a Roman Catholic convert, Niemeyer had read widely in Christian spirituality, and yet, with the exception of a few quotations from certain beloved medieval mystics like John Ruusbroec, he did not translate this interest into his published works.

As a student of Gerhart Niemeyer at Hillsdale College in the late 1970s, I had a privileged viewpoint on his life and work. In the classroom, the broader range of his interests was much more evident. For example, two of the courses he taught at the time were based entirely on fiction: Russian Writers & Totalitarianism and Modern Writers & Ideology. In the discussion that follows I will supplement my commentary on his late essays with references to the courses I took with him. Like so many of his students, I bear the indelible imprint of Niemeyer's vision. Because my own vocation has been shaped, to a significant degree, by my encounter with his teaching, I hope the reader will indulge the autobiographical notes in this present essay.

Autonomous Man

With the publication of his essay "The Autonomous Man" in 1974, the shift in the center of gravity in Niemeyer's writings became evident. Up to this point, Niemeyer had devoted his intellectual efforts to understanding how modern ideologies had moved from the realm of the mind—the fantasies or "possible realities" of alienated intellectuals—to totalitarian systems that attempted to impose these dreams on the world through organized violence.

But Niemeyer's autonomous man is not necessarily a totalitarian apparatchik or even a Western "fellow traveler." Rather, the autonomous man is Niemeyer's description of a different sort of ideologue, someone in rebellion from tradition and transcendence but detached from even the political movements of his time. In one sense, the autonomous man might arguably be called "postmodern man," though Niemeyer showed little interest in this term. The individual he describes may not be an active member of an ideological political movement, but this does not lessen his destructive potential for the larger social order. For a society of autonomous men, Niemeyer believed, tended toward anomie and anarchy. The realms in which the autonomous man makes the greatest impact are in culture and education rather than politics or government.

Niemeyer begins the essay by invoking his concept of the "total critique" in which the modern ideologue, turning the human mind into "its own place" (Milton), denounces all existing order and seeks to substitute for it dreams of utopia. From Machiavelli and Hobbes through the *philosophes* and on to Marx and Nietzsche, the modern mind found the classical and Judeo-Christian foundations of the West to be inadequate.

> As the total critique of society gathered momentum, all aspects of society being condemned as totally false and inhuman, all human authority as a sham, all norms as suspect of hidden self-interest, all power as masked violence, man was denuded of the last vestiges of order. Nothing was left to mediate between each person's subjectivity and universal reality. Universal order and meaning could no longer be found through any concrete manifestations, it had no more standing in this world and thus vanished into unreality. Man found himself isolated in a meaningless and irrelevant setting, far more isolated than Pascal in the vast cosmic spaces.[2]

The autonomous man believes himself to be self-created, and thus refuses to acknowledge dependence on a Creator. And with the disappearance of a transcendent ground for truth, Niemeyer continues, the autonomous man denies the existence of higher norms outside of himself. Thus "norm is absorbed into will." Here Niemeyer invokes Nietzsche, the tutelary spirit of the autonomous man.

Two crucial deformations follow from the ideologue's self-deification. First is the substitution of psychology for ontology. In short, instead of the human effort to probe the nature of a reality that exists above and prior to his own existence, the mind's own drives and needs—including its unconscious drives and needs—become the *fons et origo* of reality. Thus the imagination, instead of seeking symbols that are attuned to transcendence, becomes the source of abstract, disembodied, self-enclosed systems.

This, in turn, leads to the second deformation: the confusion of acting and making. Aristotle made clear the distinction between acting, which is the proper realm of ethics and politics, and making, which is the creation of new artifacts. "Acting," Niemeyer writes, "occurs in the midst of things which are what they are by nature; it means choosing conduct, or actions, bearing in mind what befits the natures of men and things."[3] But the modern ideologue looks upon politics as the realm of making, believing that wholly new structures can be created out of the mind. Hence the rise of totalist political systems.

Niemeyer was well aware that the rise of the autonomous man did not mean a society full of Nietzschean *Übermenschen*, so he introduces a distinction between two types of autonomy. The "mega-self" is closer to the Nietzschean model: it is the intellectual or activist who sees "science as power" and dreams of conquering the recalcitrance of both nature and the traditional social order. The other type of autonomous man is not such an overreacher: the "micro-self" is the isolated, alienated individual whose ambitions are more hedonistic. The micro-self, immersed in modern therapeutic psychology, seeks above all to craft a "lifestyle," which has increasingly been defined as one that defies moral and social conventions. This quest for freedom, Niemeyer concludes, devolves into hedonism.

Spiritual Restlessness

A few years later, in another important essay, "Beyond 'Democratic Disorder,'" Niemeyer extended his analysis of contemporary Western culture. Here, instead of the somewhat awkward terms mega- and micro-self, he speaks of nihilist intellectuals and a "profanized" middle class. By furthering the process of secularization, the elite make it possible for the hedonistic middle classes to pursue happiness as best they can. Living off of the last remnants of moral capital bequeathed by Christianity, these contented, urban masses do not so much engage in active rebellion as they make a pastime of petulant "whimpering" about their lives. Their desire for perfection is not the ardent pilgrimage toward holiness of the Christian saint but the tantrums of the brat whose limitless desires are not immediately met. The desire for safety supersedes the need for sacrifice and decisive action. In the political realm, Niemeyer contends, this restless desire for perfection is translated into the political correctness of never-ending quests for more equality. If that means a denigration of the very traditions and institutions that have given rise to the search for greater justice, then both the elite and the middle class are satisfied.[4]

Niemeyer notes the different spheres in which the elite and the masses live and move and have their being. For the middle class, the milieu they inhabit is that of popular culture, whereas the province of the elite is that of high culture. As an intellectual whose life was devoted to calling other intellectuals to moral and spiritual accountability, Niemeyer devoted relatively little time to a critique of popular culture, and much of what he wrote about it differs little from similar critiques over the last half-century. Nonetheless, he possessed an acute awareness of the rise of what Philip Rieff called the "therapeutic mentality." While Niemeyer tended to use the word therapy in a positive sense, indicating the sort of healing wisdom of the great thinkers and saints, he understood that a heavily psychologized West would be characterized by "spiritual restlessness." This restive spirit sought solace not only in material hedonism but spiritual hedonism, including a shallow curiosity for spiritual fads and trends, particularly those that seemed exotic and Eastern, but which made few personal demands on their adherents and which were changed as quickly as the year's fashions.

Inevitably, Niemeyer's interest in culture centered around the loftier heights of literature and the arts. In his later essays, illustrations from these realms are never far away. For example, in "The Autonomous Man," he illustrates the idea that "norm is absorbed into will" with reference to what has come to be known as serial or "twelve tone" music: a form which insists that each of the twelve musical tones be sounded before any can be repeated. Thus serial music imposes a type of order, but it is utterly abstract, ungrounded in human experience and the product merely of the will of the composer.

Nowhere does Niemeyer set out a specific aesthetic. In "The Autonomous Man" he notes that the imagination can be used for good or ill. In the broadest sense, he believed that the imagination could move either in the direction of autonomy, creating self-enclosed systems, or in the direction of participation, that is, a deepening of our sense of the mystery that surrounds our existence. So the poet William Blake represents for Niemeyer the "romantic intoxication with the imagined; he created an entire mythical world for himself, but also sought to impose new mythical meaning on various aspects of existing reality."[5] Blake's popularity, then, is directly related to the way autonomous individuals find their condition reflected in his poetry. Bad art, for Niemeyer, was not just that which promotes immorality, but, in an even deeper sense, promotes unreality—the fantasy that leaves us locked in private purgatories.

The Eternal in the Particular

Though he believed art should promote order, Niemeyer did not impose on it a merely didactic or utilitarian ethic. He recognized, for example, that "art is a territory that must not be sullied by the advocacies of politics or philosophical contention."[6] With Aristotle, Niemeyer saw art as being closer to philosophy than to history. "Art aims at understanding, which is the dimension of the eternal encountered in the setting of the particular."[7] In writing about the Southern philosopher-poet Marion Montgomery, Niemeyer says that "his focus is on poets, writers and their concern, which essentially is with nature." At its best, then, art does not lead to fantasy and abstraction but to the concreteness of daily human experience, or what Niemeyer calls "the reality given to us in time and place."[8]

Like philosophy, art begins and ends in wonder—it promotes a deeper sense of the mystery that bounds our experience. Above all, art recreates "the abode of mankind, the 'in-between,' where there is the experience of tension between the higher reality of the divine and the lower reality of created things as well as of demonic narcissism, between nature and grace, between tradition and alienation."[9]

What, then, did Niemeyer make of the literature and art of the modern era? Despite ubiquitous references to the creative masterpieces of the twentieth century, he never developed a consistent position on this subject. At times, his focus was on the way that modern art reflected the solipsistic realm of the autonomous man. In a typical passage, he might criticize such modern art movements as Fauvism, Cubism, Dada, serial music, and so on. These movements are dominated by the "laws of dissolution."

> In music, the serialist says: "Thou shalt not use any note more than once, lest it become a tonal center." In Cubist painting the law is: "Thou shalt not leave the object intact." In literature: "Thou shalt have no hero to your story," which is the first commandment followed by

the other, which is like unto it, "Thou shalt not portray any personal character, because there is no truth in any character except that of the ideology to which the person is committed." Regarding films the law forbids the depiction of reality, since it is nothing but illusions, so that only irrational dreams or actions deserve to be called real.[10]

As broad-brush criticism of modern art, these sentences might elicit agreement from a majority of people, but the very broadness of the brush is problematic.

There were several modern writers whom Niemeyer admired, including T.S. Eliot, who were pioneers of High Modernism. Eliot's poetic technique for much of his career was the literary equivalent of Cubism and in literary personae like J. Alfred Prufrock and Gerontion, Eliot created some of the most enduring anti-heroes of the modern age. There are times in his essays when Niemeyer seems close to granting that artistic forms which appear to represent dissolution may, in fact, be up to something constructive.

> Then came solitary thinkers who could supply a voice for the suffering: Kafka, Beckett, Joyce, and Canetti; Alban Berg and Schönberg; playwrights for the theater of the absurd; artists painting without object or line; and rock stars. Their function in society is to put into words, music, pictures, and action the agony of the Nothing, so that the millions of its mute sufferers can feel understood.[11]

While still largely negative in connotation, this passage lists individuals elsewhere singled out as among those who have wrestled with modernity in a fruitful manner. After singling out some of the greatest interpreters of modernity such as Eric Voegelin, J. L. Talmon, Norman Cohn, Albert Camus, and Henri de Lubac, Niemeyer goes on to cite T. S. Eliot, James Joyce, Ezra Pound, Robert Musil, Heimito von Doderer, and Elias Canetti as men of insight. Others that he names in various places include Wyndham Lewis, Thomas Mann, Joseph Conrad, Evelyn Waugh, J. R. R. Tolkien, C. S. Lewis, and Thornton Wilder. Of course, when it comes to a poet of the stature of Eliot, Niemeyer was perhaps more willing to accept his earlier poetry as diagnostic of modernity's ills, so long as Eliot's conversion to Christianity and crowning achievement, *Four Quartets*, were kept to the forefront.

Literature and Ideology

But if Niemeyer's ideas about aesthetics and modern art were far from systematic or entirely consistent, it would be wrong to see his engagement with literature and the arts to be of little importance to his overall vision, particularly in the last two decades of his life. In the classroom, as I have indicated, he was much less shy about extended considerations of modern literature. Two of the most memorable courses I took from him were "Russian Writers & Totalitarianism" and "Modern Writers & Ideology." These courses focused on two different approaches to the political and spiritual crises of the modern era. As I look back upon them, I realize just how demanding—and rewarding—they were.

In "Russian Writers and Totalitarianism" Niemeyer was able to chronicle the before and after of the Communist Revolution. We read Turgenev's *Fathers and Sons*, Dostoevsky's *The Possessed* and *The Brothers Karamazov*, Pasternak's *Doctor Zhivago*, and Solzhenitsyn's *One Day in the Life of Ivan Denisovich*, *The First Circle*, and *Cancer Ward*. Turgenev and Pasternak were studied primarily as transitional figures. In *Fathers and Sons*, a generation of liberals is succeeded by radical ideologues who have taken advantage of their fathers' relativism and decadence to seek after the goal of political revolution. In *Doctor Zhivago*, Pasternak attempts to find the answer to the question of how a ruthless totalitarian system could arise out of Russian soil; his story, while epic in scope, falls short of profound insight into the spiritual pathology of ideology. "A pall of great metaphysical sadness hangs over [Pasternak's] work," Niemeyer once wrote.[12] Without the redemptive vision of Christianity, Pasternak could only fall back on romantic individualism, which only ended in sadness.

The central figures in the course were Dostoevsky and Solzhenitsyn. In print, Niemeyer could be quite tough on Dostoevsky, who, he concluded, was limited by an existential Christianity that veered dangerously close to irrationalism and what in theological terms would be called fideism.[13] From the frightful ordeal of the radicalizing of the Russian intelligentsia, Niemeyer wrote, Dostoevsky "emerged not a radiant victor but rather a battered, bruised, and bloodied warrior whose exclamation of faith comes in his work to hardly more than a stammer."[14] In the classroom Niemeyer was less harsh, taking us through *The Possessed*—with its large cast of ideologues—as well as *The Brothers Karamazov*, the core of which is nihilistic Ivan's metaphysical challenge thrown down at the spiritual neophyte Alyosha with great energy and passion.

We paid particular attention to the story within the story—Ivan's tale of "The Grand Inquisitor"—for its incisive and compelling portrait of a Nietzschean vision, including a critique of the metaphysical freedom which is the legacy of Christianity, and the need for Supermen to relieve the masses of the freedom they don't want.

Those who know Niemeyer's work at all know that Aleksandr Solzhenitsyn was one of his heroes. Having inherited the totalitarian world prophesied by Dostoevsky, Solzhenitsyn had endured deep and prolonged suffering in the Gulag Archipelago. What struck Niemeyer as extraordinary was that Solzhenitsyn and others within the Gulag had had the experience of spiritual renewal precisely when everything had been taken away from them. Stripped of freedom, possessions, modesty, and health, at least some of the inmates of the Gulag heard the still small voice of God and rediscovered their human dignity. For Niemeyer, this rediscovery was intimately linked with the very freedom that Ivan Karamazov's Grand Inquisitor had mocked as something human beings did not desire.

> [I]n the midst of the most inhuman conditions the dozen or so main characters [in Solzhenitsyn's *First Circle*] make choices central to their humanity: whether to consent to an assignment of routine drudgery or be sent to a Siberian slave camp, whether or not to divorce a husband who is behind bars, whether to humor a warder's tyranny or resist it, whether to do honest work or mark time, whether or not to cooperate as an informer, whether or not to go along with Communist reasoning.[15]

In a world of degradation, a nihilist's dream made into reality, Solzhenitsyn's characters discover God not merely in shallow emotional conversions, but as the source of goodness. If, as Niemeyer once wrote, the "shapes of order and structure in human history manifest vectors of underlying goodness," then the protagonists in Solzhenitsyn's stories become aware, through suffering and deprivation, of just where some of those vectors lie.[16] Even in the frigid wasteland of Siberia, the goodness of creation itself can be experienced. "The soul, open to being, senses participation, the Creation is good, and our companions, for better or for worse, are of it too."[17] Thus in the Gulag, ontology replaces psychology, reversing the secularizing movement of modernity and restoring divine being as the ground of human existence. "Even in the midst of apparently bottomless defeat, [Solzhenitsyn's] characters manage to sustain faith, hope, love; they remain pilgrims on their way to man's ultimate destiny."[18]

From Under the Rubble

The other literature-based course taught by Niemeyer, "Modern Writers & Ideology," was equally absorbing, though in some ways even more dense and ambiguous. What held the course together was Niemeyer's interest in the relationship between the decay of liberalism and the rise of totalitarian ideologies and alienated elites in the West. The texts studied were Arthur Koestler's *Darkness at Noon*, Joseph Conrad's *Secret Agent*, Lionel Trilling's *Middle of the Journey*, Thomas Mann's *Doctor Faustus*, Robert Musil's *Man Without Qualities*, and Max Frisch's *Firebugs*. The settings and styles of these works are literally all over the map—from Frisch's satirical play, a morality tale about the helplessness of relativism in the face of evil, to the massive novels-of-ideas by Musil and Mann. But each contains profound insights into what Niemeyer called the "throes of mortal agony" that have characterized a decadent liberalism in recent decades. From Musil's dense novel about the decline and fall of the Austro-Hungarian Empire Niemeyer picked up the author's understanding of the way that fantasy leads to ideology. As Musil's narrator says, the ideologue is someone who prefers "possible realities" to "real possibilities":

> A possible experience or a possible truth does not equate to real experience or real truth minus the value "real"; but, at least in the opinion of its devotees, it has in it something out-and-out divine, a fiery, soaring quality, a constructive will, a conscious utopianism that does not shrink from reality but treats it, on the contrary as a mission and an invention.[19]

To take just one example from this course, Niemeyer's teaching of Mann's *Doctor Faustus* demonstrated a capacity for a close reading of literary texts. This novel, published in the aftermath of World War II, is Mann's attempt to understand the tragedy of Germany's descent into national socialism. It is written in the form of a biography: the "author," Serenus Zeitblom, is an earnest, humane liberal; the "subject" of the biography is Adrian Leverkühn, a towering genius of modern classical music, but also a man who has sold his soul to the devil in order to become the celebrated founder of a new, abstract form of composition that bears a remarkable resemblance to the twelve-tone or serial technique.

Leverkühn is essentially a composite of two modern thinkers: Nietzsche and the composer Arnold Schönberg. As Niemeyer pointed out in class, Nietzsche is never mentioned in the text, which is ironic, given his pervasive influence on German culture. But the omission is deliberate: Nietzsche has been absorbed into the people, the culture, into Leverkühn himself. The composer—whose name means "I'd rather be bold"—becomes not only a Romantic "genius" (with its overtones of the cultic worship of the charismatic leader), but a revolutionary who will bring a new, abstract order to a decadent, liberal culture. Leverkühn says to Zeitblom: "[B]arbarism is the opposite of culture only within the order of thought which it gives us. Outside of it the opposite may be something quite different or no opposite at all."

Mann's vision comprehends not only the emergence of the alienated ideologue-as-revolutionary, but a sense of how an entire culture can drift into complicity with evil. The German people, lost and alienated in a liberal culture, grow weary of freedom without direction or moral energy. So the new order promised by Leverkühn and his political equivalents becomes powerfully attractive, a magnetic force. As Zeitblom reflects at one point, the intellectuals had begun to develop a sense of inevitability about Nazism.

> But what . . . they were saying was: It is coming, it is coming, and when it is here it will find us on the crest of the moment. It is interesting, it is even good, simply by virtue of being what is inevitably going to be, and to recognize it is sufficient of an achievement and satisfaction. It is not our affair to do anything against it.[20]

Doctor Faustus ends with this sentence: "A lonely man folds his hands and speaks: 'God be merciful to thy poor soul, my friend, my fatherland.'" In German, of course, "man" can be rendered "Mann." In pointing out Thomas Mann's own intense suffering over the tragic fate of Germany, Niemeyer's own suffering as political émigré resonated in the classroom.

Vectors of Underlying Goodness

The relationship between suffering and the "positive experiences" that could bring about renewal by recovering the "vectors of underlying goodness" was one of Niemeyer's constant themes. In the case of Solzhenitsyn and others who had rediscovered their souls in the Gulag Archipelago, the suffering had been so intense that it had served as a refiner's fire, producing men and women of prophetic vision. To add just one more example, late in his life, Niemeyer encountered the music of the Estonian composer, Arvo Pärt. Pärt had been educated in twelve-tone serialism, which had been adopted by the Soviet intelligentsia who dominated the captive nation of Estonia. Niemeyer picks up the story:

> [Pärt's] way from "under the rubble" [a phrase from Solzhenitsyn] led him through the equivalent of the musician's "abyss," through complete silence, musical silence, mental silence, spiritual silence, silence observed for years, silence as the soul's recovery-regime from absolute lostness. As he began to emerge, cautiously sounding first one note, then a repetition of that note, he remained committed to silence as the point of beginning, and allowed no notes "unworthy of the underlying silence." The emerging music turned out to be strongly spiritual, and his latest composition is a Passion according to St. John.[21]

Pärt's music combines some of the best elements of minimalism with a renewed interest in ancient Christian chant and polyphony. The result is music saturated with reverence and respect for mystery, helping to bring about a renaissance of sacred choral music in our time.

Niemeyer, in his typically tough and unsentimental fashion, was much less inclined to see signs of such spiritual recovery in the West, precisely because we have experienced neither the extremity of suffering, nor the shock of societal collapse and defeat. One partial exception to this skepticism was Niemeyer's late appreciation for Southern culture and literature, especially as mediated through the critical and philosophical writings of Marion Montgomery. When the novelist Walker Percy was asked about why the South had produced so much great literature, he replied: "Because we lost the war." Niemeyer appreciated the tragic wisdom that informed writers like Percy, Eudora Welty, and, above all, Flannery O'Connor.

In his review-essay "Why Marion Montgomery Has to Ramble," Niemeyer responded to Montgomery's trilogy, *The Prophetic Poet and the Spirit of the Age*, which consists of *Why Flannery O'Connor Stayed Home*, *Why Poe Drank Liquor*, and *Why Hawthorne Was Melancholy*. The title of Niemeyer's essay is a reference to a criticism made of Montgomery's style, that it is rambling and repetitive, circling back on itself and revisiting many of the same ideas and authors. As Niemeyer's title indicates, he strongly defended Montgomery's approach. The trilogy is "a sensitive man's existential journey," and "a succession of social encounters" between the reader, Montgomery, and the authors Montgomery studies. Moreover, Niemeyer argues, Montgomery's habit of circling around core topics and writers is not repetitive, but always reveals new angles and new perspectives. The form of Montgomery's writing is that of a "quest," which is attuned to the nature of the search for meaning in the mystery of the in between (a term derived from the Platonic concept of the *Metaxy*).[22]

Montgomery helped to open a realm of literature to which Niemeyer had had little access. This is especially true in the case of Flannery O'Connor, who, it might be argued, provides an example of a Western writer whose work represents a major achievement in what Niemeyer would call "therapeutic" thought. Her writings are not a response to totalitarianism, which is a European and Eastern phenomenon, but to the "soft intellectual irrationality" that has penetrated the cultural life of the United States. Niemeyer singles out the series of "separations" that O'Connor contends have contributed to the decline of American culture: the separations of "thought from action, judgment from vision, nature from grace, reason from imagination."[23]

Critiquing the Puritan Heritage

As Niemeyer sees it, Hawthorne, O'Connor, and Montgomery (as guide) all contribute to a necessary critique of America's Puritan heritage. This religious tradition, while possessed of many virtues, also brought about deformations of central Christian themes and ideas. The danger of Puritanism lay not just in the incipient utopianism of the "city on a hill" metaphor, but in an excessively low view of nature and creation. From Montgomery's analysis, Niemeyer calls attention to the Puritan emphasis on "Industry" as chief virtue, which tends to stress the notion of mastery *over* nature, and on ceaseless activity. As further evidence of this, Montgomery points out the fascination of the Puritans with "technometria," the idea of applied science as a means to power. Niemeyer's own Christian vision moved, by contrast, in a more strongly sacramental direction, upholding the goodness of creation and its capacity to mediate transcendence.

There is one other aspect of Montgomery's trilogy that Niemeyer singles out. Twice in his review-essay Niemeyer points to Montgomery's fundamental graciousness as writer and intellectual combatant. There is no hostility, Niemeyer notes, in the Southerner's approach, even when dealing with thinkers who have arguably unleashed demonic forces in the modern era. But not all would-be culture critics have maintained this spirit. "We have had a number of books casting the acid of angry rejection over the spirit of our age. They are not in error; it is only that in many cases they do not get us anywhere."[24] Though he does not make the connection directly, I would argue that it is the very nature of the humanities, and in particular the study of literature, to help remind thoughtful people of the ambiguities and dangers of intemperate denunciations and the rhetoric of polarization.

If one looks carefully at the late essays of Gerhart Niemeyer, there are similar statements, cautions against forms of culture criticism that may become vitiated by rigidity and extremism—and perhaps even become ideological in themselves. Throughout the bulk of his career, Niemeyer felt comfortable thinking of himself as a political conservative. He even tended to support the majority of political efforts spearheaded by conservatives. But as a scholar steeped in the humanities and a deeply spiritual person, he did sound a note of caution when he felt that conservatism itself might cease to be an "up-turning" force and descend into ideology. In his seminal essay, "Beyond 'Democratic Disorder,'" written soon after the election of Ronald Reagan to the presidency, Niemeyer called on conservatives to wield power with prudence and "sobriety." (In hindsight, his hope that conservatives would heed the emphasis in Camus on the need for "limits" was not realistic, particularly in the case of Reagan, whose rhetoric shaded into the language of unlimited expansion and progress.) Niemeyer warned not only of the danger of certain intellectual strands of conservatism, such as "individualist rhetoric," but also of the whole tendency of conservative factions to act "with the air of a crusade, with fanfares of a 'final battle' being heard in the background."[25]

Capturing "Positive Experiences"

When I founded a literary and arts quarterly, *Image*, in 1989, much of the impetus behind the project could be traced back to what I had learned from

Gerhart Niemeyer. Two key concepts of his shaped the journal's editorial policy. First, it seemed to me that it was incumbent upon those who sought to uphold the tradition of the West—a tradition in which faith, reason, and imagination are grounded in openness-in-love toward transcendent truth—to avoid the blandishments of ideology, even when it appeared in conservative trappings. For me, that included the temptation to carry on "with the air of a crusade," denouncing modern art and literature as monolithically evil. In the light of Niemeyer's teaching, it was evident to me that the "culture wars" could only end in Pyrrhic victories, as the rhetoric of total righteousness battled against all enemies. Niemeyer's passion for history and tradition as the living memory of a people united not only in space but in time meant, to my mind, that the tradition had to be kept alive, not pronounced dead by those who had given up on the idea that the Judeo-Christian vision could reanimate Western culture in the present moment.

I also became convinced that it was the role of great art and literature not only to provide diagnostic insight into social and cultural decadence, but also to capture the "positive experiences"—new visions of order—that Niemeyer felt would be the basis of genuine renewal. It seemed to me that such experiences might well be found in contemporary art and literature, precisely, as Niemeyer had pointed out, because in America a spiritual hunger was leading many people—including both makers and receivers of art—to explore once more the richness of the Western religious heritage of Judaism and Christianity. It seemed to me then (and still does) that we must be willing to look for these "positive experiences" in a variety of places. Niemeyer's own life history predisposed him to art that engaged political and philosophical issues, which was why he responded so powerfully to writers like Solzhenitsyn, Eliot, and O'Connor. But in founding *Image* I felt that the aesthetic net had to be cast wider, and that we might need, in these postmodern days, to be willing to bring in many hauls of smaller fish, rather than wait for new "prophetic poets" like Solzhenitsyn and O'Connor to emerge.

In the course of researching this essay I have come to believe that the mission of *Image* is close in spirit to Niemeyer's ideas about education, which are captured in one of his most passionate essays, "The Glory and Misery of Education." In that essay he sets out some of his familiar themes—the modern rejection of the classical-Christian synthesis, which has led to positivism, fragmentation ("the wine-tasting approach"), and the loss of memory that comes with the abandonment of tradition as a living thing. At the heart of his argument, however, is a plea for educators to once again seek out Heraclitus's *koinos*, the realm of being that can be known and held in common by what Marion Montgomery calls "the larger body." This is impossible unless educators are free to teach about what human beings have believed over the centuries. This is particularly true in the case of transcendent beliefs, which "transcend man's subjectivity, both personal and collective," because they "regard the whole of which we acknowledge ourselves to be a part." The need to understand ourselves as part of a larger whole brings us back to Niemeyer's concept of "participation," that loving openness to the divine that bounds our existence in the in-between.

> The whole, then, has no context: there is no place beyond which we could stand, even in imagination, to look on the whole as if it were an object. Our wonderment about the whole therefore can have no end. The whole has inescapably the character of a mystery.[26]

The role of education, then, is helping students understand beliefs "not as if they were alien objects, but rather from within, the beliefs as well as their study being seen as an integral part of the 'serious play' of life in which we are involved."[27] The connection with *Image* comes in at this point, because it is in literature and the arts that we are able to enter the "within" of others. There may be no better definition of art than that of "serious play." So for *Image* the goal has been to provide imaginative visions of what it is like to struggle with Judaism and Christianity at this moment in history.

Late Reflections

I was nervous when I sent the pilot issue of *Image* to Niemeyer. His response was swift, and, as I feared, in his "tough" mode. He wrote on April 28, 1989:

> What struck me first was the "and" between the arts and religion. Try to apply this to Homer, or Sophocles, or even Mallory. One could not squeeze an "and" in here any place, could one? Thus the unspoken premise for your magazine is still the "dissociation of sensibility." Now Eliot himself dropped this formula relatively early in his life. Why? Would it be because his own life had moved on beyond this condition? Then the question comes up whether to include in your journal only those of whom it was never true (e.g. David Jones).

This present issue [#1] seems to go the way of the first possibility. You then come up with strenuous efforts to discover God, or "religion," where the artistic message at first glance seems not to speak of God, or even to be incompatible with such speech. The article about Updike struck me as such an effort. It mentions that Updike read Karl Barth and is knowledgeable about Gnosticism; but that leaves one still wondering whether he read the Bible and knew the Church Fathers. And how about such speech about God which celebrates the "new freedom" as being the "new message of God"? The work of [painter Steve] Hawley seems to be another example of what I mean, for it is necessary to bring out, with considerable effort, the meaning of his various pictorial symbols, after which one holds in one's hand a message that could better be expressed in discursive language.

In other words, the "and" in your title turns out to stand for a distance of considerable magnitude. Is that your editorial intention? If so, it reminds me of all the parents who, in the 'sixties, spoke of their hopelessly rebellious children with the words: "He is trying to tell me something." Forgive me if I seem unreceptive to your ideas. Still, I wish the new Journal every good thing.

While it wasn't the most encouraging of letters, I had to grant that Niemeyer had put his finger on one of the central theological and aesthetic problems for *Image*. The "and" in our subtitle pointed out an awkward fact: that we were pointing, rather self-consciously, to a relationship that ought to be unselfconscious. In the great works of art and literature, the relationship between art and religion is that of a seamless garment, and not the yoking of two "themes" or realms of discourse. The response to this, of course, is that we don't live in the time of Homer or Sophocles or Mallory; we live in a postmodern world in which pluralism and diversity have been elevated above the ideas of cultural and spiritual unity. Of course, Niemeyer was aware that a number of modern artists, including Eliot and O'Connor, had found ingenious ways to avoid the problem of the "and"—to use indirection, violence, and the grotesque to reconnect the deepest purposes of art and religion.

My own conviction was that, despite his skepticism, *Image* represented a vision inspired by Niemeyer's late concerns with Christianity and culture. I knew that most of the content in the journal would not have the same stark experience of life-after-totalitarian-ideology that characterizes the work of Solzhenitsyn and Pärt, but I hoped that the more subtle approaches in the pages of *Image* would transcend the self-consciousness of the "and." Five years after his first letter I heard from Niemeyer again on the subject of *Image*. In a letter dated September 29, 1994, Niemeyer wrote:

> You probably noticed that my attitude toward the *Image* idea was defi-
> nitely lukewarm. I cannot give you an explanation therefor, except that
> I had not found anything attracting me in modern art.
>
> Let me tell you that this attitude of mine has made a 180 degree
> turn, as a result of reading *Image*. The magazine is an astonishing
> accomplishment. I say this explicitly without the addition "of yours." It
> is an accomplishment tout court, and it would be an accomplishment of
> anyone else. First, its selections are authoritative. Secondly, the articles,
> each of which is most substantial, are written in a tone that bears wit-
> ness to the title of the magazine no less than the pictures or other works
> of art do. In my mind—which of course may be doing some repenting
> of its erstwhile lack of respect—*Image* must be attributed a very high
> rank among all the publications of this century. And you deserve a deep
> bow of admiration for what you have brought into existence.

Niemeyer's later, more reflective, response to *Image* indicated that he had expanded, yet again, his awareness of where in our culture the "positive expe-riences" might be found—a flexibility and openness that I continue to find astonishing in a man of his age.

In devoting much of the last two decades of his life to writing and reflect-ing on matters of culture and education, Gerhart Niemeyer demonstrated an abiding concern for the concrete ways that the deepest philosophical, theo-logical, and political concepts can be embodied by the imagination and find resonance in the human heart. He once wrote that perhaps the most crucial thing for people to do in the current social climate is to heed St. Paul's call to "discern the spirits," the process of sorting out "what is from God and what is evil." To be sure, philosophy, with its conceptual and rational orderliness, can do much to help us learn discernment. But the greatest and most endur-ing creations of culture, as well as of the liberal arts tradition of education, combine to train our sensibilities so that we can discern the spirits in trying times.

20

Malcolm Muggeridge:
Slow Pilgrim

On November 27, 1982, in the Chapel of Our Lady, Help of Christians, in the English village of Hurst Green, Malcolm Muggeridge (1903–1990) and his wife Kitty were received into the Roman Catholic Church. The event merited a few small articles in the media outlets of the English-speaking world, and a certain amount of interest among those who had read Muggeridge's writings, but it had little impact on the intellectuals and leaders of Western nations. Unlike the conversion of John Henry Newman over a century ago, Muggeridge's reception did not cause a wave of converts to the Church of Rome nor did it fundamentally change the position of the church in Britain. Yet this little-noticed event may in the long run have far-reaching consequences, for Muggeridge was a twentieth-century man and his conversion involved a long and weary effort to cast off the causes, ideologies, and obsessions of our time in order to embrace a faith that in the words of St. Augustine is "ever ancient, ever new."

Who was Malcolm Muggeridge, and what is meant by calling him a "twentieth-century man"? This is an important question, for his liberal, secularist critics have denied that Muggeridge is in any way a representative figure of our times. What is the evidence?

A Socialist Household

Muggeridge was raised in a socialist household. His father was an earnest atheist, a man of modest means and little education who nonetheless entertained many of Britain's leading Fabian intellectuals in his home. He accompanied his father during his campaigns to be elected a Labour MP, revelling in the utopian rhetoric that promised a happy, enlightened world managed by a paternalist state. After a lackluster career as an undergraduate at Cambridge University, Muggeridge went to a remote town in India as a teacher in a Christian school. There he came to see the moral bankruptcy and fraudulence of the British Empire, and there he also witnessed Gandhi's efforts to stir the Indians to moral and political independence.

As a young man, Muggeridge was an avid reader of D. H. Lawrence, whom he saw as a prophet of free, uninhibited sexuality. His own marriage, to a niece of Beatrice Webb, one of the Fabian intellectuals, was intended to be a modern marriage of sexual convenience, without permanent commitments.

While working as a teacher in Cairo, Muggeridge discovered his primary vocation: journalism. After working as a correspondent for the *Manchester Guardian*, the bastion of progressive liberalism, he was invited to join the staff as an editorial writer. In Manchester, Muggeridge for the first time began to have doubts about the ability of liberalism to preserve order in the West. He saw the liberal mind as enmeshed in a series of abstractions, complacent and out of touch with intractable human problems; the liberal naïvely thought that *more* education and *more* money would improve all society's ills. But instead of rejecting the political left, he went to the Soviet Union as Moscow correspondent for the *Guardian*, hoping to start his life afresh in the Worker's Paradise. Within the space of a few weeks his hopes were dashed. Muggeridge not only witnessed the beginning of Stalin's show trials, but he was able to go into the Ukraine and witness firsthand the brutal violence and famine brought about by Stalin's forcible collectivization of agriculture. The articles he wrote about his trip to the Ukraine were smuggled out in a diplomatic bag; he knew they would spell the end of his time as a journalist in Moscow.

Ironically, Muggeridge's articles had almost no impact on the West, where intellectuals like George Bernard Shaw and journalists like Walter Duranty of the *New York Times* assured everyone that the Soviet Union was a thriving, successful experiment in socialist planning.

During World War II, Muggeridge worked for the newly-formed British Intelligence service, meeting such famous traitors as Kim Philby, Guy Burgess, and Donald Maclean. In "liberated" France, he saw corruption, injustice, and violence as everyone accused everyone else of being a collaborator with the Nazis—a Hobbesian war of all against all.

After the war, Muggeridge became one of the pioneers of television broadcasting. In the 1950s and 1960s he rose to fame as a talk-show host, maker of documentaries, and TV personality. But throughout this time he was becoming convinced that the media constituted the single most destructive force in the West; it dealt in fantasy, not reality, a constant stream of abstractions which glossed over the reality of evil and the necessity of moral standards. By the late 1960s, Muggeridge had become a Christian, though he did not join any church until that day in 1982, when he ended his lifelong pilgrimage by joining the Church of Rome.

A Twentieth-Century Man?

Is Muggeridge a representative of twentieth-century man? If not, it would be hard to imagine anyone with better qualifications. Whether as a participant or an observer, he witnessed the decline of the British Empire, the rise of state socialism, the catastrophe of totalitarianism in Russia, the cult of sexual "freedom," and the rapid rise of the power of the media. He had been a correspondent in Moscow and Washington, and had known and interviewed most of the major politicians, writers, actors, and celebrities of the last half of the twentieth century.

Of course, it would be wrong to imply that Muggeridge passively accepted all of these movements and ideologies. From the beginning he was not only a journalist but a formidable satirist—one of the finest prose stylists in English and a master of black comedy. Whenever he joined an institution—the British Empire, the Army, or the British Broadcasting Corporation—Muggeridge saw its failings and mercilessly satirized them. He often jeopardized his job and his reputation in order to speak what he considered to be the truth. When he wrote about collectivization in the Ukraine, he knew that his chances of getting a senior position in British journalism would be impossible.

From the outset his career was marked by a relentless realism, a quest for truth beyond the pleasing illusions with which we surround ourselves. Muggeridge's honesty often included a capacity to acknowledge his own failings, even when he found himself unable to reform those failings.

In his memoirs, *Chronicles of Wasted Time*, Muggeridge defended his career as a satirist and at the same time indicated how his dark vision about the death of Western civilization is compatible with—indeed, is necessitated by—a belief in the transcendent:

> How can I ever explain to those who insist that we must believe in the world to love it that it is *because* I disbelieve in the world that I love every breath I take, look forward with ever-greater delight to the coming of each spring, rejoice ever more in the companionship of my fellow humans, to no single one of whom—searching my heart—do I wish ill, and from no single one of whom do I wish to separate myself, in word or thought or deed, or in the prospect of some other existence beyond the ticking of clocks, the vista of the hills, the bounds and dimensions of our earthly hopes and desires? To accept this world as a destination rather than as a staging-post, and the experience of living in it as expressing life's full significance, would seem to me to reduce life to something too banal and trivial to be taken seriously or held in esteem. The only thing that could make me falter in taking a position of extreme, if not demented, optimism about our human condition and prospects would be if one of the prospectuses for an earthly paradise—whether Scandinavian-Styled, British-Beveridge, old Stalin-Ware, Dollar-Reinforced, Mao-Special, Tito- or Castro-ised—looked like providing a satisfying or fulfilled way of life. On this score I see no cause for present anxiety. To attempt to expose and ridicule the fraudulence of such prospectuses is no more life-denying than exposing the fraudulence of one for building an housing estate on the slopes of Etna would be shelter-denying.

Muggeridge's disillusionment with the political prospectuses for utopia led him to the conclusion that two forces are at war in this world; he called them Love vs. Power, or Imagination vs. Will. In *Chronicles of Wasted Time*, he recounts that his friend, Hugh Kingsmill,

> saw the imagination and the will as contending impulses, and he liked to recall an inscription on a stone found in North Africa: "I, a Captain of a Legion of Rome, serving in the desert of Libya, have learnt and pondered this truth: 'There are in life but two things, Love and Power, and no one has both.'" The will was the dynamo of action and the fuel

of lust; the imagination was a window, to look out of, and dream of escaping. On the one hand, the men of the will—Caesar, Cromwell, Napoleon, Hitler and Stalin; on the other, the men of the imagination—Jesus, St. Francis, Blake, Bonhoeffer, Solzhenitsyn. The will belongs to time, the imagination projects time into eternity.

This is the ultimate conflict, according to Muggeridge, not East vs. West, First World vs. Third World, or Capitalism vs. Socialism. Such is the conclusion a long pilgrimage, with many wrong turnings, led him to embrace.

Love and Power

In the struggle between love and power, only the Incarnation can make sense of our confused world. Muggeridge came to accept the Christian faith, but his acute sense of the evanescence of human institutions led him to remain aloof from any particular denomination. Throughout his life, he had been the outsider, the prophet who stood outside of institutions in order to reveal their weaknesses and hypocrisies. At the same time he had a desperate desire to find peace and acceptance with his fellow Christians. After his profession of faith in Christ, Muggeridge began to feel the call to join the Body of Christ—the church.

The process of conversion to the Catholic Church is different for each person who undergoes it—there are as many paths to Rome as there are pilgrims on the road. Muggeridge's conversion was influenced by three important elements: 1) His sense of moral decay—particularly in the area of sexuality and the family—including the prevalence of abortion, euthanasia, divorce, pornography, and contraception; 2) his ability to reconcile his criticisms of human institutions with the divine foundation of the church; and 3) his admiration for Catholics who practice active charity—primarily Mother Teresa of Calcutta and Father Bidone—thus dealing with the problems of the world in a supremely realistic way, yet motivated by supernatural love.

Over the years, Muggeridge came to believe that order and freedom are not achieved by economic or political means, but are grounded in the moral issues that affect the most intimate aspects of our lives: sexuality, and the relationships between man and wife, parent and child. Far from claiming any natural moral superiority on these matters, he said that his own marital infidelities would have ruined his marriage had not a residual Christian morality stood in the way. The early proponent of D. H. Lawrence came to believe that sex without a fundamental commitment to enduring love and to the sanctity of human life inevitably leads to violence, exploitation, and alienation.

In turning to organized religion for support on these issues, Muggeridge could find no help in the Anglican Church, which had reversed the universal Christian ban on contraceptives as early as the Lambeth Conference of 1930. The Anglicans, with their lack of a central teaching authority, seemed to him ready to capitulate to social trends rather than fight them.

What attracted Muggeridge to the Catholic Church was the very radicalism and absolutism of its position on the sanctity of life and on artificial birth control. With his vivid awareness of the human tendency to avoid responsibility for sin by acquiescing to the *Zeitgeist*, he naturally gravitated to the church, which stood as a "sign of contradiction" to the age. Thus Muggeridge was an early and ardent supporter of *Humanae Vitae* long before he became a Catholic. For him, the separation of eroticism from procreation is an event of catastrophic consequences. In a powerful passage from *Chronicles of Wasted Time*, he describes his own participation in the modern mysticism of sex:

> Kitty and I . . . were children of our time. How could we be otherwise? We looked to our bodies for gratification, which we felt they owed us, and that we now owned one another. . . . It was inevitable that this pursuit should become the prevailing preoccupation, the obsessive quest, of our restless and confused generation. Sex is the only mysticism offered by materialism, whose other toys—like motor-cars and aeroplanes and moving pictures and swimming-pools and flights to the moon—soon pall. Sex pure and undefiled; without the burden of procreation, or even, ultimately, of love or identity. Just sex; jointly attained, or solitary—derived from visions, drug-infused; from spectacles, on film or glossy paper. Up and down moving stairways, with, just out of reach, legs and busts and mouths and crotches; ascending to no heights, descending to no depths, only movement upwards and downwards, interminably, with the trivial images of desire for ever in view, and forever inaccessible. . . . Our moving stairway, as we hoped, climbed into a paradise where ecstasy was attainable through sensation pure and undefiled. The Blessed Orgasm itself leaned out from the gold bar of heaven; and, rubber-stoppered against any adverse consequence like birth, sealed and sterilised and secured for *coitus non interruptus* that

is guaranteed *non fecundus*, we pursued happiness in truth twentieth-century style.

For Muggeridge, the transition from the contraceptive mentality to the approval of abortion on demand is clear and inevitable. Abortion is merely the logical outcome of the hedonism which sacrifices love and responsibility to immediate gratification. On the issue of abortion, as in the case of contraception, the Catholic Church, Muggeridge found, was the only bulwark of sanity.

The Outsider and the Church

As he discovered his own ideas coinciding with the moral teachings of the church, he was forced to confront his relationship to it. Always the outsider, the satirist of the follies of human institutions, Muggeridge found himself hesitating before the human elements of the church—hypocrisy and brutality in the past, trendiness and liberalism in the present. He often expressed the belief that Vatican II was ill-timed, that it opened a Pandora's box of heresy and apostasy threatening the very survival of the Catholic Church. Though he had been aware of the theological arguments concerning the divine foundation of the church, and therefore its guarantee against error on matters of faith and morals, what enabled him to make his submission took the form of more concrete things: the church's stand on moral issues, and, most importantly, the orthodoxy and intellectual incisiveness of Pope John Paul II.

Actions had always spoken louder than words for Muggeridge, who freely confessed his lack of interest in systematic theology. Ever since his days as an undergraduate, he wrote in *Chronicles of Wasted Time*, "what appealed to me [in Christianity] were the wild extravagances of faith; the phrases about God's wisdom being men's foolishness, St. Francis of Assisi rejoicing at being naked on the naked earth, the sublime paradoxes of *The Marriage of Heaven and Hell*." Hence he had always been drawn to mystics, whose "extravagance" bears witness to their communion with the transcendent and their ability to see this world in a proper perspective. The spiritual writers who appealed to him over the years include St. Augustine, the author of *The Cloud of Unknowing*, Pascal, Blake, Kierkegaard, Simone Weil, and Bonhoeffer.

The greatest saints for Muggeridge were undoubtedly those who combined mysticism with effective and transforming activity in the world. Here his models are St. Francis and St. Teresa of Avila. In his long career as writer and satirist, he mocked the pretensions of both the socialist centralized state and the individualism of the capitalist economy to minister to men's deepest spiritual needs. The secular state is forever mired in abstractions, bureaucracy, and corruption, in spite of slogans about democracy, justice, and freedom. The activist mystic, on the other hand, is the supreme realist: moved by supernatural charity to see the preciousness of each individual, aware of evil and its many guises, willing and able to comfort the suffering with the assurance of divine love, the saint is the only effective "social worker."

Thanks to the examples of Father Bidone and Mother Teresa, Muggeridge came to understand the church as the womb of saints. Only the saints know how to maintain that precarious balance of being in the world but not of the world. Father Bidone, an Italian priest who belonged to the order of the Sons of Divine Providence, worked extensively with handicapped children. Mother Teresa's work with the destitute of Calcutta and dozens of other nations around the world are well known, thanks in large part to the film and book which Muggeridge made about her entitled *Something Beautiful for God*. In his last book, a memoir tracing his spiritual journey, *Confessions of a Twentieth Century Pilgrim*, he wrote of Mother Teresa:

> One the one hand, she makes mystical concepts seem an integral part of day-to-day living; on the other, she, as it were, transcendentalizes our most ordinary conclusions and expectations. Thus, she persuades aspiring helpers who are too incapacitated to become active members of her order, that somehow or other their fortitude in accepting their affliction gives her additional strength and courage for her work; that their endurance of suffering is her powerhouse. I have myself seen a lady preparing to undergo her umpteenth operation all shining and joyful because she is convinced that thereby Mother Teresa will acquire extra muscle in the service of Christ. At the same time, she managed to induce high caste Indian ladies to minister to derelicts brought in from the streets of Calcutta— something that, as someone who has lived, one way and another, a number of years in India, I should never have believed possible.

He also wrote that "Mother Teresa is a living conversion" and that simply to be near her was to be converted.

At the end of his life, in and through the church, Malcolm Muggeridge returned to his youthful ideas about transforming the world. No longer an exponent of utopian abstractions, he came to hold what Miguel de Unamuno called "the tragic sense of life." His vision of social reform is of Christian saints who quietly go about their works of compassion while all about them the world succumbs to barbarism. Muggeridge was widely considered a gloomy, pessimistic thinker, but he responded to that accusation with a story. When Archbishop Fulton Sheen, the popular Catholic evangelist, lay dying in New York, he summoned Muggeridge (who had never met him) to his bedside. The urgent message which Sheen said he must impart to Muggeridge was this: "We are witnessing the end of Christendom but not of Christ." There is, he said, no more hopeful message in the world than that.

21

Marion Montgomery:
Being and Metaphor

In the history of Western literature since the Middle Ages, one of the most noticeable trends has been the extent to which poets have felt the need to become critics, and not only critics in a general sense, but authors of works defending their vocation as servants of the Muse. However self-conscious Dante was about his poetic style and the nobility and suitability of the Italian language as a medium for great poetry, and however chaotic were the internecine political struggles of his day, he certainly did not need to defend the value of poetry to his intended audience. Chaucer may have been a customs officer, but he assuredly did not suffer bouts of angst over his passion for literature and its place in civilized life. But with the Renaissance and Reformation we find Sir Philip Sidney, the humanist and courtier, writing *A Defence of Poetry* against charges of immorality and frivolity. Later, Shelley will pen a book with the same title, defending not only the "morality" of poetry, but its prophetic role in an industrial society. Shelley himself drew heavily on the work of Wordsworth and Coleridge, who were at such pains to promote their theories of the imagination.

In the modern era, we take all this for granted. Indeed, we have come to expect the programmatic rhetoric of the manifesto, rather than the genteel defense of poesy. It is evident that in the modern era the artist has become increasingly estranged from his audience and so oppressed by the conditions of modern consciousness that he must in essence clear a space for his imaginative vision through his critical writings. Even if the artist himself is not racked by alienation or class hatred, he will feel the need to somehow explain and justify his work to his society, or perhaps only to himself.

In coming to a proper appreciation of Marion Montgomery's achievement in his trilogy, *The Prophetic Poet and the Spirit of the Age*—consisting of *Why Flannery O'Connor Stayed Home*, *Why Poe Drank Liquor*, and *Why Hawthorne Was Melancholy*—it is important that we remind ourselves that the author is, first and foremost, a poet. Before his first critical work was published, Montgomery had written three volumes of poetry, as well as two novels and a novella. Except for a novel published in 1974, his books since 1970 have consisted of critical evaluations of T. S. Eliot, Ezra Pound, English poetry, and, now, the trilogy. This shift from creative writing to criticism cannot be ascribed simply to a loss of imaginative drive, given the quality of his long poem, "At Al Johnson's Lake," which appeared in 1982. Like so many modern artists, Montgomery has found it necessary to come to grips with the crisis of our time, to embark on what he calls a "reflective journey toward order."

American Literature and the Crisis of Modernity

The trilogy, then, despite its philosophical dimension, is a poet's book, proceeding "more suggestively than exhaustively," as Montgomery states in his preface. The author humbly acknowledges his debt to the work of philosophers, theologians, and historians; to a great extent, the trilogy is a work of synthesis, a bringing together of insights on modern ideology and the first principles of art and philosophy. As Professor Niemeyer has claimed in an essay, much of the value of the trilogy lies in its relation of the crisis of modernity to the realm of literature, and, more specifically, to American literature.[1]

Though the literary aspect of the trilogy is its obvious point of departure, it often appears submerged by the seemingly more urgent problems of philosophy and political theory. In addition, the very diffuse, meditative style of the trilogy tends to make it difficult to see as a whole Montgomery's insights into the nature of literary form and creative intentionality. It is my conviction, however, that the most vital and original achievement in the trilogy is Montgomery's understanding of metaphor and the imagination. For if Montgomery uses philosophy to develop a critique of modern ideology, he turns from this negative work not to a philosophical answer, but to an imaginative response that offers us a pattern of order. Unlike most contemporary critics, Montgomery persistently clings to the belief that art relates to life, that the highest art is a form of therapy for the soul. Art, he says, along with his mentor Flannery O'Connor, doesn't prove anything; but it does enact an imaginative vision that can move us in the direction of order.

Any attempt to extract a single theme or subject from Montgomery's suggestive prose risks turning subtle moments of understanding into flat, rigid propositions. But with that risk in mind I propose to sketch out Montgomery's key concepts concerning imagination and metaphor, and to place those concepts in the context of the trilogy's third volume, where they are given their most extensive treatment.

Montgomery has let it be known that he considers his earlier book, *The Reflective Journey Toward Order*, to be a "prelude" to the trilogy, though of course it stands perfectly well on its own.[2] Like the trilogy, *The Reflective Journey Toward Order* consists of a series of essays or meditations grouped around common themes. The book's thesis, in its simplest form, is that the Romantic age, far from being confined to the first decades of the nineteenth century, actually extends from Dante's time to our own. With Dante, for the first time in Western art, the problem of the artist's relation to tradition, nature, and to his own creative productions becomes acute. Discussing primarily Dante, Wordsworth, and Eliot, Montgomery examines the poetry of spiritual quest, in which the artist seeks to move from his painfully self-conscious fall from innocence to a higher innocence, a point of rest. Dante reached this state because of his confidence in nature as a window onto the transcendent, and because his *Comedy* encompasses his own stumbling efforts to comprehend his relation to the mystery of being. Wordsworth, on the other hand, inherits the Renaissance dichotomy between mind and nature; he struggles awkwardly, scanning his native Lake District, unsure whether nature actually speaks to him or is merely illusion. Finally, Eliot, more Wordsworthian than he himself understands at first, undertakes a long and arduous pilgrimage, from the solipsism of a Prufrock to the final surrender of the poet before the divine source of being, a surrender "costing not less than everything."

The guiding spirits in *The Reflective Journey Toward Order* are principally Coleridge and Eliot. Montgomery's crucial conclusion is that Eliot's early attempt to divorce the personality of the artist from his art, though a well-intentioned effort at escaping the Romantic poet's self-preoccupation, was a false start. Instead, he contends that the modern poet can only participate in transcendent being through what the philosopher Michael Polanyi calls "personal knowledge." Art is not a hermetically sealed, self-sufficient kingdom, but must open out to spiritual experience. The question is not whether the poet is present in his work, but in what manner he addresses the mystery of the world beyond his self.

The Reflective Journey Toward Order deals almost exclusively with lyric poetry, and its guides are more literary than philosophical. The change between this book and the trilogy reflects Montgomery's intensive study of such authors as Eric Voegelin, Leo Strauss, Mircea Eliade, Josef Pieper, Jacques Maritain, and Etienne Gilson. More importantly, it reveals how much he learned from his friend and fellow Georgian, Flannery O'Connor, and her philosopher of choice, St. Thomas Aquinas.

If *The Reflective Journey* dealt with lyric poetry and the more private world of the poet, the trilogy turns to fiction, the overarching political and intellectual matters concerning Western society, and particularly the American experience. *Why Flannery O'Connor Stayed Home* sets out to describe both the nature of modernity and how O'Connor brilliantly responded to modern consciousness. In a sense, Montgomery begins in the "present," only to go back in American history in the next two volumes. Poe serves as a locus for an understanding of nihilism, presaging the philosophy of Heidegger. It is in the third volume that Montgomery stretches the broadest canvas, taking in the intellectual and literary influences on American culture from Puritanism and Transcendentalism to the modern masters of the grotesque, Flannery O'Connor and Nathanael West. Montgomery discusses the problem of the imagination more theoretically in the first two volumes, and applies that theory concretely in the third.

From Knowing to Thinking

The fundamental temptation for both the reason and the imagination is the belief that the mind is its own place. "The wonder of mind's participation in time . . . may easily distract it from the question of abiding cause, and the mind's attention be thus secretly transformed into cause, even before thought itself becomes so bold as to argue itself the cause."[3] The temptation is as old as, and perhaps equivalent to, the original fall from grace in Eden itself. But with the rise of nominalism in the late medieval era, the very nature of modern consciousness and thought is conditioned by the mind's isolation from transcendent being. Here Montgomery benefits from the distinctions bequeathed to us most especially in the thought of St. Thomas Aquinas. Several times in the trilogy, he quotes Etienne Gilson's basic rendering of the "problem of problems" for the philosopher.

In Thomas's technical language, actual existence, which he calls *esse*, is that by virtue of which a thing, which he calls *res*, is a being, an *ens*. It is the being-hood or being-ness of being. It is *be* in being. It is *to be* that makes a certain thing to be a being. *Esse* is defined by its essence, namely that which the thing is.[4]

The pitfall for the mind is the conviction that it can create or be the self-sufficient ground of *esse*. This is to deny that man is a contingent being, an *ens*, who is not responsible for the act of being, or *esse*, which maintains him in existence. Both the philosopher and the poet go about their true business when they contemplate the mystery of being.

Thomas holds that man is a union of soul and body, that his knowledge of reality comes through the senses. It is the power of reason which enables man to abstract from sense experience and contemplate reality. Both the Nominalists, and Descartes after them, discarded this unity of perception by positing a radical break between man's mind and his knowledge of reality. Montgomery is also fond of quoting Anton Pegis's comment that "what we call the decline of medieval philosophy was really a transition from man as knower to man as thinker—from man knowing the world of sensible things to man thinking abstract thoughts in separation from existence. What is thinking but dis-existentialized knowing?"

When man separates himself from a knowledge of being, he no longer participates in it, but rather seeks to manipulate it to his own private ends. From this initial separation, this aboriginal schism, numerous sects arise, for man is now free to reject existence (nihilism), or see nature as a blind, determining force (naturalism), or proclaim that the mind may create its own reality (idealism or solipsism).

Montgomery's originality and importance lies primarily in the way he applies these philosophical concepts to the history of the imagination in Western literature since Dante. As he writes in the introduction to *Why Hawthorne Was Melancholy*: "For the poet, the mystery of *esse* lies in his perception of *ens* and the challenge to his art is to embody his vision of being."[5] The poet in the modern world has largely followed the philosophers in believing that he can be the source of *esse*. He becomes the creator of what Robert Musil has called "Second Realities," not "real possibilities" but self-contained kingdoms of art which are their own way of salvation. The true poet attends to the concrete world of beings, and in his encounter with the sensible world he may come to an apprehension of their Cause. To embody one's vision of being is to create an "incarnational art." But this creation is "secondary," an imitation of God's primary creation. That imitation is accomplished through the use of the intellect, that which in man is most akin to God's being. Flannery O'Connor puts it this way:

> St. Thomas called art "reason in making." This is a very cold and very beautiful definition, and if it is unpopular today, this is because reason has lost ground among us. As grace and nature have been separated, so imagination and reason have been separated, and this always means an end to art. The artist uses his reason to discover an answering reason in everything he sees. For him, to be reasonable is to find, in the object, in the situation, in the sequence, the spirit which makes it itself. This is not an easy or simple thing to do. It is to intrude upon the timeless, and that is only done by the violence of a single-minded respect for the truth.

With the help of O'Connor and Thomas, Montgomery is thus able to improve upon Eliot's famous notion of the "dissociation of sensibility." More than a separation of "thought and feeling," as Eliot would have it, the prior division between grace and nature leaves the artist with a natural world no longer continuous with its cause. Inevitably, a distancing and estrangement between poet and world grows into alienation. John Donne still had access to scholastic philosophy in elaborating his metaphysical analogies, but after his time nature increasingly becomes emptied of meaning and is used to suit the fancy's whim.

From Window to Mirror

Montgomery focuses on the change which metaphor and symbol undergo as the logic of modernity progresses. The Dantean symbol is a window on the world, a sensible thing representing through itself something beyond itself; in short, it possesses meaning. But in the modern era, metaphor is seen as a mirror, a cipher skillfully manipulated to evoke emotion or thought. Taken to its logical conclusion, the symbol as mirror may be seen in the Symbolist school of poetry (a school, incidentally, to which Eliot, Pound, and Yeats were all initially attracted, only to reject in favor of an older understanding of metaphor). Montgomery describes the nature of the Symbolist's symbol:

> The symbol in this sense must function as a projected satellite for intra-self communication; against the symbol the closed self bounces its

emotional unrest and receives it back as sensual response, maintaining thereby its closed world as inviolate against threats of revelation. The "poem" becomes a moment's solace to the alienated man, performed through images dissociated from any response other than a subjective reaction to the existence of the self.[6]

The irrationality and arbitrary playfulness spawned by this approach to metaphor led from Symbolism to Dada and Surrealism, and underlies much of our contemporary fascination with art as a closed system of signs, as in the French *nouveau roman* of Alain Robbe-Grillet and Nobel Prize–winner Claude Simon.

The hardening of metaphor into the plaything of the fancy is precisely what occurred in the eighteenth century and was what the Romantic movement sought to counter. Both Wordsworth and Coleridge struggled to restore the imagination to a more epistemologically accessible reality. We have alluded to Wordsworth's difficulties in finding that anchor for the imagination. Coleridge, whose Christian vision was more firmly grounded, is largely responsible for our distinction between fancy and imagination. The fancy deals with "fixities and definites," that is, it rearranges dead things, whereas the primary imagination is the "repetition in the finite mind of the eternal act of creation in the infinite I AM."[7] But if Coleridge hoped to reestablish the imagination on a metaphysical base, most of the other Romantics glorified the imagination as creator of a self-contained universe, the new god of liberation from human limitation. Thus Montgomery notes that in the Romantic imagination, Satan, the archetypal rebel against transcendent order, is transformed into Prometheus, the rebel against the gods who brings fire, and hence civilization, to mankind. Shelley unbinds Prometheus from his rock, and Blake comments that Milton was of the Devil's party without knowing it.

By championing the Promethean imagination, the more radical Romantics intensified a problem that had been affecting the poet since the time of the Renaissance: that of casting the poet in the role of high priest of art. Thus the poem becomes a religious ritual and the aesthetic high points or "epiphanies" (as they would come to be known in the context of Joyce's fiction) are the equivalent of receiving the Eucharist. In *Why Hawthorne Was Melancholy*, Montgomery distinguishes two types of art based on two different modernist approaches to being. The "naturalist," who believes that "the stark immediate moment of the senses [is] the ultimate reality," sees the world as ruled by mechanism and cultivates despair or a Nietzschean "tragic joy." On the other hand, the "transcendentalist" or "idealist," whom Montgomery calls "the ultimate solipsist, the creator of a supreme fiction of the self," will inhabit a bizarre fantasyland, either nihilistic (as in Poe), utopian (as in Emerson), or merely absurd (as in the surrealists).[8] What the naturalist and idealist have in common, Montgomery asserts, is an assumption of power, a positing of mind over being.[9] The poet might be better seen as alchemist rather than priest: half magician, half scientist, he sets out not to encounter and understand a mystery, but to impose his private reality on the world.

Puritans and Transcendentalists

Such, in a brief and abstract form, is an overview of Montgomery's understanding of the imagination and its temptations as they have developed in modern literature. In turning now to *Why Hawthorne Was Melancholy*, it will be possible to see these phenomena in the perspective of American literature, and to better perceive how two major artists, Nathaniel Hawthorne and Nathanael West, swam against the current of modernity.

Why Hawthorne Was Melancholy is in some ways the most ambitious volume of the trilogy. Montgomery attempts nothing less than an interpretation of the Puritan, transcendentalist, and Lockean influences in our culture, tracing these strains of thought in Emerson, Jonathan Edwards, Hawthorne, Henry James, and Nathanael West, with side glances at the Stoic tradition in the South, the Puritan poet Edward Taylor, and that Emersonian gone native, Walt Whitman. But it is important to remember that Montgomery's method is "suggestive," not "exhaustive." Nor should we assume that the final volume of the trilogy is part of a linear progression that will culminate in a grand synthesis. In fact, two thirds of the way through this volume, Montgomery shifts his attention to the growth of the grotesque in modern literature. By ending with a section on West, however, he can claim in some sense to be arriving at the place from which he started and knowing it for the first time. That is because West, master of the grotesque and incisive critic of our contemporary decadence, acts as something of a secular alter ego to Flannery O'Connor, who is the focus of the first volume and a constant presence throughout Montgomery's reflective journey in the trilogy. In West, Montgomery can see more clearly O'Connor's breakthrough, her lifting of West's despairing vision into the divine comedy of redemption.

A hundred years before West, Hawthorne confronted the rise of the American popular spirit, that strange mixture of vaguely optimistic progressivism and a restless desire to conquer and appropriate nature. Hawthorne's immediate concern was with two strands of thought, each oddly entwined with the other: the Puritan inheritance, especially as it is influenced by Locke, and the liberalism of the transcendentalists epitomized by Emerson.

Montgomery is adept not only at criticizing the ideological deformations of these traditions but also in relating them to the deformations of language and vision they produce. Thus he notes that in denying the natural world the goodness that enables it to become sacramentally representative of grace, the Puritans reduced ritual to mere ceremony, excluding the numinous from the public realm and exalting functionality. Here he cites O'Connor's comment that when Emerson broke with the Unitarian Church because he refused to participate in the Communion service so long as bread and wine were used, he contributed to the "vaporization of American religion."[10] Montgomery notes that the Puritans' Manichean alienation from nature leads them to elevate Industry as the highest virtue, paving the way for the pragmatic spirit to come. And with a unique insight, he claims that for the Puritans, allegory was seen as useful for instruction, and is therefore "spiritually pragmatic art."[11]

Hawthorne treats Emerson with deference and lightly veiled irony in his public allusions to the former tenant of the Old Manse, but in his notebooks and fiction, Emerson is a significant antagonist. Emerson shared with the Puritans something Montgomery calls "inverted Platonism": the belief that the world is the shadow of the mind. But Emerson "transfers Calvinistic election from the province of God to that of Nature."[12] Dispensing with evil, the past, and human institutions, the Emersonian "great man" divinizes himself. But to maintain his divinity, the "great man" must abandon passive faith and engage in a constant round of activity and domination.[13]

Though Emerson ostensibly considers every person capable of this self-divinization, he assumes that some are more equal than others. Indeed, as Montgomery points out, Emerson's creed is extremely compatible with the laissez-faire ethic of ruthless individual competition. As with most ideologies, Emerson's thought is infected with progressivist urgency, a frenetic becoming that pushes away from an isolated present.[14] Here again, one can see that in the course of American history the transcendentalists and the Puritans become "folded in a single party."

Hawthorne's Response

Needless to say, Hawthorne set himself against these forces, even as he feared his own attraction to them. Unfortunately, it must be said that Montgomery's exploration of Hawthorne's oeuvre is weak and often misdirected. He spends an inordinate amount of time examining Hawthorne's personal state of mind as revealed in his notebooks. To be sure, by doing this, Montgomery is able to show how experiences that troubled Hawthorne privately are downplayed when transferred into public prose, as in the sketches about his experiences in England published as *Our Old Home*. But Montgomery seems to forget that for some artists, the truest response to doubts and fears is worked out, not in journals or diaries, but in the art itself. Far from wanting to downplay Hawthorne's own artistic weaknesses and spiritual uncertainty, I nonetheless feel that Montgomery misses opportunities to see in that dark romancer the many flashes of imaginative vision which raise him to the status of prophetic poet.

Montgomery stresses the clumsiness of Hawthorne's allegory, that "spiritually pragmatic art" he inherits from his Puritan forebears. He contrasts it to what Flannery O'Connor called the "anagogical imagination," which involves the ability to see multiple levels of meaning within a single realistic or possible image or event. And yet we have the example of Dante to show us that highly elaborate allegory is not incompatible with anagogical density. Without having to put Hawthorne on a level with Dante, we can see where he is able to achieve a symbolic density beyond rigid one-to-one correspondences. O'Connor also once said that Protestantism lends itself to dramatic treatment because it is open-ended: on the one side it is open to Catholicism, and on the other it is open to atheism. In this sense, Hawthorne at his best is able to dramatize the Puritan world and subtly transform it into something beyond itself. Of course, this is most ably done in *The Scarlet Letter*. That novel is given a taut structure through the use of three scenes which take place on the public scaffold, that place of punishment and reproof and suffering. At the outset, Hester Prynne stands on it in the full light of day, vividly aware of the presence of her lover, Dimmesdale, and her husband and enemy, Chillingworth, one at the heart of society and one at its periphery, whose identities are unknown to all but her. Later, Dimmesdale goes to the scaffold in the dead of night in an agony of remorse, and there meets Hester, Pearl, and Chillingworth; in this scene the characters meet but do not truly repent. Finally, the novel's climax involves Dimmesdale's public confession and death on the same scaffold: the instrument that is used to enforce society's hypocritical standards becomes the locus of a freely chosen act of penitence and potential redemption. Hawthorne, in transforming the scaffold, takes it from its one-dimensional, literal function and raises it to a mysterious sign of grace, reminiscent of Golgotha and the cross of Christ.

Even in this most schematic of novels, Hawthorne is able to find realistic touches that lend psychological and moral depth to his vision. For instance, as demonic and cold as Chillingworth may be, at the moment he discovers the scarlet letter on the chest of the sleeping Dimmesdale, the narrator says that "what distinguished the physician's ecstasy from Satan's was the trait of wonder in it."[15] It is that human trait of wonder that enables Hawthorne to hint at Chillingworth's possible redemption. Montgomery sees this as an unwillingness on Hawthorne's part to judge his character. But I would prefer to see it in much the same light cast by O'Connor on her character the Misfit, who appears in her story, "A Good Man Is Hard to Find." She wrote: "I don't want to equate the Misfit with the devil. I prefer to think that, however unlikely this may seem, the old lady's gesture, like the mustard-seed, will grow to be a great crow-filled tree in the Misfit's heart, and will be enough of a pain to him there to turn him into the prophet he was meant to become." This vision is shared by Hawthorne, however close he may come to sentimentality.

Montgomery again and again notes that Hawthorne is unable to make a complete surrender of the self in the certitude of faith, and yet nearly all his protagonists must make a surrender which admits human limitation. As R. W. B. Lewis writes in *The American Adam*, the constant rhythm of Hawthorne's novels is one of attempted escape and the absolute necessity of return.[16] Hester and Dimmesdale, in the heart of the forest, think they can throw off their past and escape the reality of their transgression. In a pathetic and comic variation, Clifford and Hepzibah in *The House of the Seven Gables* flee on the train, only to return after traveling a couple stops to confess a crime they did not actually commit. Emerging from his mountain retreat, Donatello in *The Marble Faun* returns to Rome to admit his act of murder. But beyond the return, there is a pattern of penance and sacrifice. Miriam, whose life is linked to that of Donatello, begins a pilgrimage at the end of the novel which will last as long as Donatello's imprisonment. After Dimmesdale's death, Hester lives a life of sacrifice, ministering to the sick. Montgomery sees Hester's fate as evidence of Hawthorne's stoicism; but why could it not equally be penance? Hazel Motes embarks on a penitential journey at the end of *Wise Blood*, and if it gains dramatic force by its symbolic richness and brief time span, it is not a difference of kind when compared to *The Scarlet Letter*. Hawthorne's artistry is undoubtedly more labored, but his mythopoetic and psychological powers at least shine through a faulty narrative. His rhythm of escape and return is predicated on the need to accept the limitations of time and to live within those limitations, working out one's salvation in fear and trembling. In its emphasis on the lifelong pilgrimage of suffering, Hawthorne's vision is closer to that of Eliot of *Ash Wednesday* and *Four Quartets* than to that of O'Connor.

Montgomery is most effective in demonstrating the way in which Hawthorne struggled with the problem of the place of the artist in relation to the community, particularly in his reading of the "Custom House," that essential preface to *The Scarlet Letter*. Hawthorne's many scruples about becoming a "cold observer" indicate his own fear of becoming a manipulator of being who violates the sanctity of the human heart. By setting Hawthorne against Henry James, Montgomery is able to show that the weaker artist refused to take art as the path of salvation the way the great master of fiction did. For Hawthorne, as for Montgomery, art must continually open the reader and the poet himself onto a larger world, and if there is perhaps more of a conflict within James than Montgomery admits, the thrust of his critical analysis remains sound.

Nathanael West and Flannery O'Connor

Hawthorne's choice of romance as his fictional vehicle testifies, as O'Connor says, to his intuition that the novel needed to steer clear of false types of realism based on reductionist worldviews. Montgomery concludes his trilogy with a study of another fictional compensation for ideological narrowness: the grotesque. In one sense, art is always striving to hold up a mirror to society, but that mirror may be distorted in such a way as to disturb the individual, making him see an image he prefers not to confront. Art may function as doppelganger, enabling one to see oneself as if for the first time, without any pleasing illusions. (Hawthorne uses mirrors constantly, such as the incident in which a suit of armor makes Hester's scarlet letter seem grotesquely large.) Montgomery traces the rise of the grotesque in European literature, rightly pointing out that it parallels the rise of rationalism. He writes: "When reason's measure of nature becomes so severe as to make it an intellectual sin to believe in any country save nature's . . . nature itself becomes a most unsettling fairyland. . . . The nineteenth century grotesque which trenches upon the void appears . . . as an older imaginative vision now blinded and made desperate in its entrapment by modern gnostic thought. Its cry of emptiness is a cry for rescue; its destructive resistance is that of the spirit cornered."[17] When the rationalist mind eliminates the realm of myth, in which the imagination forms "deep images" bespeaking man's position as inhabitant of Middle Earth, nature returns in nightmare form.

It is in the twentieth century that the grotesque is taken up by major artists and loses its Gothic, haunted-house flavor. But Montgomery's interest is not in the images of horror concocted by believers in the absurd; his concern is for the artists who use the grotesque as part of a clear-headed critique of modern consciousness. He finds two such artists in Nathanael West and Flannery O'Connor. Despite his bleak outlook, West, like O'Connor, is principally a comic writer. West's America is a land which continues to spout Emersonian optimism on the surface, but which suffers from inner spiritual chaos. Violence is so endemic to society that it can only draw people's attention if it possesses some form of ghastly aesthetic grotesquerie about it. A headline like "FATHER CUTS SON'S THROAT IN BASEBALL ARGUMENT" is not imaginative enough as a crime to merit front page treatment; it would have to be a father killing three sons with a baseball bat, not a knife, according to West. In such a culture, the satirist despairs of his craft. So, at the end of West's lacerating satire of Hollywood, *The Day of the Locust*, the painter Tod Hackett, who is injured in a mad-mob scene at a film premiere, is reduced to mimicking the ambulance siren as he is carried off to the hospital. He cannot find a vantage point from which to satirize the chaos he witnesses and is reduced to neurotic participation in disorder.

Both West and O'Connor find that language is in decay, and that cliché acts as a kind of mental salve to deaden the pain of existence. The immense challenge they faced as artists was to take violence and cliché and transform it into vision. (The extent to which this effort of transformation can be pushed is evident in West's comment that he originally considered making his novel *Miss Lonelyhearts* into a comic strip, and that this medium still underlies the narrative method of the book.) For West, the decay of mind and word is exemplified primarily in the mass media, in his age dominated by the newspaper and (as in ours) by Hollywood. Miss Lonelyhearts, along with Tod Hackett, is an image of the artist's reduced role in a mad world: Hackett is a set designer and Miss Lonelyhearts (the only name this character is given) writes the agony column for a metropolitan newspaper: both are implicated in society's decay, while struggling to break free from it.

Miss Lonelyhearts writes in a completely abstract medium; he is largely cut off from any true community and can only receive messages of despair and send out messages of bland comfort. A job that started off as a joke turns into a sanity-threatening labor. Montgomery writes: "Miss Lonelyhearts' territory is enlarged as the inner life becomes public property in a new socialism of the spirit."[18] But like most other modern artists, Miss Lonelyhearts conceives of his role in salvific terms; as he says, "I've got a Christ complex." His one attempt to get involved with his readers leads to his death. He is described, significantly, as having the look of a "New England puritan," and later, his nihilist colleague, Shrike, calls him "a swollen Mussolini of the soul." These descriptions, though far removed from the Emersonian "great man," are still a faint echo of the totalitarian direction of the self-divinizing individual. The novel ends with Miss Lonelyhearts going partially insane and attempting to become a savior. He dies in a mock Passion when trying to embrace the man he cuckolded, a wimp who would probably have been too weak to fire his gun in any case. Montgomery sees West as arranging his ending so as to eliminate any possible "meaning" in it, since the death is accidental.[19] But accident or no accident, West at least shows the folly of the artist's mad quest for godhead.

Intimacy with Creation

W. H. Auden used the phrase "West's Disease" to describe the inability of West's characters to turn wishes into desires. They cannot move beyond velleities; they ask, with Prufrock, "Do I dare to eat a peach? . . . Do I dare disturb the universe?" Auden's comment immediately brings Rayber, of O'Connor's *The Violent Bear It Away*, to mind. Tarwater's accusation against the paralyzed intellectual, caught up in his deterministic worldview, is that he can't act. So, too, a comment by West that Miss Lonelyhearts is engaged in "self-torture by conscious sinning" conjures up the figure of Hazel Motes, that Nietzschean so earnestly bent on denying existence to his conscience. But these comparisons with O'Connor in themselves indicate the distance that separates her from West: for the debilities and rebellions of West's characters are seen in her fiction against a broader and more inclusive backdrop. If Rayber cannot act, Tarwater can, and finds that his murder of the idiot boy Bishop contains within it a grace he cannot deny. Hazel finally discovers, to use a cliché O'Connor might approve of, that you can run but you can't hide.

O'Connor's wholeness of vision stems from her conviction that she is not the creator or the redeemer of her world; those actions she knows to have been accomplished for her. As Montgomery puts it, "the distortions of the world in her fiction reflect distortions of the world by her characters; their grotesqueness is presented by an imaginative art as an effect whose cause, within the imaginative vision, is in the character's own act of will."[20] In the same vein he writes: "Her prophets, she says, come to see what they do not wish to see, and in that ultimate vision have their eyes burned clean. For in seeing an Ultimate Grotesque, there occurs a loss of that life we have believed our own. . . . If nature became, in the sweep of naturalistic thought . . . impersonal and indifferent to man . . . we might say that Miss O'Connor rather makes nature terrifying because it becomes too personal."[21]

West could not reach that state of "intimacy with creation," but O'Connor admired the integrity and passion with which he approached his art. To end *Why Hawthorne Was Melancholy* with West is for Montgomery the best way to understand O'Connor's breakthrough. But Montgomery is honest enough to admit that O'Connor's way is not the only way; he even says that her very confidence makes for a lessening of dramatic tension in her work.

It is clear that for the trilogy Montgomery has taken O'Connor for his Virgil, or perhaps his Beatrice. I have no quarrel with this. But in coming to a just estimate of Montgomery's critical contribution to our current crisis, we should remember his equally important studies of Eliot. One of my few criticisms of the trilogy is that O'Connor is omnipresent but Eliot is not fully integrated into the work; that is why the earlier book, *The Reflective Journey Toward Order* is not so much a prelude to the trilogy as a complement to it. O'Connor had the grace of a confident vision and the artistic advantages that vision afforded. But for someone like Eliot, for whom the "awful daring of a moment's surrender" was long and painful in coming, the personal dimension in art becomes another crucial breakthrough for the imagination. Given the penetrating and hopeful insights Marion Montgomery has been able to give us into these authors and their world, we can only hope that he will return to his own art with a sense that he has arrived at the place from which he began, seeing it as if for the first time.

Notes

Chapter 7:
After This Our Exile: The Christian Poet in the Modern World

1. Jacques Maritain, *Art and Scholasticism and the Frontiers of Poetry* (Notre Dame: University of Notre Dame Press, 1974), 135.

2. Flannery O'Connor, *The Habit of Being* (New York: Farrar, Straus, Giroux, 1979), 90.

3. T. S. Eliot, *Selected Essays, 1909–1932* (New York: Harcourt Brace, 1932), 248.

4. Hans Urs von Balthasar, *The Glory of the Lord: A Theological Aesthetics,* vol. 3, *Studies in Theological Style: Lay Styles* (San Francisco: Ignatius Press, 1986), 353–399.

5. Austin Warren, *Rage for Order* (Ann Arbor: University of Michigan Press, 1948), 57.

6. von Balthasar, *The Glory of the Lord*, vol. 3, 365.

7. Ibid., 375–81.

8. All references to Hopkins's poetry are from *Poems and Prose* (New York: Penguin, 1953).

9. Marion Montgomery, *T. S. Eliot: An Essay on the American Magus* (Athens: University of Georgia Press, 1969), 7.

10. Anne C. Bolgan, "The Philosophy of Bradley and the Mind and Art of T. S. Eliot," in *English Literature and British Philosophy*, S. P. Rosenbaum, ed. (Chicago: University of Chicago Press, 1971), 265–66.

11. Gerhart Niemeyer, "Reason and Faith: The Fallacious Antithesis," in *Aftersight and Foresight: Selected Essays* (Lanham, MD: University Press of America; Bryn Mawr, PA: Intercollegiate Studies Institute, 1988), 238.

12. For an introduction to Hill, see my "True Sequences of Pain: The Poetry of Geoffrey Hill," *The Hillsdale Review* 6 (Fall 1985): 3–10. Reprinted in this volume.

13. Geoffrey Hill, *The Lords of Limit: Essays on Literature and Ideas* (New York: Oxford University Press, 1984), 3.

14. Geoffrey Hill, *Collected Poems* (Harmondsworth, UK: Penguin, 1985), 177–79.

15. von Balthasar, *The Glory of the Lord*, vol. 3, 487.

Chapter 9:
Evelyn Waugh: Savage Indignation

1. Martin Stannard, *Evelyn Waugh: The Early Years, 1903–1939* (London: J.M. Dent, 1986), 1.

2. Ibid., 2.

3. Christopher Sykes, *Evelyn Waugh: A Biography* (Harmondsworth, UK: Penguin, 1977), 181.

4. Stannard, *Evelyn Waugh*, 3.

5. Evelyn Waugh, *The Essays, Articles, and Reviews of Evelyn Waugh*, ed. Donat Gallagher (Boston: Little, Brown, 1983), 161–62.

6. *Essays, Articles, and Reviews*, 206.

7. Evelyn Waugh, *A Handful of Dust* (Boston: Little, Brown, 1934), 38.

8. Ibid., 79.

9. Ibid., 287–88.

10. T. S. Eliot, *The Complete Poems and Plays, 1909–1950* (New York: Harcourt, Brace, 1971), 143.

11. Evelyn Waugh, *Brideshead Revisited* (Boston: Little, Brown, 1945), from a preface that was suppressed in later editions.

12. Waugh, *Essays, Articles, and Reviews*, 304.

13. Waugh, *Brideshead Revisited*, 89.

14. Ibid.

15. The author heard Thomas Howard make this statement during a public lecture.

16. Waugh, *Brideshead Revisited*, 309.

17. Ibid., 133.

Chapter 11:
Geoffrey Hill: True Sequences of Pain

1. This essay, written and published in the early 1980s, covers what is now clearly the first half of Hill's poetic output. After a difficult period in which he himself largely fell silent, Hill in recent years has shifted into a prolific mode, publishing half a dozen volumes in the last decade.

Chapter 12:
Andrew Lytle: Myth and Memory

1. Andrew Lytle, *I'll Take My Stand: The South and the Agrarian Tradition*, 75th Anniversary Edition (Baton Rouge: Louisiana State University Press, 2006).

2. Lytle, *Bedford Forrest and His Critter Company*, reprint edition (Nashville: J. S. Sanders & Co., 2002).

3. Lytle, *A Wake for the Living*, reprint edition (Nashville: J.S. Sanders & Co., 1992).

4. William C. Havard and Walter Sullivan, eds., *A Band of Prophets: The Vanderbilt Agrarians After Fifty Years* (Baton Rouge, Louisiana State University Press, 1982), 16.

5. Reprinted as "The Local Universality of Andrew Lytle," in *The Form Discovered: Essays on the Achievement of Andrew Lytle* (Jackson, MS: University & College Press of Mississippi, 1973), 79–80.

6. Lytle, "The Image as Guide to Meaning in the Historical Novel," *The Hero with the Private Parts* (Baton Rouge: Louisiana State University Press, 1966), 7–8.

7. Stephen J. Tonsor, "Myth, History and the Problem of Desacralized Time," *Continuity: A Journal of History* 4/5 (Spring/Fall 1982): 26.

8. Lytle, "The Image as Guide," *Hero*, 6.

9. Lytle, "The Hero with the Private Parts," *Hero*, 42–59.

10. C. Hugh Holman, *The Immoderate Past: The Southern Writers and History* (Athens, GA: University of Georgia Press, 1976); and Thomas Daniel Young, *The Past in the Present: A Thematic Study of Modern Southern Fiction* (Baton Rouge: Louisiana State University Press, 1981).

11. Lewis P. Simpson, *The Dispossessed Garden: Pastoral and History in Southern Literature* (Athens, GA: University of Georgia Press, 1975).

12. Quoted by Louis D. Rubin Jr. in "Southern Literature, The Historical Image," in *South: Modern Southern Literature in Its Cultural Setting*, ed. Louis D. Rubin Jr. and Robert D. Jacobs (Westport, CT: Greenwood Press, 1974), 33.

13. Quoted by Simpson, *The Dispossessed Garden*, 74.

14. Lytle, "Regeneration for the Man," *Hero*, 132.

15. Simpson, "The Southern Republic of Letters and I'll Take My Stand," *A Band of Prophets*, 72–73.

16. Lytle, "The Momentary Man," *The Hillsdale Review* 1 (Spring 1979): 10.

17. Lytle, "The Hero with the Private Parts," *Hero*, 46.

18. Lytle, "Afterword: A Semi-Centennial," in *Why the South Will Survive*, ed. Clyde Wilson (Athens, GA: University of Georgia Press, 1981), 229.

19. Lytle, *A Wake for the Living*, 7.

20. Lytle, *The Long Night*, reprint edition (Mobile, AL: University of Alabama Press, 1988), 33.

21. Ibid., 70–71.

22. Ibid., 187.

23. See Harold Weatherby's fine essay, "The Quality of Richness: Observations on Andrew Lytle's *The Long Night*," in *The Form Discovered; Essays on the Achievemetn of Andrew Lytle* (The Mississippi Quarterly Series in Southern Literature) (Oxford, MS: University & College Press of Mississippi: 1973), 35–41.

24. See Lytle's comments on the Battle of Shiloh in *A Wake for the Living*, 168–71.

25. Lytle, *The Long Night*, 295–96.

26. Ibid., 278.

27. Ibid., 14.

28. Ibid., 17.

29. Lytle, "Foreword to A Novel, A Novella, and Four Short Stories," reprinted in *Stories: Alchemy and Others* (Sewanee, TN: University of the South Press, 1984).

Chapter 17:
Makoto Fujimura: Refiner's Fire

1. T. S. Eliot, "What Dante Means to Me," in *To Criticize the Critic, and Other Writings* (Lincoln: University of Nebraska Press, 1988), 134.

Chapter 19: Gerhart Niemeyer: Discerning the Spirits

1. Gerhart Niemeyer, "Forces that Shape the Twentieth Century," in *Within and Above Ourselves: Essays in Political Analysis* (Wilmington, DE: Intercollegiate Studies Institute, 1996), 187.

2. Niemeyer, "The Autonomous Man," in *Aftersight and Foresight: Selected Essays* (Lanham, MD: University Press of America; Bryn Mawr, PA: Intercollegiate Studies Institute, 1988), 5–6.

3. Niemeyer, *Aftersight*, 9.

4. In the light of the recent terrorist attacks on the United States, one can't help but think that Niemeyer would be intensely skeptical about America's revived spirit of patriotism, since it is not accompanied by any real desire for personal sacrifice and is unlikely to spur a deeper appreciation for the principles at the roots of our political order.

5. Niemeyer, *Aftersight*, 9.

6. Ibid., 305.

7. Ibid., 316.

8. Ibid., 316.

9. Ibid., 303.

10. Niemeyer, *Within*, 75–76.

11. Ibid., 338.

12. Niemeyer, *Aftersight*, 290.

13. To be fair I should mention that in a later essay, "Recovering History and Redeeming the Time," published in 1986, Niemeyer was less harsh on Dostoevsky, and more open to the idea that he was a major "prophetic poet."

14. Niemeyer, *Aftersight*, 289.

15. Ibid., 291–92.

16. Niemeyer, *Within*, 205.

17. Niemeyer, *Aftersight*, 296.

18. Ibid., 290.

19. Robert Musil, *The Man Without Qualities* (New York: Capricorn Books, 1965), 12.

20. Thomas Mann, *Doctor Faustus* (New York: Vintage Books, 1971), 371.

21. Niemeyer, *Within*, 87. The title of Pärt's work is *Passio*. It was published in 1982.

22. Niemeyer, *Aftersight*, 301, 303.

23. Ibid., 317.

24. Ibid., 318.

25. Ibid., 333.

26. Ibid., 342.

27. Ibid., 343.

Chapter 21:
Marion Montgomery: Being and Metaphor

1. Gerhart Niemeyer, "Why Marion Montgomery Has to Ramble," *Center Journal* 4 (Spring 1985): 71–95.

2. Marion Montgomery, *The Reflective Journey Toward Order* (Athens, GA: University of Georgia Press, 1973).

3. Montgomery, *Why Hawthorne Was Melancholy* (La Salle, IL: Sherwood Sugden & Company, 1984), 12.

4. Etienne Gilson, *The Spirit of Thomism* (New York: Harper Torchbooks, 1966), 64.

5. Montgomery, *Hawthorne*, 18.

6. Montgomery, *Why Poe Drank Liquor*, 155.

7. S. T. Coleridge, *Biographia Literaria* (New York: E.P. Dutton, 1975), 167.

8. Montgomery, *Hawthorne*, 480.

9. Ibid., 481.

10. Ibid., 34.

11. Ibid., 127.

12. Ibid., 25.

13. Ibid., 49.

14. Ibid., 63, 26.

15. Quoted in F. O. Mathiessen, *American Renaissance* (New York: Oxford University Press, 1941), 306–7.

16. R. W. B. Lewis, *The American Adam* (Chicago: University of Chicago Press, 1955), 110–26.

17. Montgomery, *Hawthorne*, 404, 406.

18. Ibid., 519.

19. Ibid., 522–23.

20. Ibid., 514–15.

21. Ibid., 382.

Acknowledgments

The first round of thanks must go to the many individuals at the Intercollegiate Studies Institute who have offered me support and encouragement over the course of three decades. In particular I honor the memory of two men—John F. Lulves Jr. and E. Victor Milione—who not only showed extraordinary kindness to me when I was just a lad but who also helped build ISI into an enduring institution. My thanks also to ISI's current president, T. Kenneth Cribb Jr.

Jeffrey Nelson, when he directed ISI Books many years ago, invited me to gather the material for this collection. He, too, is a builder and a visionary, and I am honored to be his friend. Thanks also to his successors at ISI Books, Jeremy Beer and Jed Donahue, for patiently waiting for me to complete the project.

My colleagues at *Image* journal and the Master of Fine Arts in Creative Writing program at Seattle Pacific University have done more than I can say to create and sustain a vibrant community that has nourished me in countless ways. My gratitude to Mary Kenagy Mitchell, Julie Mullins, Anna Johnson, and Beth Bevis.

Sara Arrigoni helped me finally get this collection off the ground, providing invaluable editorial, organizational, and moral support. I owe her big-time.

I am so grateful to Jim and Bev Ohlman, who graciously extended their hospitality to me when I needed to get away to finish editing this volume.

There is no way that I can adequately thank all those writers and thinkers with whom I've carried on conversations that have been central to my own development. At the risk of leaving many out, I would like to acknowledge Scott Cairns, Robert Clark, Annie Dillard, Ron Hansen, John Lukacs, Thomas Lynch, Paul Mariani, Barry Moser, Virgil Nemoianu, Kathleen Norris, Theodore Prescott, Santiago Ramos, Richard Rodriguez, and Robert Royal.

The quartet of essays in Part Five serve as a token of my gratitude to the four men who were my mentors; each of them convinced me that the tradition of the Man of Letters was not quite extinct.

Thanks to my agent, Carol Mann, for her continuing support.

I dedicate this book to my wife, Suzanne, who has acted as Virgil *and* Beatrice (and occasionally Cerberus) on this slow pilgrimage of mine.

Once again I thank my children—Magdalen, Helena, Charles, and Benedict—for their forbearance, mercy, and love.

In preparing these essays for publication, I've attempted to reduce some repetition of ideas and phrases, but I hope the reader will forgive what remains.

Index